SEAGULLS IN THE ATTIC

Also by Tessa Hainsworth

Up With the Larks

SEAGULLS IN THE ATTIC

Tessa Hainsworth

preface
publishing

Published by Preface Publishing 2010

10 9 8 7 6 5 4 3 2 1

First published in Great Britain in 2010 by Preface Publishing
20 Vauxhall Bridge Road
London SW1V 2SA

An imprint of The Random House Group Limited

www.rbooks.co.uk
www.prefacepublishing.co.uk

Addresses for companies within The Random House Group Limited
can be found at www.randomhouse.co.uk

The Random House Group Limited Reg. No. 954009

A CIP catalogue record for this book is available from the British Library

ISBN 978 1 84809 263 1

The Random ... ncil (FSC), the
leading inter ... re printed on
Greenpeace- ... procurement

Ty ... ted,

Still Giddy on Cornwall's champagne air . . .

To Richard, Tom and Georgie – I count my
blessings everyday!
Thank you to all my family and friends.
Special thanks to Karen Hayes and Jane Turnbull.

To Uther, Tom, Marley,
and their parents, uncles and aunts,
with love as always.

Prologue

The beach is empty; only I and Jake, my liver and white spaniel, are making footprints in the pure white sand. It's early spring, just after sunrise, and the sky is the colour of apricots on the horizon. The sea is perfectly still; the tide is nearly full out and the rock pools and formations that disappear when the tide is in have appeared again. I love the way the coves and beaches transform themselves unrecognisably with each tidal event: stones, rocks and tiny inlets come and go, creating a seascape that seems magically elusive.

I stand watching the sea change from a deep indigo to emerald and back to blue, as the sun begins to lighten the day. Tiny waves sparkle like dewdrops and up above me high white clouds are turning amber and gold.

Jake runs along the pristine sand, chasing the delicate waves lapping at my feet. Seagulls soar, greeting the morning with their joyful cries. The smell of salt, the birdsong, the primeval thrumming of the ocean makes me feel at one with the sky and earth.

Every morning now I can do this, tumble out of bed and take an early morning walk with Jake, long before anyone else is awake. The beach is near our house in Cornwall, so near that although I'm a postwoman and have to be at work early, I still have this time to myself to start the day.

I stop walking, take deep breaths. Everything seems to be waking up on this spring morning; even the sea is swelling with promise. On my way here all my senses were buzzing with nature waking up: the scent of rich earth; the singing of robins, blackbirds, skylarks, thrushes; the richness of colour in the dazzling yellow of the wild daffodils and the rich creaminess of the lush magnolia.

The smell of the sea is heady at this hour of the morning and almost intoxicating. Out of sheer exuberance I ruffle Jake's damp fur then begin to run along the shore, the dog racing alongside me, delighted with our game of tag.

I don't stop until I'm at the rock pool at the edge of the beach. It's half hidden by a massive outcrop and behind this and the pool is my secret spot, the place where I find cowrie shells. I love these tiny pinkish shells, no bigger than my little fingernail. They're lucky shells, the Cornish equivalent to the Irish four-leaf clover. Crouching down and sifting my fingers through the wet sand, I know that today, this incredibly beautiful day, I'll find one, and within minutes, I do. Not just one but two cowrie shells, pearly and perfect. It's an omen, I think. Today I'm beginning work on my allotment, starting for the first time to grow vegetables to feed my family, taking the first step towards self-sufficiency. Finding the lucky shells is a fortuitous start to the venture.

Clutching my shells I retrace my steps, watching the light strengthen, making the sea glow. I'm still not used to it, still can't believe I'm here, even though it's my second year of delivering the post in Cornwall. Sometimes I look around for the person I was not so long ago, the high-flying career woman, and I wonder how this barefoot postie making footprints in the untouched white sand, made such a metamorphosis. However it happened, I'm grateful for it.

I take one more look at the sea, inhale another deep breath of the ozone and listen for a few moments more to the evocative cries of the herring gulls as they skim the water looking for fish. Then I call Jake and head for home – to my family, to work, and to the start of another magical Cornish day.

Chapter 1

How does my garden grow?

The day is idyllic, perfect for what I plan to do. The March winds at the beginning of the month have died down, as have the squally showers of the last few days. The sun, as I leave the house, is beaming as brightly as I am as I skip down the lane; it's like summer even though spring only officially begins today. I cross the short distance to the other side of the village, grinning and nodding at the occasional person – or dog or cat or bird – that I pass. What a day to start a garden!

I've never grown vegetables before. We hadn't the land in London, nor the time. I was trying to combine a managerial position with The Body Shop along with giving quality time to Ben, my husband, and our two children, Will and Amy aged eight and six. It didn't leave much free time for things like growing your own food.

Here in Cornwall, where we've lived for over a year now, I still don't have any land for a vegetable garden, which is why I'm on my way to the other side of the village. There I've not only got an allotment, but a place to keep my six hens. We did keep the chickens in our back garden, but it was really not the right place for them, being much too near the house and attracting vermin of all kinds. The hens, and our allotment are now situated on land belonging to Edna and Hector Humphrey, a couple in their nineties. They both seem remarkably spry and fit despite being rather skinny and slight. The Humphreys have let me use some of their acreage in return for eggs and produce from the allotment, which is enormously kind of them. They live in a wonderfully massive house surrounded by what was once a beautiful garden now gone to rack and ruin. I'm using a plot between their front garden and an ancient apple orchard, a walled area less ramshackle than the rest of their land.

My hens are delighted with the move, made only a few weeks ago. Instead of a basic run they can now grub about in most of the overgrown orchard, which we've partitioned off with chicken wire. I have a fabulous hen house for them on a tall stump, three feet off the ground so that no hungry predators can get at them. There is a plank leading up to it, rather like a bridge over a moat, a pitched roof with corrugated iron and a portcullis-type door. Inside are two sweet nesting boxes each with its own little roof.

'Oh happy hens!' I cried as I watched them coming out of their new house that first morning. They clucked and clacked back at me, agreeing I'm sure. They are quite used to my chatting to them and always answer back politely.

Now that the mornings are lighter I can let them out of the hen house and feed them on my way to work as a postwoman. Edna and Hector insist on shutting them up in the evenings, saying it will put a spring in their steps, having chickens around the place again.

'Reminds me of the old days,' Hector had mused as the hens arrived at their new home.

'Ah, to be sure,' Edna had sighed and nodded her head. 'We had all sorts of wayward creatures sharing our place in the old days.'

Despite my eagerness to get started on my garden, I can't help slowing down as I walk, stopping here and there to look and admire. The entire village is a rainbow of colour, the daffodils still determined to bloom on despite arriving here long before anywhere else. Primroses stare out from every hedgerow and garden, as do other wild flowers whose names I don't know. Colours assail me: indigo blues, sunset pinks and oranges, wine reds. Last month the camellias were in full bloom and we were treated to a month-long carnival of pink, red and white petals floating through the air like confetti. That, plus the blissful scent of the magnolias beginning to stir, made February, usually the dreariest, most tiresome month in London, a joyful delight in south Cornwall.

'Why are you sounding so bubbly?' asked my best friend Annie in London during one of our frequent phone conversations. 'It's February. Cold, slushy, grey, dark, endless.'

'Oh really?' I replied. 'Actually today I ate my lunch outside. I parked the post van on the estuary at Creek and sat on the sea wall with a seagull. Bliss.' She nearly hung up on me.

I forget about Annie, about London, as I cut through the churchyard on my way to the Humphreys' place. The church squats in the centre of Treverny, like a great fat hen, with the houses surrounding it her little chicks. There are bouquets of fresh hothouse flowers on the tombstones but to my mind they are not a patch on the wild profusion of blooms and colour everywhere else in the village.

Glutted with all these delights, I saunter past the Humphreys' house, a large, rambling farmhouse which was originally medieval but with bits added on as parts of the old building disintegrated over the centuries. Most of it is now Victorian shabby, rather like Edna and Hector themselves who seem to live in layers of clothes bought decades ago on their many travels, or else dug out from musty, old trunks stored in their attic. Somehow they manage to look both bizarre and elegant in their odd assortment of clothing, which is especially interesting to me as I too am trying to manage on clothes from charity shops or hand-me-downs from friends and family. Since moving to Cornwall money has been scarce, and though I'm lucky enough to have a full-time job, the salary of a postal deliverer is not huge. With the debts we still have from the move, the work on the house, and all the expenses of those early days when neither Ben, my husband, nor I could find work, money is scarce. Things have eased a bit, as Ben, an actor, is 'resting' with several part-time jobs locally, but we still have to watch every penny.

One thing I do have now that I didn't have in London is peace of mind, tranquillity and time. When my post deliveries are finished, I don't have to stress about my work as I did in London, I can totally forget about it. There's also no more stressing about things I've left undone, no more worrying that the children aren't getting enough quality time with their mother, no more tears because Ben and I seem never to have a chance to sit down and talk. My off-duty hours are mine alone, not the Royal Mail's.

And as an added bonus, my time actually at work is mine too. As long as the post gets delivered at more or less the usual hours, I'm free to stop for a moment or two and stare at a sunrise coming over the water when I deliver to one of the seaside villages, or wait until a blackbird has finished its song before moving on to my next delivery. I remember the crazy wonder of seeing newborn lambs in December and stopping to watch them play in the still green fields as I delivered van loads of Christmas cards and parcels. The milder weather of this part of the world jumbles the seasons in the best possible way, and still manages to spring delightful surprises on me every month.

But today is my day off, it's all mine. Though it's not even ten o'clock the morning sun is strong. The name of the Humphreys' house is still etched on a wooden plaque nailed onto the ancient oak tree at the entrance, looking as if it has been there for as many years as the owners. 'Poet's Tenement' is what it says and when I first read it I got quite excited, loving the romantic idea that generations of poets had lived here in poetic squalor, existing on words alone as they penned their verses in this rural idyll.

Hector put me right when I asked him about it. 'Don't be daft, maid,' he said smiling kindly at me. 'The deeds may say what they like but my father looked up the history when he bought this place as a young man. Seems decades ago some feller called Pote, or Poat lived here, and the name got corrupted through the generations.'

'Oh. So no real poets then?'

'Well, maid, not that I've heard tell. But my father's brother used to tell limericks at the local in his day, so I suppose you could consider him a poet,' he smiled enigmatically.

'But Hector, what about the tenement part? It's such a fantastic house, with such massive gardens. How could it ever be called a tenement?'

Edna, who had joined us during this exchange, said, 'It's an old English word, used to mean a few acres, a smallholding, something like that. So hence the name, my dear. Someone called Pote, or Poot, or whatever owned a bit of farmland to go with his house and there you are.'

I must have looked crestfallen for she added, 'You'd have preferred a Cornish Wordsworth, wouldn't you? I must say, so would I, once. Until I went to Japan with a poet many years ago.'

As usual, Edna changed the subject after this cryptic remark, and I shall never know a thing more about her Japanese poet. Always curious about people, I've asked numerous folk in Treverny about the Humphreys, but no one seems to know much about them, even though they are certainly Cornish and have lived here off and on since they married. Hector was born in Poet's Tenement and Edna came 'from the north somewhere', a local told me once, which I took to mean the north of England until I found out later that he meant north Cornwall. It's taken me some time to realise that anywhere north of the Tamar River is referred to as 'Up Country', just as I thought an 'emmett' was some kind of Cornish insect until I realised that that was the local word for tourists.

Hector is sitting on the bench outside Poet's Tenement so I stop to say hello. He is totally bald, has been since he was young, according to those who knew him then. He usually wears an assortment of hats but today he's got his shiny head exposed to the sun, 'airing it out after the winter', he chuckles to me as I sit beside him for a chat. His face is as wrinkly as dried fruit and as sweet; his smile, like Edna's, is genuine and warm despite a missing tooth or two.

Hector and I look out over the front garden as we chat. An ancient stone wall, crumbling in spots, surrounds the jumble of flowers and plants all crammed together every which way. The wild daffodils are mixed with heather and rosehips alongside a bit of gorse and all sorts of things whose name I couldn't begin to even guess. Once a week a local man, Doug, comes out to clear the path which runs around the inside of the wall so that it doesn't disappear beneath the foliage, but that's all the help they have.

After I've admired the colourful chaos of the garden, Hector says, 'I see you're all spruced up to start sowing.' He's noted my wellie boots, my gardening gloves, my basket full of seeds and some tiny plants.

'Yes, I'm all set to go. Joe up the road brought his rotivator and prepared the ground for me. I'd never have been able to dig it all up, and nor would Ben with his bad back.'

'How is he?'

'Oh much better and back at work, but he's not supposed to do any heavy lifting for a while.' Ben had been hurt in a fall down the stairs a month or so ago and had only just recovered, which is why I didn't want him near the garden. He would try to do too much and injure himself again. Besides, the garden, for this year anyway, is my project. Ben is juggling such odd and long hours at his part-time jobs that he's got no time to take on anything else.

I ask Hector about Edna, worried that she might be ill. Usually the two sit together on the semi-rotten wooden bench in the front garden on a sunny morning, winter or summer.

'Edna? Couldn't be better. She'll be out by and by. Had a spot of bother getting out of bed this morning. Says she wants to take her time getting dressed and I wasn't to fuss but to warm the bench for her.'

I'm immediately concerned. The woman is in her nineties after all. 'Oh goodness, is there anything I can do? Do you want me to look in on her, check she's all right?'

He is indignant. ''Twould make her madder than a March Hare, maid. She likes her independence, that one.'

I'm reluctant to leave when for all I know, Edna could have fallen down those long stairs in the house, or slipped on one of the rugs scattered indiscriminately on the old slate floors of the hall and kitchen. But Hector is the picture of ease, having closed his eyes again and lifted his face to the sun, politely but soundly dismissing me. Worried though I am about Edna, there's nothing I can do but say goodbye and carry on.

I pass through the tangled front garden and on through a gate into 'my' piece of land. I can get there from the road as well, but I decided, when I took on part of the field next to the house, that it would be good to check on the Humphreys when I go by. I've learned that they have no relatives in the area – their one son emigrated to New Zealand years ago. He visits when he can, but it's not often. He's nearly seventy and is in very poor health apparently. I assume from the way they live that Edna and Hector have to be careful about their money. They won't take any cash for the allotment though and from the look of them, they can't eat much so they won't be taking many eggs or vegetables. I know I've got a very good deal and I'm so grateful that I'm hoping I can repay the couple by doing whatever odd jobs they might need done. At least with my hens here, I have to come everyday so I'll be around to keep an eye on them.

But now I've got my own job to do. I stand still for a few moments taking in the rich earth, dug and waiting to be planted. Birds are giddy with song on this first real spring morning – there are skylarks, robins and thrushes singing their little hearts out, with the blackbird joining in lustily and blue tits twitter away, a kind of background sound to the others. A song keeps coming into my head, the old nursery rhyme I used to croon to the children, 'Mary, Mary, quite contrary, how does your garden grow? With silver bells and cockleshells . . .' Well, I don't know about bells and shells, but how about, 'With spinach, beans and lettuces, and pretty leeks all in a row.'

The earth smells lush and rich, as if it's so full of secret growing things, you can almost feel it humming with life. Beyond my allotment is a field of ewes and new lambs, the grass they're grazing on a dazzling contrast to the blue of the sky. There's not a trace of March wind in the air, and in fact it's so warm I take off my old patched jacket and sit down on a flat stone by the side of the gate to the field, for no other reason than to gaze at my garden-to-be. 'Postie, postie, warm as toastie, how does your garden grow?' I sing to myself. 'With parsnips beet and more to eat, and runner beans all in a row'.

I'm about to go into a third verse when I hear a voice. 'Tessa m'dear, are you all right?' I turn to see Edna peering at me through her huge, round, old-fashioned specs with the tortoise-shell frames. She's standing on her side of the gate into the field which is my allotment.

'Oh fine, thanks, just fine.'

'That's good, dear. I thought I heard you talking to your-self; it worried me slightly. You don't want to start that at your young age.'

I make some kind of gurgling noise in reply, indicating that I appreciate her little joke even though I'm not sure it is a joke. 'But what about you? Hector said you weren't feeling well this morning.'

She looks cross at this. 'Hector talks rubbish sometimes, I'm right as rain. Now, can I do anything to help you with that? You look a trifle flummoxed. Hot and bothered, my dear.'

I assure her that everything is fine, that I'm just about to begin planting. I show her my basket with the onion sets, the dried pea seeds ready to go straight into the ground and the tiny leek plants I got from Daphne, who lives and farms with her husband, Joe, just outside the village.

Edna looks at my prize specimens solemnly through her owl glasses that cover half her face. I've never seen such enormous ones. She is like a tiny bespectacled wren with her little legs encased in old sheepskin boots, her wisp of feathery hair, her small beak-like nose. She's wearing something brown and non-descript but instead of a jacket or coat, she's put on a waist-length, blue velvet cape with a silver clasp at the neck. It looks like something her great-grandmother might have worn to a ball.

9

After she's examined my seeds and plants, she says, 'If you're sure you don't need help, I'll leave you to it. But do call Hector or me if you get into any difficulty, dear.'

She walks away, stately as an ancient queen and I'm left feeling rather bemused – isn't it supposed to be *me* helping *her*? But I've got work to do, and it's time I began. I start with the five leek plants, diligently making a hole for each one and tenderly putting it in. I've taken off my gardening gloves as I love the feel of the earth between my fingers. Bliss, I think, sheer bliss.

Next the onion sets. I plant out each one separately and lovingly cover it with dirt. A robin perches on the ash tree next to the gate to watch and I stop what I'm doing to gaze back, admiring its rosy little breast and perky face. Finally, I plant the peas. I've bought a packet and put them right into the ground. I hope it's not too early, but the weather forecast is good for the next week and by then March will be nearly over. At least I'll have made a start.

When I finish, I sit back down again to admire my work. Admittedly, all I can see is a cultivated field and five little leek plants, but hey, it's my very first vegetable garden. I can't count the window box I had in London where I tried to grow herbs. The basil died before its life even began, no doubt because of the cold, and the coriander was a nonstarter. Only the chives survived. We used them in everything.

I leave by the road gate as I've seen Hector and Edna today, and know that they are both alive and well. On my way back I stop at the village to buy milk and run into Daphne. She and Joe are a couple in their late forties who have been farming here since they were first married and they've both become friends during the last year. Our children are all the same ages and go to school together.

'How's it going?' Daphne asks.

I tell her in great detail about planting out the leeks and sowing the peas. Oh dear, I'm becoming a gardening bore already. Daphne listens politely but her eyes are starting to glaze over. After all, she's been growing food for years. We walk out of the shop together as we speak and now stand talking on the road. An old yellow Labrador walks by, out for his morning constitutional alone. The woman who owns him has terrible arthritis in her knees and can't take him out much, so he's decided to walk himself. He goes up and down the village twice, keeping to the side of the road to avoid the odd car, and never soils anyone's garden.

Daphne and I stop chatting to make a fuss of Old Yeller, as the Labrador's been called since puppyhood. He's sometimes joined by Annabel, an apricot poodle whom Annie mistook for a stray with embarrassing consequences on one of her visits here. She hadn't learned village dog etiquette which maintained that if an animal is well behaved and road trained, it can wander freely around Treverny without interference.

When Old Yeller leaves us, he goes over to a low garden wall covered with soft green moss where a grey cat sits sunning herself. The dog knows this cat and wants to start a dialogue. He nudges her softly but the cat won't have it. She smacks Old Yeller soundly across his nose but he doesn't yelp; she's kept her claws in. Daphne and I watch with amusement as the dog makes a movement that almost seems a shrug, as if to say, oh well I'll find someone else to play with.

Daphne goes back to our conversation we were having before being interrupted by animal antics. 'What you should do, Tessa, now that your vegetables are all planned, is raise your own animal for food. You're living in the country after all.'

'I'd love to – all that wonderful organic food. But we just don't have the room. Can you imagine a cow in our small back garden?'

Daphne rolls her eyes. 'Knowing you, if you wanted a cow badly enough you'd probably keep it in the house if there was no room outside. Actually, I was wondering about a lamb. You can keep it on our farm; we've got plenty of room and we're close enough that it won't be a problem for you or one of the family to come out to feed and, look after it.'

I'm dumbfounded. 'What a kind offer, Daphne. Are you sure?' I'm beginning to feel excited about this. 'It would be amazing for the children, learning how to raise their own food supplies, having some responsibility for their own survival. Great lessons for the future.' I look at her closely. 'But are you sure?' I repeat. 'Why don't you talk it over with Joe before we decide anything.'

'Joe will be fine about it. The reason I thought of it is that there are a lot of sock lambs about this time of year; you know, the orphan lambs that the farmers have to bottle feed. They're a nuisance, so sometimes you can pick one up cheap. We've done that before, raised a sock lamb for the meat.'

'But it's a lot of ask of you.'

'Not at all. We keep sheep as you know and yours can live with ours. No problem. And it'll be great for my kids, having Will and Amy over all the time, looking after their very own lamb.'

I run all the way home to tell Ben who is there now, having worked an early shift at the café in St Geraint, the seaside town only a few miles from our village. 'Ben, we're going to grow our own lamb chops!' I shout as I rush into the kitchen. He nearly drops the cup he is holding when I crash in on him.

'Steady on, Tessa. Calm down and have a cup of tea, the kettle's just boiled. Then tell me what on earth you've come up with now.'

I explain Daphne's idea and after some initial questions about the management of it all, he's as excited as I am. I feel giddy with new ideas about feeding the family with our own produce. 'Think of the money we'll save, Ben. But even better, the healthy eating we'll be doing. And the satisfaction! Oh, it'll be heaven. Maybe we could even see if Daphne and Joe would let us keep a pig on their farm. Or a cow? For the milk?'

But Ben quite rightly baulks at this and I know I'm getting carried away as usual. He says, 'We're both working, Tessa, and the children are at school. We can't tie ourselves to milking a cow once a day. Besides, it's extremely difficult apparently when you've not done it before.'

'OK, but what about a pig? Maybe the Humphreys would let us keep at pig on their land, what do you think?'

'Let's just stick to a lamb for now. At least we've been around sheep and know a bit about them, thanks to Daphne and Joe and some of the other farmers around here. But we know nothing about pigs.'

I agree he's right. Still, first lamb chops, then who knows what next: pork roasts, bacon, fresh ham. The sky's the limit.

The next morning I'm up before dawn as usual, to get to the sorting office, pick up the post and get on with my round. Though it's still quite chilly in the morning, I can feel that the day will warm up beautifully as it did yesterday. The days are lengthening quickly it seems and soon there will be that wonderful summer spell when I actually go to work in the early light. Creeping out quietly as I always do, my postie uniform having been laid out the night before, I'm tempted to drive the short distance to the Humphreys' place to flash the torch across my garden, admire the newly planted leeks and the neat rows where the onions and peas have been sown. But even I know this is daft; I'll take a look later.

I jump into Minger, our old car, a white Peugeot that used to be a police car. It doesn't want to start but then it never does on a chilly morning. I've learned to be patient, for in the end it never fails me. Turning off the engine for a moment to give it a rest, I look out at the sleeping village. A nearly full moon casts a luminous sheen on the grass as well as the trees which are budding up ready to burst into glorious spring leaf. All of the village is clearly visible in the moonlight; it looks as if it's been sleeping for years and is waiting for a magic wand to wake it. I think about the couple from London who bought a second home here a year or so ago and tried to bully the local council to put streetlights on our one quiet main road. The man said it was awkward holding a torch when walking his dog at night. When all his arguments, threats and pleadings failed, and the streetlight idea was given a firm veto, he got into such a huff that he sold the house, much to everyone's relief. I suppose he's now in Devon or somewhere else in the West Country, making trouble for the locals there.

Thinking thankfully about the absence of streetlights in Treverny, I start Minger's ancient engine again and this time it grumbles into action. I drive along silent roads to St Geraint where I pick up the postal van which is parked behind the boatyard. Once again I linger, savouring the moonlight on the calm sea. My job, I think. The sea is my office. I still can't believe it sometimes, that I and my family actually did it, moved from what had become for us a nightmare of commuting, juggling family and job, to this place where I am learning to live again, take deep breaths, stop and look at the stars as I am doing now.

When I get to the sorting office in Truro, where today I'm picking up the post for St Geraint and Morranport, another, smaller seaside village, things are not so tranquil. It is never peaceful, with the huge sorting office teeming with postmen and women rushing to pick up their deliveries and load them into the waiting vans, but today there's another crisis.

Susie, the Cornishwoman who has been my lifeline as I

learned this new job, finds me and says, 'Eddie's off sick, maid. Only just phoned in, so you and I got to split his round. No one else about who can do it today.'

Eddie joined us as a relief postie about a year or so ago but now has his own round. He's young, freckle-faced, cheeky and endearing, always up for a joke and a laugh. He's not often off work so he must have the flu that's been going around the villages.

Luckily we all know each other's rounds, so it's not that bad but just makes a longer day. And it's one of those days when everything seems to go wrong. For a start, the indicators on my van aren't working so I have to use hand signals. This would be fine if I'd been right about assuming it would be a fine sunny day like yesterday. As the sun comes up the rain rolls in, the horizontal kind that blows right into my face every time I roll down the window to make a hand signal.

As if I didn't have enough trouble with the postal van, my old car also gives me grief when I finally finish, wet and soaking and hungry. I didn't bring any lunch. I thought I'd be home in time to have a late one with Ben, but it's too late now. Minger, after all my faith and patience, decides to be fickle and rewards me by absolutely refusing to start. I finally get out in the rain which is now a downpour and luckily find Mickey who sometimes works in the boatyard. He's an ace mechanic and kindly does something magical to get me going again. As I thank him profusely he says in warning, 'Maid, you need to be taking this old heap in. I've patched it up but it won't last. It do be needing some serious work.'

Serious work. More money. What we desperately need is a new car but we can't afford it although this one is costing us a fortune. I drive home feeling rather less euphoric than I did this morning. But after a hot bath, dry clothes, and a great helping of a lasagne Ben has made, I'm feeling more optimistic. Maybe we can get a second-hand car with all the money we will save this year growing our food, producing our own meat. I've learned how to make bread and not with a bread-maker either, but with my bare hands. Apart from a few things like tea and milk, and maybe rice and pasta and a few dried beans now and again, we'll hardly have to spend a penny on food.

Or so I dream. But why not? I've already learned how to nose around junk stores and charity shops, picking up wonderful bargains for less than a pound or two. Luckily vintage clothes are very trendy now and I've been able to find some amazing clothes. The library is great for renting DVDs at cheap prices. I not only save money but I'm feeling good about it, recycling not just paper or bottles but clothing, books and other house-hold items. It gives me a kind of contentment that all my previous spending on designer shoes or meals out in trendy restaurants never did – a contentment that isn't just a fleeting buzz but something deeper and more lasting.

I'm also determined to forage for edible food in the wonder-fully lush Cornish countryside. I went on a day's outing last summer to learn about food foraging. A few of us spent a couple of hours on the cliffs above Morranport, one of my favourite seaside villages. An amazingly knowledgeable woman from Truro taught us all the tricks about foraging, how to find edible plants such as hawthorn, 'fat hen' or muckweed as it's commonly called. I learned that the old English for fat hen is *melde*, and that the 'fat' in the other name comes from the greasiness of the seeds. Then there is the horseradish plant and of course nettles, sorrel, chickweed, dandelion and wild mustard – I'm getting excited all over again, thinking about all the food lying about the countryside just waiting to be eaten.

What with the extra load at work, the rain, and Minger inconveniently being mended, the next few days are hectic, so there's a great sense of relief when Eddie finally comes back to work, the rain stops, and I get my car back. The warm Cornish sun drying out the landscape even makes me forget the bill from the garage and the worry about how we're going to pay it. I've got a walking round today and it's idyllic, the local folk out and about, friendly and chatty, all of us happy as larks in the sunshine.

By early afternoon I'm on my way back to my garden, once again chanting softly to myself, 'Postie, postie, dry as toastie, how does your garden grow?' Naturally I'm not that much of a townie that I expect any obvious growth, but it's lovely just to be able to look and imagine all the vegetables that will be grown there. And I've got some lovely little cauliflower plants to put out, grown in a customer's greenhouse. She assured me they were 'sturdy as a baby oak, my handsome', and that it was safe to plant them out now in the early south Cornish warmth.

Edna and Hector are both outside 'Poet's Tenement' looking like meditating monks as they walk up and down on the uneven stone path through their front garden. I can never get over how that wild and unkempt garden always manages to look charming, rather like the couple themselves. Edna has on her royal blue velvet cape and Hector wears something that looks like a cardinal's cloak – it's deep red, hooded, long and flowing. Perhaps one of his ancestors was the Pope's right-hand man; with those two you never know. I find it interesting how, despite their oddity, their eccentricities and their reticence, they are still embraced by the local community. I think they've already become legends in their own lifetimes, the villagers being proud of having something to add to the mystery, myth and folklore which is rampant in this county.

I stand for a moment and watch them walking back and forth on the rough path then around and around the inside path along the stone wall. They walk slowly, contemplatively. I've seen them do this before; it's their form of exercise. Apparently they've done it for years, ever since they got too old to ramble over seaside cliffs.

The first thing I see when I get to my garden are my onion sets, which instead of being planted firmly under the earth as I left them, are scattered randomly on top of the ground. I'm both bewildered and indignant. Who did this? Who dared vandalise my garden? All I can do is stand there and gape. What happened? Why?

As if I've spoken aloud, a voice answers my silent question. 'It's those blackbirds, maid. They think there's something tasty under there and peck the onions out. Too bad. You'll have to sow them all over again.'

I turn and see Hector nodding at me. He's barely taller than his wife and just as bird-like only instead of a tiny beak for a nose, his is long and bony, more like a hawk's. Covering his bald head today in a straw hat which appears to have been run over a few times by a horse and cart. He looks distinguished, though goodness knows how he manages it with that ruby red drapery and an old straw hat; perhaps it is his manner. Both he and Edna never seem flustered or fazed by anything. Though old and fragile-looking, they both stand ramrod straight, which gives them the appearance of always being in control despite their whacky clothes and advanced age.

I look at him quizzically. 'Blackbirds? But I like blackbirds. They have such a lovely song.'

A glimmer of amusement passes over Hector's face. 'So do we all, maid, but that doesn't mean they can't be pesky at times. Best make the most of it and get on with replanting. Shall I give you a hand?'

'No, thanks, Hector. I'll be fine.'

I've just replanted the onions and am investigating my leek

plants which look a bit beaten down after all the rain. At least the peas seem fine. Carefully I plant out the cauliflowers that were given to me, with a cursory nod at the blackbird watching me in the tree.

'Leave my patch alone,' I mutter. As if in answer the black-bird bursts into song. I listen for a minute then grin. 'OK, I forgive you. Just don't do it again.'

I'm about to go when someone calls to me from the other gate, the one leading onto the road. It's one of the farm workers from Daphne and Joe's farm, a middle-aged man called Doug, who also works a morning a week strimming the Humphreys' front path. 'Great day for gardening, ain't it? Great day all around, if you ask me.' He leans over the gate, surveying my allotment.

'Oh hi, Doug. Yes, it's gorgeous isn't it. I thought I might have planted too early but it looks like spring is here to stay.'

'Hmm, mebbe, mebbe not. Them leeks don't look too good. A bit early I'd have said for leeks. And you've put the cauli in. Hmm.'

'Oh? Oh dear. But it's so warm and sheltered, I thought they'd be fine.'

Doug purses his lips and sucks air through them, making a whistling sound. I've seen Cornish farmers do this many a time, especially when they're about to pronounce something horrific, like the price of feed rising exorbitantly or the impos-sibility of selling an animal for the price the buyer is asking. 'Don't know who told you that, my lover. If you ask me, peas are the only crop hardy enough to sow now.' He makes that air-sucking noise again and shakes his head.

'What's the matter? What is it?' I ask. He's not saying anything and I'm beginning to get a bit nervous. After all, Doug's been working on the land since he was a boy and he should know what he's talking about.

Finally he speaks, 'Peas is all very well, my handsome, but even then, you got to be careful, if you ask me. You see, I hear tell that there's gonna be a frost tonight.'

'What?' I nearly shriek the word. 'This is south Cornwall, look at the sun. There can't be a frost.'

'I feel it in my bones. If you ask me,' he folds his arms stubbornly across his chest. He's a burly man, rugged and jowly.

I stare at him. 'OK, Doug, so what do I do? Everything's already in the ground. I'm not about to dig it up because you think there might be a frost.'

He looks chuffed at being asked. He makes that whistling sound again as if the answer is going to be tough and then says one word, 'Fleece.'

'Fleece?'

'Yep, that'll do it. Get a bit of fleece and put it over the peas, that'll give 'em some protection. Yes, that'll do just fine. Best get on now, see you again.' He walks away, no doubt quite pleased with himself, telling the city gal a few facts about the land.

Fleece, eh? Well, that's no problem. I know where to get some fleece, with all the sheep around here. Doug said just a bit would do. I have plenty of time to get some as Ben is picking up the children from school today.

So instead of going straight home, I wander down the lane leading out of the village and down to some local farms. It's such a golden day that I'm delighted to have an excuse not to go straight home. The narrow road is lined with hedgerows beginning to green up with the coming of spring. Pink, blue and yellow wild flowers peep between twigs and a robin is watching me from a beech tree. The warmth is soporific, I can feel it filling my body, warming my bones as it's warming the earth. Spring in Cornwall has got to be one of most entrancing seasons of the year.

After ten minutes of walking I come to a field of sheep. I've passed by here lots of times and noticed how, towards the end of winter and spring, before the sheep are shorn, their wool sometimes gets a bit straggly, catching on bits of fencing, brambles and low tree branches. A public footpath runs along the sides of this field which is ideal. I walk all around it, gathering bits of wool here and there, dropping it into my basket. There are more pickings in the field opposite. The sheep gaze at me from a distance, placid and undisturbed.

By the time I finish collecting, I have a basketful of wool. Put together it must be almost as much as a whole sheep's fleece. This is what Doug meant, I assure myself, for even I, townie that I am, know not even Cornish farmers shear in March, so finding an entire sheep's fleece would be impossible. In fact, with my basketful of wool straight off the sheep's back, I'm feeling quite on top of this gardening lark. Doug cannot resist poking fun at us city folk at times when we struggle to make sense of country ways so I wish he'd pass by now to see how enterprising I've been.

This is the life. I begin to whistle as I saunter back to my allotment, going in through the gate from the road and noting with satisfaction that all is as it should be. I've replanted the onion sets and they remain untouched by birds. The little leeks are perking up and the cauliflower plants I've just put out are fine. It might be only an hour or two since I was here last, but I can't help feeling relieved that everything still looks the same.

I take the fleece from my basket and painstakingly drape it over the row of peas. It looks sparse when it's all spread out like that but Doug said it would do the trick. It looks pretty on the dark brown soil, like a light coating of snow or frost, or a delicate spider's web, shining with dew, perhaps. The patterns the wisps of wool make are so intriguing that I can't help rearranging them so that the sunlight can shine on and through the wool making lovely swirls and intricate designs. Just because my garden is meant to be functional, I decide, it can still be aesthetically pleasing.

I turn to gaze with admiration at my new cold frame, which I made with a top from a window and frame I found at the local tip and bits of wood. It's extraordinary, the delight one can have in such simple things. Instead of a designer handbag or an exquisite new pair of shoes, I've got a cold frame.

The clucking of the hens demands my attention next. It's too early for them to go in for the night so I take them a handful of corn from the feed bin. They bustle up around me, fussing and making the friendly confidential clucking noises that I love. Originally we had only the brown Rhode Islands but a couple of them died and I've replaced one with a light Sussex, a white hen with black feathers on her neck and tail. I've learned that these Sussex hens were bred white so that no dark quill marks showed up on their skin when they were plucked. Her eggs are pale brown, not like my other replacement, the Maran hen, whose eggs are a rich dark chocolate colour.

While my hens cluck and peck at the corn I've tossed them, I check the nest boxes to see if they've started laying again. They stopped over winter, and then with the move to their new home, they're a bit slow getting started again.

I put my hand in the straw. The first box is empty, but eureka! The other one has a single egg in it. I peer at it and see that it's one of the brown Rhode Islanders. I'm so tempted to run home with it to show Ben, Amy and Will, but I know I have to leave it there. Even when there's no need, when there's no cockerel around to fertilise a hen's eggs, she's still massively protective of them. If I take this one away, whoever did the laying will decide the nest box isn't a safe place and take her future eggs somewhere else. I don't want them to start laying all over the orchard.

I go out and croon over the hens. 'Wonderful job, girls, you're brilliant! Great start, whoever it was. I'm sure you'll all be laying before the week is out. I can't tell you how we're all looking forward to fresh eggs for breakfast again.'

They cock their heads to one side as chickens do, looking at me with one beady eye, following me around. As I walk through the old orchard, I feel, as I do each time, that I'm in some kind of fairy tale, an eerie yet benign story of ancient elves, sprites and spirits. The pear trees mixed in with the apples are old, gnarled and well past their prime. Emerald green moss grows up the battered trunks and on the odd rocks strewn seemingly randomly here and there. Branches have broken off throughout the years and been left to lie where they fell, some beginning to rot and split. From here you can see neither the road nor any house other than Poet's Tenement, which, from this side, looks like a whimsical castle fit for a magnificent Elfin king.

With great satisfaction I once again head towards home, stopping on my way to pick the tops off a bunch of nettles growing at the edge of the lane, making sure I don't pick any leaves dog-pee height as I learned from the Truro lady in my food-foraging class. I've been reading up on how to find and identify food that can be picked for free. Apparently the early spring nettles are the best, and there are masses growing now. I pick enough to steam for our dinner tonight, wearing the thick gloves I bought especially for this purpose. Last time I picked nettles I wore my yellow Marigold gloves, learning the hard way how painful nettle stings can be. That time I obviously steamed the nettles too lightly as they were still a bit tough and stingy. Will and Amy will groan when they see me walk in with this next batch but I'm ever hopeful. Nettles are supposed to taste a bit like spinach when cooked properly. Trial and error, I decide, though this year might be more error as it's my first attempt.

Back home, Ben has made a delicious stew from cheap but nourishing cuts of lamb from the butcher at St Geraint, potatoes and veg from local producers. The gravy is his own perfect blend of herbs and spices. We've both learned how to make tasty meals at half the cost of our London meals, back in the days when we bought any ingredient we fancied no matter what the cost. None of us would say we enjoyed our food more in those days than we do now.

To top off our meal I steam the nettles to go with the stew. This time I only picked the top leaves as I was supposed to, and steamed it until it was just right. To everyone's surprise, it's delicious, a bit like spinach only with its own distinct taste. This food foraging does pay off, I decide. I vow to carry a basket or rucksack with me everywhere I go from now on, along with some thick gloves.

Next day I'm in my allotment when Susie comes by with a few more leek plants someone's given her which she can't use. I show off my hens, my new homemade cold frame. 'I've bought some lettuce seeds,' I burble with excitement. 'I can't wait to sow them in the cold frame tomorrow.'

'They'll be doing nicely there. But remember, my bird, once they begin to grow, take the top off that frame in the morning if it's going to be a really sunny day so they don't shrivel and die of the heat. Then back on in the evenings for those cold spring nights.'

'Thanks, Susie. You're a star.'

She shrugs this off and turns to take a proper look at my garden. 'Tessa, what on earth is *that*?'

'What?'

'That white stuff. All over that part of the garden.'

'Oh, that's the fleece.'

'Fleece?' she looks perplexed. Maybe there's something about gardening I know that she doesn't, thanks to Doug.

I try not to sound smug as I explain. 'You see, even though peas are the first seeds that can go into the ground because they're quite hardy, there's still a chance of night frost. So it's best to put some fleece over them to protect them.'

She's staring at me as if I were a madwoman, 'Who told you to put sheep's wool down?'

I'm beginning to feel something is not quite right. 'It's fleece. Sheep's wool is their fleece, right? It was Doug, you know, works up at Daphne and Joe's farm. Said the peas could do with some fleece over it for protection.'

Susie is grinning before I even finish my explanation. I ask, 'Was Doug having me on? Aren't you supposed to put fleece on your garden?'

She has to catch her breath before she can answer for by now she's giggling like crazy, 'No, my bird, Doug was absolutely right about the fleece. The thing is, gardening fleece does not come off sheep. It's a roll of thin fleecy material. You get it in gardening or farming shops, not from sheep.' At this she has to sit down she is laughing so hard.

As usual Susie's laugh is infectious and it's not long before I start giggling too. We flop down on the warm grass by my new cold frame and cackle like a couple of crows, tears streaming down our faces. I look up when we've just about exhausted ourselves to see Edna and Hector staring at us over the gate that leads from their garden to the allotment field. 'Oh, hello, don't mind us, I just did the dumbest thing,' I begin.

Edna stops me, 'Don't explain, m'dear, please. And don't stop. Hector and I do so love to see young folk enjoying themselves.'

'We certainly do,' Hector adds. 'Please carry on.'

But of course when someone tells you to go on laughing hysterically, it's practically impossible to do so. Susie and I give them apologetic smiles, mumble something about getting on and get up quickly, wiping grass and loose dirt from our clothes. Edna and Hector look disappointed, as if someone has turfed them out of the cinema in the middle of a favourite film.

'Please,' I say to Susie before she goes. 'Please, please, please don't tell Doug. Anybody but Doug. He'll never let me hear the end of it.'

Susie promises, but a few days later I'm in my garden again when Doug stops by. He too is guffawing as he looks over at the sheep's wool covering my peas. 'Your veggie garden do be looking like one of them weird displays I hear tell about over at St Ives, that Tate place. Mebbe you should be charging admission, my lover.'

'Susie told you, did she?' I ask him.

'Nah, my handsome, 'twere not Susie. Don't rightly recall who told me, as all the village was talking about it last night in the pub. Your garden's not exactly hidden, y'know.' I take his point. He goes on, 'So are you going to get it off and get some proper fleece? Nights still might get pretty cold, if you ask me.'

I stand up straight, trying to get back at least some shred of dignity. 'The kind of fleece you're talking about costs money, Doug, and mine was free. It might not be the right kind but it's wool and it's warm, and hopefully it'll do at least some good in protecting my peas.'

He looks at me and shakes his head, rolls his eyes. 'Right you are, my lover, whatever you say. And good luck to you.'

He ambles off down the lane while I turn back to the allotment. Whatever Doug or Susie say, the cobwebs of swirling virgin wool does look lovely draped over the deep, rich, glorious Cornish soil.

Chapter 2

A rose by any other name . . .

It's hard to tear myself away from my new project to go to work, but of course I must. Eddie has recovered from his bout of flu and we're all more or less back to normal. With the clocks going forward the day seems even longer, though the mornings are slower to lighten. I'm still overwhelmed by the amount of light in Cornwall. In London, it seemed that the buildings, the crowded streets, the crammed nature of the city, made it hard for light to penetrate. And when it did, I was often unaware of it. Living inside, in offices and the underground, coming home when dark or nearly dark, I was completely out of touch with light and air and sky.

Here, though, it's totally the opposite. Even on grey over-cast days there is a sheen of light I never noticed before. It changes every hour, too. Sometimes it's silvery grey and silky, like the sky just before a misty dawn, or a deep velvety grey like the sea before a squall. Often when there's a storm brewing, there's an eerie yellow tinge everywhere, highlighting the trees and countryside in a sulphurous light before the storm actually descends and the light turns a rich plum purple.

This morning, though, there are few clouds, no mist, and an amazing sunrise. The colours of the sky seem to be competing with the colours of the flowering trees and bushes, and I find myself singing out loud with the sheer beauty of it all. There's not another car on the road as I drive along the main road out of Morranport, and certainly nothing on the narrow lane going up to a tiny cottage belonging to the Yellands, a Cornish couple who used to live in Falmouth. Mr Yelland worked as manager in a shop in Falmouth, as he told me once, but when they realised how much they could get for their house in town, which they'd lived in for forty years, they sold up and Mr Yelland took early retirement. 'The wife can support me now,' he said as he told me this but when I asked what she did, they both roared with laughter as if I'd said the funniest thing in the world. Mr Yelland, it transpired, doesn't believe in a wife of his going out to work; it would be 'demeaning' he told me once. Mrs Yelland, neat permed grey hair, a tidy face and body, wearing a clean apron over her flowery house dress, obviously agreed, as she beamed at her husband. As far as I can see, she cooks, cleans, waits on Mr Yelland hand and foot while he enjoys his retirement, with the local paper and an old pipe that I rarely see alight but that is always wobbling in the side of his mouth.

As I jump out of my van, parked by a tiny creek on the Yellands' property, I see a mass of hawthorn shoots growing near the gate to their garden. On the other side, there are dandelions. I can't resist; I begin to pick. For some reason I leaped out of the van with my empty postie bag still on my shoulder, though I'm carrying the single letter for the Yellands in my hand. Putting the letter on the stone gatepost, I thrust the shoots and young dandelion leaves into my postbag.

Luckily I remember to grab the letter as I go through the little gate leading into the garden. And there, growing wild in front of the Yellands' flower borders, is what I'm sure is garlic mustard. But is it? My book says it comes out in April, but then it's nearly April now, and anyway everything comes early in south Cornwall.

I've been dying to find this plant, which is supposed to grow profusely all over the English countryside. It's called garlic mustard because the leaves, when crushed, give off a garlicky smell and taste. Could this be it? I'm so thrilled that I kneel down on the grass, still damp with dew, to take a closer look. Plucking a few of the pale green leaves, I crush one, smell, taste – yes, it definitely is mustard garlic! I grab a handful, stuff it in my bag, and shuffle over, still on my hands and knees, to another patch further down.

'Mrs Hainsworth, are you all right? Have you fallen?' I look up to see Mr Yelland staring down at me. From this angle his face, pale and completely round, looks like the moon. His silver hair, smooth and flattened to the side with a nifty part, gleams like moonbeams.

I scramble up quickly. 'Uh, no, I'm fine. I was just, uh, admiring your roses.'

For the life of me I don't know why I said that. True, there is a rose bush by the gate, and true I have noticed it in the past, particularly last summer when the Yellands first moved in and it was in bloom. But it's not in bloom now and in fact looks rather stark at this moment in time.

Mr Yelland looks at me, his bland moon face expression-less. I look back at him, for once at a complete loss for words. Then he looks down. So do I. Because of the mild weather I've worn my baggie, official Royal Mail shorts. Is this what he's staring at? Or is it my knees, black and filthy with mud from his garden?

'Ha ha,' I trill, finding my voice at last. 'Didn't realise the ground was still so wet.'

We both turn our gazes to the ground, shaking our heads. I suddenly remember his letter, thrust in the pocket of my shorts, and hand it to him. He doesn't even look at it. 'Mrs Hainsworth,' he says politely. 'There are no roses.'

Now we both look at the rather naked-looking rose bush. I say, 'I realise that, but there will be soon. Look at all the buds.'

By then Mrs Yelland has joined us. 'Is she all right, dear?' she says to her husband. 'Oh Mrs Hainsworth, look at your knees! Did you fall?'

'No, no. I'm fine. Just a bit dirty.' I give a another little trill of laughter as I brush my knees nonchalantly, as if it's no big deal for a postie to be scrabbling on hands and knees in a customer's garden.

Mr Yelland says, 'Mrs Hainsworth was admiring our rose bush.'

'Oh, are you interested in roses? Mr Yelland is, always has been. Oh, how happy he'll be that he has another rose lover to talk to.'

I can't get over how Mrs Yelland always calls her husband Mr Yelland. I stifle a giggle, wondering how Ben would react if I began calling him Mr Hainsworth. He'd probably love it. Maybe he'll start asking the children to address him as Sir.

My knowledge of roses is zilch so I try to come clean. 'Uh, actually, I was also looking at those leaves on the other side of the rose bush. They look like garlic mustard. Supposed to be great for cooking.' I want to confess that I've picked a bunch of them and they're now in my post bag but I'm too embarrassed. I can't believe I forgot I was on someone's private property when I started foraging. I do manage to mutter, 'I'm afraid I picked a few leaves. Sorry, I should have asked.'

Mr Yelland smiles expansively which makes his face rounder than ever. It looks odd somehow, naked. I realise his pipe isn't in his mouth. Seeing me kneeling by his rose bush must have sent him rushing outside without it. Perhaps he thought I was worshipping it.

'Now, is that so, my maid? Well, we can't begrudge our postie a leaf or two now can we, Mrs Yelland.' He stoops down and in a larger-than-life gesture, plucks a couple of leaves of the mustard green and hands it to me with a flourish.

I thank him profusely while his wife beams at this gallantry. He goes on, 'Mrs Hainsworth, I can't begin to tell you how delighted I am that you share my interest in roses. Only an aficionado like myself would have known, without a bloom to identify it, that the rose bush you were admiring is an Old Garden Rose.'

He's waiting for me to say something. 'Ah, yes. Yes, of course.'

'And you know without my saying, that the Old Garden Roses are the predecessors of all the roses we have today. Some even date back to the Roman Empire, where they were revered for their beauty and fragrance.' He takes a deep breath. Mrs Yelland does the same and I feel as if I must follow suit. The Yellands have a rapturous look on their faces as if they can smell the non-existent rose blooms but all I get is a far-off scent of manure from a dung-spreading farmer.

After we've all sniffed the air like a pack of inquisitive terriers I say, 'Lovely talking to you both, but I must get on delivering the post.'

I start to go but before I get away, Mr Yelland says, 'I'm so looking forward to your next delivery. Mrs Yelland enjoys looking at the roses, and inhaling their scent, but she's not a connoisseur like you and I.'

I'm still trying to explain that I'm not really as they follow me to my van, waving aside my objections. As we all wave an enthusiastic farewell, Mr Yelland calls out, 'I'll be waiting for you on your next delivery!'

I groan silently, thinking I'd better read up on roses before I see them again.

March turns to April and I'm in love with the magic of spring in this part of the world. Cherry blossoms are rampant, turning the village into a fairy tale of scented pink. All over the church-yard and in the beech wood alongside the village the wild garlic is out and the earthy scent of it mingles with bloom and blossom. The ground is carpeted with the white garlic flowers which then mingle with the stunning blue of early bluebells. I pick the first showing of the wild garlic and make a favourite soup with garlic and nettles, frying a clove of garlic with a chopped onion and a couple of potatoes, adding the trimmed nettles and garlic leaves to the pan, then some chicken stock. It only needs about fifteen minutes of rapid boiling, then I liquidise it, add salt and pepper, a touch of nutmeg, some single cream and I've got a soup that's both scrumptious and economical. The bliss of it is, both the garlic and nettles are at their best all through April and May so there are dozens of wonderful soup meals ahead.

In my hens' orchard the old scabby apple and few pear trees amaze me by making a huge effort putting out blossom which dots the branches like little wisps of cloud, transforming the hens' area. The hens seem to take it all for granted, but I spend ages sitting with them and imbibing the magic of the land stir-ring, growing, surprising me with something new every day.

From the hens I check out the allotment. The lettuces I planted in my cold frame are growing beautifully. I can't wait to transplant them into the garden but we've had some chilly nights and days, too. But for the last few days the sun has been quite hot and I've had to take the glass top off the frame so that the delicate plants don't roast. Every evening before twilight I come down and replace it. Sometimes Will or Amy come with me, or Ben. Or we all go together, and if it's decent weather we finish off at the beach nearby to give Jake a run. I love these spring evenings, balmy with the promise of summer. The sea air smells rich in ozone and ocean scents just as the earth smells warm and full of healthy growing things. There's one beach we go to where the scent of the wild garlic mingles with the smell of sea and ozone and we inhale it like a drug, it's so potent, so special.

Tonight the cove is exceptionally beautiful. You can see the stars, galaxies of them, over the sea and sand, and there's a full moon which strikes a reflection like a golden path straight down the water. We linger until dark, throwing sticks for Jake, taking off our shoes and paddling even though the water is icy.

It isn't until late that night when we're getting ready for bed that I remember we have not put the glass back on the cold frame this evening.

'It'll be fine,' Ben says. 'It's a warm night.'

He's right. Our bedroom window is open and the chilliness of the past few nights is gone. I fall asleep happily, secure in the knowledge that not only are my lettuces safe, but also that I have a day off tomorrow.

It's nearly noon by the time I get to the garden. After dropping the children at school, I have shopping and other chores, but now I have time to plant out my lettuces. Having consulted Daphne, Susie and other knowledgeable gardeners, I know what to do next. The plants in the cold frame have grown and the timing is right. The weather forecast is for blissful days at least till the end of April, not far away now.

It's so warm I'm wearing shorts and a T-shirt. It really feels like summer, though I know by now that the weather can, and will, change again many times before summer really comes. But what a day to be in the garden! I've bought some runner bean seeds, and Martin and Emma Rowland, two of my customers who have now become friends, gave me some courgette plants. Then there is spinach, more leeks, and parsnips – so many things to plant. What a lark this gardening is.

I wave to the Humphreys, sitting on their bench in the sun. They look odd, somehow bleached, but it's only because they're wearing identical white tunics or some kind of robe, sort of Gandi-ish. Lord knows what trunk they came out of, or what country they were bought in, but they do look cool and comfortable.

They wave back so that I know they're alive – they sit so motionless sometimes that I'm not quite sure – then I rush up to my cold frame. To my horror, the lettuce plants are gone. I stand staring, frozen to the spot. Has someone vandalised them in the night? I look closer. They've not been pulled out by the roots, it's just the tops that are missing. The leaves, the whole plant, gone.

I'm dazed, stunned, not knowing how to react to this wholly unexpected disaster as I can't begin to understand how it happened. Edna and Hector appear at the gate. Hector says, 'You look distressed, maid. Is something wrong?'

'My lettuce,' I cry. 'All gone.'

They come through the gate and peer into the cold frame, then nod sagely. 'Rabbits,' Edna says.

'Plenty of them around this year,' Hector adds.

'Rabbits? They ate my lettuce? All of it?'

Hector points to some little black things that look like small marbles. 'You see? Rabbits for sure.'

'But how did they get in?' Then I remember, 'I left the top off last night but it was so warm . . .' my voice trails off sadly.

'It's not very high, you see, dear,' Edna says as if explaining things to a child.

'Quite easy for a bunny to jump over,' Hector agrees.

A *bunny*? He calls that creature which ate my prized lettuces a *bunny*? I'm so crestfallen that suddenly Edna and Hector are on either side of me, holding on to my arms and steering me out of the gate, through their front garden and into their vast kitchen.

'A cup of tea is what you need,' Edna says as she fills an old brown teapot with an even older kettle which has been boiling on an ancient Aga. 'Nice old-fashioned ordinary tea.' I'm relieved at this. Though I often drink various herbal teas myself sometimes at home, the kind Edna makes are really off the wall. I've never heard of half the herbs she uses. Most of the time they are completely heavenly but at other times the taste is either bitter or rusty, like drinking water that's been sitting in an old iron trough for a decade or two. 'I like to experiment with my brews,' she's said to me more than once. 'I'm always trying something new.' My pioneer spirit does respond to Edna's concoctions and I usually enjoy them, but after rabbits have eaten all your lettuce plants, a good strong cup of PG Tips is just what you need.

Though it's still warm and sunny outside, it's cold inside despite the Aga in the kitchen. The long corridor leading to the other rooms is lined with books. Some are in massive old wooden bookcases but many more are on the floor, piled in great rows lining each side of the hallway. Some are ancient hardbacks, others have shiny new covers that look as if they came out recently. There are paperbacks too, all sizes and shapes. All the books look well read.

The floors in both the corridor and the kitchen are slate, and the few wool rugs lying about in the kitchen look lethal, frayed and loose, an invitation to be tripped over. They take turns fussing over me, bringing me tea and digestive biscuits from a tin, and I get this weird feeling that I'm the doddering one and they're the carers, when it should be the other way around.

I feel much cheerier after tea with the Humphreys and go back to my garden. At least the peas are beginning to come up, which is something. The onion sets were dug up a second time, this time by pigeons, Hector told me. He'd seen them on my garden and ran to shoo them away but it was too late. I shudder to think of Hector running anywhere. I hope the birds stay away, not only for my sake but for his and Edna's.

As I leave by the other gate, I see not one rabbit but two staring at me from the other side of the field. I used to love watching the little creatures playing in the meadows in the evening. First blackbirds, then rabbits – once friends, now enemies – how ambivalent nature is, I'm beginning to realise!

I make a face at those cheeky predators, stick my tongue out in a half playful, half serious gesture. Poor things, I chide myself, a rabbit's got to do what a rabbit's got to do. But then again, my poor lettuce. Oh dear, who ever thought gardening would be such a battle? I go home wondering what other hitherto beloved little furry or feathered creature will turn out to be another Enemy of the Allotment.

It's gratifying how sympathetic all my customers are about the rabbits. Losing not just one lettuce plant but the whole lot is certainly discouraging, as all the gardeners amongst my customers agree.

My colleagues are less inclined to sympathy. 'A garden's hard work, bird,' Susie says, 'and if you will insist on growing, when there be loads of food in shops, you'll find they be lots more setbacks yet, believe me.'

Eddie goes a step further. Creeping up on me in the

St Geraint post office, he shouts, 'Catch, Tessa!' The next thing I know he's thrown what I think is a pale green ball at me but as I catch it, I see it's an iceberg lettuce from the Spar shop, still wrapped in plastic.

He grins. 'I was going to get to your allotment, stick the lettuce in your garden, but I got up too late this morning. T'would've been a right laugh, seeing your face.'

I can't help grinning back at him as I juggle the lettuce in one hand, some post I'm sorting in the other. 'But you wouldn't have seen my face when I found the lettuce, Eddie.'

'Mebbe not, but I'd have seen it as you told us next day how one sturdy lettuce plant survived the rabbits against all odds.'

I laugh. I know he's teasing me but sometimes I wonder just how naïve and gullible they think I am about country matters.

Later, I'm up at Poldowe, the village above Morranport, talking to a fiery middle-aged woman named Ginger. It's not a nickname either; apparently her parents were great Fred Astaire and Ginger Rogers fans and she was conceived after a night at one of their films. Or so she told me once with a rueful grin. Her hair isn't ginger but brown with silvery grey streaks and she wears it pulled back in a ponytail high on top of her head, which makes her look like a high-spirited pony. Her manner is gingery, though. Widowed at an early age – her husband was a fisherman who died at sea many years ago – she raised their two kids on her own and then had a series of live-in partners but none of them lasted more than a year or two, according to local history. The story goes that there was nothing wrong with them that the locals could see, they just couldn't live up to her husband. The children are gone now, neither lad became a fisherman but live way Up Country somewhere.

Ginger talks tough and looks tough, but I have a feeling it

hides something vulnerable and soft inside her. I don't often see her as she works in Truro as a receptionist in a dentist's office, but today she's home and comes to the door for her post. 'Hey, Tessa,' she says, taking her mail. 'Nell down at the Morranport post office says the rabbits ate all your lettuce plants.'

'Goodness, word gets round! I only mentioned it to Nell because she asked how my garden was growing.'

Ginger, dressed in jeans and a faded denim shirt, puts her hand in her back pocket and extracts a rather squashed-looking packet which she thrusts into my hand. 'Here, take these,' she says gruffly. 'I bought 'em last year but never got around to planting them in my tiny patch. You might as well have 'em.'

I take a look. It's a packet of lettuce seeds. Before I can thank her she says hurriedly, 'Not too late, to try again. Shouldn't give up, y'know. Keep trying.'

She's shut the door and I haven't been able to get in a heart-felt thank you.

It's not until the next day that I'm back at the Yellands' cottage again. Strongly resisting stealing any more garlic mustard, or for that matter his dandelion leaves and hawthorn shoots, I knock at the door clutching a half dozen eggs. I'm feeling so guilty for foraging in their garden without permission that I'm giving the Yellands some of my precious eggs. The hens are all starting to lay again which is brilliant, but we seem to be eating as many as they lay. I use them in everything – quiches, cakes, Spanish omelettes, Italian frittatas – you name it, I've probably put eggs in it. I've had to curb myself to have enough to give away.

Mr Yelland opens the door, pipe in his mouth. I say, 'These are for you and Mrs Yelland, for giving me the garlic mustard the other day.' He looks a bit bemused, as if wondering how two paltry leaves warranted a half dozen fresh, free-range eggs. Perhaps he didn't see me stuff the rest into my bag, before he came out. I'll never know.

'By the way,' he says now. 'Thanks for putting us on to that mustard stuff. The missus has been using it in her Oxo gravy for the Sunday roast, and 'tis smashing, it is. Isn't that right, Mrs Yelland?'

She appears beside him, as if waiting for his call, 'Oh yes, it's so flavoursome. I wish we had more of it growing.'

So much for me cadging some more from them, as was on my hidden agenda. I haven't been able to find another cache of it, not so far, anyway.

I'm hoping I can get away before he remembers the roses, but no such luck. 'Mrs Hainsworth, now tell me, what is your favourite rose? Or do you have several favourites?'

I'm tempted to ask him again to call me Tessa, especially as we now seem to be rose buddies, but the time I did before he seemed offended so I guess I'd better let it go. Really, they seem to live in a 1950s' time warp, these two.

I say, 'Oh, uh, I love climbing roses.' I never had time to google roses so I can't think of anything else to say. This seems to satisfy him though.

'Ah yes. Climbing roses. Come out in the back garden, I've got a prize one there. It's called Bright Fire and is about to come into bloom. Look at all those buds! It's a heavy spring bloomer as I'm sure you know.'

He shows me some of his other roses, his pipe juddering up and down at the side of his mouth as he speaks. Mrs Yelland, in her usual pristine apron, follows us about, beaming.

As I leave Mr Yelland says, 'Mrs Hainsworth, I wonder if you could do us a favour. When we first moved here, we had a daily newspaper delivery but that has since been stopped. Mrs Yelland and I feel quite deprived without the local paper.

Would it be too inconvenient if you picked one up for us every day and delivered it with our post? We could take George, of course, but he's getting on now and we don't like to take him out too often.'

George? Who's George? I'm about to ask when I see that the Yellands have turned away from me and are looking fondly at their old car which has been taken out of the garage, surrounded by chamois cloths and other equipment indicating it is in the middle of being lovingly cleaned and polished. I've seen it before and it certainly is ancient, an old Morris Minor Traveller, a tiny white estate car with wooden window frames. George is in immaculate condition.

Mr Yelland turns back to me. 'We would pay you in advance for the newspapers, of course, and add something for your trouble.'

'Goodness, of course I'll do it, no problem at all, but I wouldn't hear of accepting anything but the price of the newspaper. And no need to give it to me in advance.'

The look of gratitude on their faces is matched by their effusive thanks which I brush away quickly. As a matter of fact, the Yellands aren't the only couple I deliver goods for. So many local services have stopped – milk and newspaper deliveries, the fishmonger calling once a week – that many people, especially the elderly or those without vehicles, feel cut off. I take a few pints of milk every week to more than one customer, and often I deliver fresh vegetables to folk without transport. As one of them said, some things you can stock up with but others need to be fresh.

As social services become scarcer and scarcer, I know I'm not the only postal deliverer who has taken on the mantle of a social worker. Just recently I've had to change the bandages on a woman with a sprained ankle, help a pensioner down his stairs when his hip went 'wonky' and he couldn't get down, and chase a wasp from the kitchen of a woman who was highly allergic to the stings.

In fact I'm going now to a woman called Delia Davenport, and taking, along with her post, a warm, freshly baked Cornish pasty that someone in Poldowe had made that morning. 'I did an extra for poor Delia,' the woman said. 'I know she do love her pasties.'

Delia, though an octogenarian, is unlike many of the other tough old octogenarians I deliver to who live independent and active lives. Though Delia lives alone in one of the villages, she's fragile, in delicate health, and never leaves her house. Her neighbours think there's nothing terribly wrong physically with her, but that she just gave up on life when her husband died ten years ago. Now she just sits, watches television, and relies on the neighbours to do her shopping, and Meals-on-Wheels to provide a hot dinner. And on her postie to light a fire for her every morning. It started last autumn, when Delia had a little fall getting her tiny bucket of coal into the house to start her morning fire. Though the house has storage heaters, Delia likes, and needs, her small coal fire every day but after the fall, has been afraid to light it. I volunteered one day as I was delivering her post and I've carried on doing it. Like the neighbours, I don't mind helping out. Delia's self-imposed helplessness is so sweet-natured that I can't help but like her.

She's sitting in her armchair as I come in, greeting me with her wispy smile. She looks old, older even than Edna Humphrey. 'Morning, Delia,' I say as I take the empty coal bucket, fill it up from the supply at the back of the house and begin to light the fire. 'You've got a fresh pasty for your dinner today.'

The coal bucket hardly holds much but it's enough to keep the fire glowing in the tiny fireplace all day. It's so warm now it's not needed at all, but Delia likes it burning winter and summer. 'It's the comfort of it,' she told me once. 'Warms the heart as well as the hands and feet.'

Delia is so delighted with the pasty that she writes a little note then and there, asking me to give it to the pasty baker when next I see her. Then she says, 'Oh, and I wonder, could you please give this newspaper clipping to Sally down the road? There's a photo of her little boy in the local paper, on a school trip, and I know she'd like an extra copy.' She hands me a carefully cut out photo then spends another five minutes looking for an envelope to put it in. I take it and promise to pass it on.

As I leave I think how this job has escalated since I started. As my customers have got to know me, they've begun to trust me, and for many I'm not only a confidante but someone they can rely on for help if necessary. I get asked both big or little questions folk might once have asked a doctor, in the days when home visits were a norm, or there are requests to buy items they'd get from the tiny village shops if so many hadn't closed.

I remember how in London I never even knew my postman's name and saw him only occasionally, fleetingly, on a rare Saturday. Yet all over rural England there are others like me, performing all those services that have sadly been abandoned as we plunge into a frantic modern world. This is, I think, the best part of my job, getting to know my customers, giving help when I can, and having the time and space to be able to do it.

Chapter 3

Snakes and ladders

A snake has entered our household. If there's one creature in the animal world I cannot bear, it's a snake.

'Elvis is a reptile, not an animal,' Will says.

'Besides,' Amy adds, 'You've gone off rabbits after they ate your lettuce.' She doesn't much like snakes either but she's siding with her brother on this one. Solidarity between siblings, it's the only way to outwit the parents.

'You know I haven't gone off rabbits, I adore them. I was only cross that day when all my lettuces were eaten in one night. It's nature. It was my fault for not protecting my plants. I've learned my lesson now.'

'You'll get used to Elvis,' Will says philosophically and wanders off to play with his pet.

I'll never get used to snakes, I think disconsolately. I not only can't bear snakes, I also have an irrational fear of them. I mentioned it to my doctor once, years ago just in passing while talking about other things, telling him about this fear.

His answer didn't exactly inspire confidence. 'It's not irrational, Tessa. The world is full of poisonous snakes that kill
people. Your fear is perfectly rational.' Thanks, I thought to
myself, that's a big help!

How did I let myself get talked into this? It all began when
Will started saving his pocket money and doing extra jobs
around the house to buy his 'very own pet'. Ben and I thought
it was a good idea; it would give him a sense of responsibility,
looking after what I assumed would be a small furry creature.
We have Jake, of course, but our dear Spaniel is a family pet,
not Will's alone. So we agreed.

Will spent hours on the Internet, researching various sites
to find the kind of pet he wanted most. Unfortunately, the
one he fell in love with was not a cute fuzzy kitten, or a tiny
sweet bunny, but a snake.

I begged, pleaded, bribed. All to no avail. Will stood his
ground. 'You promised I could choose my own pet,' he said
over and over.

So I had to give in. 'All right, Will, but only on the proviso
that you assume full responsibility for it. I want nothing to do
with it, ever.'

Off we trotted to a garden centre which is also a reptile
centre. I tried not to run screaming from the place as we
kneeled down in between twenty odd plastic boxes the size of
a sandwich. The 'snake lady' took out one reptile at a time to
introduce Will to the various hatchlings while I looked about
for the nearest exit should one of them escape and begin slithering towards me. All the hatchlings looked horrifically alike
to me, but Will knew immediately which one was special, the
best looking, the best personality, the one that would live up
to its name.

'This is the one,' he said proudly, holding up this six inch
long horror. 'This is the king. I'm going to call him Elvis.'

Thinking of that day, the day a snake entered our house-hold, I say to Ben as we're preparing dinner together, 'Why did I agree to it? Why did I ever permit it?'

Ben carries on chopping onions. He's heard me say this a dozen times since Elvis became ensconced in his glass cage, called a vivarium I soon learn, in Will's bedroom.

'We agreed because in the end we had to. We couldn't persuade him that a rabbit or guinea pig or even a rat might be better, if he wanted a pet in his room.'

I shudder. At least I've been spared a rat. But my fear of snakes is so ingrained that even a horrid rat would have been better than Elvis. I peek through the door of Will's bedroom, watch him as he takes his baby snake out of its home, holds and strokes it. The look on his face is rapturous, and despite the fact that even seeing it from this distance makes me shudder, I'm glad my son has his snake.

The next day I'm on my walking round in Morranport, stop-ping first at the tiny post office/shop perched on the edge of the sea. The tide is out and the few boats anchored on the sand look as if they're snoozing in the sun. Little water birds are pecking amongst the rock pools and so are a few toddlers, their mums and dads fondly hovering over them. You can tell these are second homers from their brand new pink, green and blue polka-dotted Wellington boots, their smart pushchairs and designer clothes. Most likely they own one of the sweet Georgian fishermen's cottages just up the road, the ones with the wrought-iron balconies, facing the sea. All of them are owned by out-of-towners now, used only for holidays. They were packed and bustling over Easter which has just passed, and it was a joy to see the houses come to life for a brief week or two. A few of them will be occupied off and on now throughout the summer, by couples who are either childless or whose children are still under school age. In winter it's a different scene and it saddens me to see the houses empty and desolate, the soul gone out of them.

Nell, the perky eighty-something-year-old who runs the shop and post office, greets me with a huge grin. 'You look like the Cheshire Cat,' I say.

Her smile gets wider. While Delia at the same age looks over ninety, Nell looks no more than sixty. Delia also acts how one used to expect old people to act, while Nell refuses to be pigeonholed as a pensioner. How weird this age thing is, I think not for the first time since I became a postwoman. I adore Nell, as does everyone, especially the men of all ages who know her. Though she doesn't suffer fools and gives short shrift to anyone she thinks deserves it, she's got a warm heart despite her sometimes gruff manner.

'You'd be grinning too, my maid, if you'd just sold out of all your kiddies' beach toys. They was all a'standing there waiting for me to open up the shop, they was that keen. Bought fishing nets, balls, toy boats, the lot. And you be telling me I shouldn't be grinning?'

I start to protest that I never said anything of the sort then remember that's just Nell's way of speaking, often ending sentences on a challenge. I shake my head to indicate that she should go on.

'Made all me day's profits in ten minutes,' she points through the window at the family outside. The two little ones are clutching nets on sticks and poking them into rock pools. 'Me favourite folk from Up Country are parents who spend far too much money on their spoiled offspring, so long as they spend it in my shop.' She gives me a fierce look, 'And I reckon now you be telling me I be getting too consumer-oriented?'

I laugh. 'Nell, I wouldn't dream of telling you anything like that.'

She offers me a cup of tea from the kettle in the back of

the post office and I accept. Though sunny, there's a chilly breeze outside. The sea looks ruffled, rather like Nell's hair which is thick and white, standing up all over her head. That and her solid, no-nonsense bosom, huge on her rather small frame, are her most prominent features, along with the clothes she wears – ordinary old cord jeans topped with a marvellous array of jumpers, all vividly coloured, form-fitting and usually of some kind of fuzzy material, mohair, angora, or indescribable home-knitted wear.

As I take my post bag and get ready to go, Nell asks, 'So how's the snake then? Has Will brought it home?'

I groan. 'Yep, two days ago. Its name is Elvis. Because he's The King, like Elvis was. Elvis, King of Snakes.'

Nell looks dreamy. 'Good name, that. I did fancy Elvis something fierce, when I was a girl.' She sighs then pulls herself together. 'So what d'you feed it? What do they eat?'

'Oh Nell, it's awful! It has to be fed mice. Tiny newborn baby mice, poor hairless things, they look like pink jelly babies. We have a bag of them in our freezer next to the ice trays. And it gets worse. As the snake gets bigger, so do the mice. There will be the fluffies next, a bit bigger, with hair. Ugh! Later it'll be big mice or small rats. All in my freezer.'

Nell grimaces, 'Well, my handsome, mebbe you could write a recipe book, one of them new-fangled ones for folk who like to try something different. How to use leftover snake food. Mice mince, stuffed mouse.' She cackles away, delighted with her joke.

With a slight shudder I say, 'Nothing about snakes makes me laugh.'

'So you still be nervous of the creature, even though you've seen your boy handling it? Can't be that frightening, can it? 'Tis only a baby, you said.'

'It still gives me the creeps. I've tried to rationalise the whole thing, tell myself logically it's only tiny, can't hurt me, can't get out of the cage, but I'm still terrified. I've got a snake phobia, not uncommon apparently.'

'Well, mebbe having your own snake in your own house will cure it once and for all. Though I reckon you be telling me now that I don't know what I'm talking about.'

'It hasn't cured me yet, Nell, but you're right, maybe it will. I can hardly bring myself to go into Will's room but I take a deep breath, tell myself it's only a poor harmless creature, and plunge in there. I'm determined to get over this.'

'Good luck to you then, my lover.'

Walking along the seafront is a joy, as usual. The breeze has not turned into a howling gale as predicted but is gently being warmed by the sun. I pass the happy little family but they're not so happy now, the toddlers are squabbling and throwing sand at each other and their parents are trying to reason with them, explain why the oldest child should not throw things back at her younger brother even though he started it. You can tell the explanations don't mean a thing to the little ones: they keep slinging sand even as the parents talk and plead.

Happy holidays, I think as I smile to them as I walk past. They don't even notice me, they look too fraught. God help them if it starts to rain for a week, as it can do at times. But not today. I saunter along, delivering my post, and because it's just that kind of day, I stop for a cold drink at the old stone house at the end of the seafront, one perched overlooking the sea. It's the home of another older couple, Archie and Jennifer Grenville. Though a retired teacher, Archie comes from a couple of generations of fishermen and this house, once a fisherman's cottage, has been in his family for decades. Jennifer is upstairs having a lie-in, Archie tells me. 'She had a restless night, couldn't sleep.' I follow him into the kitchen, warm and cosy, and with a window overlooking the sea. Around the walls are Jennifer's paintings; she's a talented artist, doing mostly portraits. I accept a glass of apple juice and sit down at the table with Archie for a few moments. Books cover it, some opened, some with pages marked with Post-it Notes. He's an amateur historian and knows everything there is about Cornish life both past and present.

After he's handed me the drink he says, 'Has your son brought the snake home yet?'

'Goodness, Nell just asked me the same thing.' I'm feeling embarrassed. Have I been obsessing over this snake to everyone? No, I remember, I only mentioned it to a couple of people, but the rural grapevine is in full growth as usual. I tell him what I told Nell, about my phobia. 'It's only a harmless corn snake,' I finish. 'But that doesn't make me like it more.'

Archie nods, 'Snakes are rare in Cornwall, but we do have some. There's the adder, of course, and the snakes in legend. All those pre-Christian sites were known as dragons' dens, or serpents' lairs. And there's the legend of St Michael slaying the poisonous serpent on St Michael's Mount. The story goes that he put great stones on the body of the huge reptile and that's how the stone circles got there.'

'Well, thank God for St Michael then. A poisonous serpent on my rounds is just what I need.'

Archie smiles, 'And then there's the Morgawr.'

'The what?'

'The Morgawr. Haven't you heard of him? The name means "sea giant" in Cornish. He's the giant sea serpent of many local legends.'

'You mean like our own Cornish Loch Ness monster?'

He nods, 'There have been many sightings around Falmouth Bay, you know. The first recorded one was in 1876 when a fisherman claimed to have caught a twenty-foot sea serpent. The more recent eye-witness accounts describe a great prehistoric snake rearing out of the sea.'

I make a face. 'Yuck. Could put you off swimming for life.'

'Poor serpent, he's blamed for everything, or has been in the past. Bad luck, bad weather, bad catches when the boats go out.'

I start to leave, 'Well, it makes little Elvis seem harmless anyway.'

I can't get away just yet though. Archie, the Cornish historian, is still talking and I love his stories. He's told me so many about local people both past and present, as well as the myths and legends of the county. 'Snakes were also thought to slither under the earth in Celtic times, symbols of the mysterious forces of the underworld,' he begins.

'Oh dear. Prehistoric serpents in the sea I can just about cope with since I'm not a fisherman and don't have to go out on boats every day. But snakes slithering under my feet as I walk? No thanks, Archie. I don't want to hear another thing.' I grin then go on, 'Just teasing, you know I love your stories. But I've got to get on now. Give my love to Jennifer.'

Archie walks me to the door. Before I leave I ask him about his godson Wayne who has just joined the crew of the Falmouth lifeboat. Wayne's a fisherman and works on one of the big boats now as his father had to give up fishing; there's no money in it anymore for the little boats. The couple are like second parents to the lad and are as close to them as any son. Proud though Archie and Jennifer are of Wayne volunteering to be on the lifeboat crew, I know they worry. It's a dangerous job.

'Wayne's fine. He had his first call out the other day, a yacht in trouble. They took out the inshore lifeboat.'

Archie has told me that the inshore lifeboat is called out for rescues closer to shore as the name suggests. It's a big inflatable boat that rights itself if it tips over. With more and more pleasure craft out on the seas these days, the inshore lifeboat is used often. The all-weather lifeboat is bigger, can hold up to thirty survivors, and is used in gales and storms, whatever the weather to help those in trouble further out to sea. The boats are manned by volunteers and I'm in complete awe of all those who risk their own lives to save those of strangers. I've always had a lot of time for the RNLI, the Royal National Lifeboat Institute, but even more now after talking to Archie and Jennifer, learning about the Falmouth Station.

The rest of the day passes smoothly. As usual I succumb to the short cuts taught to me by the other posties who have been doing the job for years, the short cuts that save time and a great deal of effort. Since there are sections of the route on the walking rounds which entail climbing up and down long drives to private estates and walking through hilly gardens, I straddle hedges, cut across tennis courts and climb over walls to save myself time and energy. These antics are not appreciated by the Royal Mail because of health and safety implications, but a blind eye is usually turned as it gets the job done quicker. However, every postie knows that no compensation would be given if an accident happened when she was not following the correct procedure.

Trying to be a good little postie, I did try to do it properly at first, but a few wet and rainy walking rounds quickly changed my mind, and I now take the short cuts without a second thought. In the van too, I've learned to use every tiny back lane in south Cornwall, which is why I'm one of the world's ace reversers now.

Another trick I've learned is how to cope with loo stops. This was a bit of a pain when I started, as I soon realised. For the chaps it was no problem, they could hide behind a hedgerow for a quick pee but for me it meant taking a ten-minute diversion in a van, or a long hike of fifteen to twenty minutes back to the village, just to find a public loo. So I had to learn to start the day with half the amount of tea I was used to and then make sure I had a loo stop at the sorting office before setting off. Finally, I've learned the whereabouts of every building site and house that have extensive renovations going on – in an emergency, the workmen can always be relied upon to let me use their loo if I'm caught short.

After Morranport I go to St Geraint where Margaret, who runs the post office there, asks me how I'm getting on with the new snake in the house. I know I never mentioned Elvis to Margaret either, but by telling one or two people, most of south Cornwall seems to know within twenty-four hours. What is endearing to me is how open and up front everyone is about it. The news isn't whispered, no one pretends they're not going to tell everyone else and nearly everyone is sure that you'll be delighted to know that word of your business has got around so satisfactorily.

Well, maybe not quite endearing. When I get back to St Geraint, Eddie is behind the counter with Margaret. It's barely large enough for two let alone three, so I only stay briefly to check out my rounds for the next few days and have a quick chat with a mate of mine, Harry, who has come in to buy a newspaper.

I'm about to leave when Eddie, passing by, says, 'Hold on a minute, Tessa. What's that on your foot? Stop, you're treading on it!'

I look down to see my foot about to step on a snake nearly a metre long. 'Aaargghhh!' My scream is heard throughout the shop and the customers freeze. All Archie's tales of giant sea serpents and snakes slithering under the earth crowd my imagination as I leap away from the snake and hide behind Harry who came rushing up to me when he heard me cry out. He looks at the snake, at me, then back at Margaret and Eddie.

I'm still shaking. 'Get it away please,' I mutter. I can't bear to even look at it again.

Margaret shrugs her shoulders at Harry and shakes her head. 'Nothing to do with me. Ask Eddie.'

Eddie says sheepishly, 'It's only a joke.'

I say, 'Joke or not, Eddie, please get it out of here, you know how I feel about snakes.'

Now all three are looking at me. Harry says, 'Tessa, it's not real. It's made of rubber or something.' He picks it up to show me.

It looks so alive that I leap away and bump hard into Eddie who says, 'Sorry, maid, 'twas only a bit of fun. Belongs to a mate of mine. He went as a snake charmer to a Halloween party last year. Looks real, don't it?'

While I try to calm my pounding heartbeat, Eddie takes the snake around the shop to show admiring customers. 'Well, I never seen nuthin' so life-like,' says one, and 'You be a right tease, Eddie me handsome,' sniggers another.

Finally Eddie, seeing my pale face, says, 'Sorry, my bird, I'm truly sorry. 'Twas only a joke. Didn't know you'd take it to heart like that.'

I take a deep breath, 'That's okay, Eddie.' I give him a wobbly grin.

Harry says, 'Tessa, do you have time to share a pot of tea? You look like you could do with one. Besides, I haven't seen you for a proper talk for ages.'

There's only one small table outside but there's no one at it. It's warm enough to sit in the sun so I plop down while Harry goes inside to order. 'I feel a bit of fool, making such a spectacle of myself,' I say with a rueful grin, when Harry returns. 'But goodness, that thing looked real.'

He grins back. 'Best entertainment I've had all week. I wish Charlie could have seen it.'

Charlie is Harry's partner, the son of a Cornish fisherman. Harry, like me, had a high-powered and stressful job in London. He worked at one of the top accountancies in the country and moved here around the same time I did. Charlie's parents, fisherfolk all their lives, were more upset about Charlie giving up the sea than they were about the fact that he is gay, but they've come around now. Charlie is doing well selling his artworks based on the sea and the Cornish landscape, while Harry has settled into a small accountant's office in St Geraint.

We watch a couple of cormorants diving down into the blue-green water of the undulating sea. It's not long before our tea is brought out by Millie and Geoff, the owners of the café. Millie carries the brown pot of tea and Geoff the cups and saucers, and they stop to talk to us for some time. Geoff in fact, after about five minutes or so, pulls up a seat at our table, and before long Millie joins him.

We catch up on all our news and goings-on then Millie says, 'There now, Geoff, fancy us sitting here cavorting with the customers. They be wanting to talk on their own now.'

We assure them that we're happy to share our table but Millie takes Geoff off and goes back into the shop, coming back almost at once with some saffron cakes she has just baked.

The sea is wrinkly today, tiny delicate ruffles that hardly move the boat just sailing out past the harbour. Seabirds fly and call to each other, suddenly diving down to snatch a small fish. The sky, reflecting the sea, is ruffled too with little urchin clouds speckling it, like a dog's fur ruffled the wrong way around. The sun's warmth is soporific. I could fall asleep sitting here, but I rouse myself to ask Harry about Charlie's new art gallery which he's opening soon to show not only his own art work but also that of other Cornish artists and craftsmen and women. It's going to be in Poldowe, where Charlie is renting some space which used to be a grocery store until it could no longer compete with the supermarkets.

'We're having a big opening in a month's time,' Harry says. 'Loads of my old friends from London are coming.'

'Let me know the date and I'll make sure Annie is here that weekend. She can spread the word about Charlie's talent to all her colleagues at the BBC.'

'How is Annie? I'd love to see her again. Since she's got involved with that Cornish bloke I've hardly seen her.'

Harry met Annie, my dearest London friend, a few months ago when she was visiting us and they discovered they had actually met before, a year or two earlier in London. Last summer at the Royal Cornwall Show Annie met Pete, an agricultural merchant, and on her Cornish weekends she spends most of her time with him.

'I don't see Annie as often either these days,' I tell Harry. 'She and Pete are quite the item. If she's not in Cornwall, he's in London.'

'Well, tell her to call around to see me and Charlie. She can bring her man, he seems a nice guy. I've met him now and again at the pub in his village, it's one of our favourites.'

We leave soon afterwards. As Harry says goodbye to Millie and Geoff, I can't help watching him. He's enormously good-looking and charismatic, especially when he smiles. There have been plenty of young women in St Geraint who have sighed over Harry and bemoaned the fact that he's gay. As he walks towards his office I notice how he's changed since moving to Cornwall, how relaxed he looks these days, how contented. It affects all of us, I think. Maybe you have be from Up Country to realise what extraordinary changes this place can make in a person.

By the time I get to the allotment that afternoon, my car is filled with courgette, runner bean and broad bean plants that

my customers have given me. Knowing I've begun my very
first attempt at vegetable growing, my customers have been
vying with each other to see who can offer me the most. Their
kindness as usual overwhelms me. So does their produce, actually, as I have far too much and end up trying to offload it on
others. It's like the old system of bartering. Maybe one day we
can all live like this and not need money at all. What bliss that
would be!

I park my car by the gate near the road but don't have time
to unload my plants before Hector is standing in front of me
waving his arms like a demented scarecrow with his straw hat
perched on his bald head, baggy trousers and a yellowing white
dinner shirt which must have been purchased around 1949.

'Stop, maid, do stop, I say!' He's got an old cane which he
seldom uses but he's waving it at me now.

I jump out of the car and he's so excited he nearly
thumps me with it. 'Steady on, Hector. What's the matter? Is
it Edna?'

He gives me a perplexed look as if to say, Now why should
I be worried about her? and shouts, 'No, no, it's the Venerable
Bede! Oh do come quickly, Tessa.'

The Venerable Bede was an Anglo-Saxon monk, born around
673 AD who lived in the wilds of Northumbria in monasteries
at Wearmouth and Jarrow. He wrote an Ecclesiastical History
of the English People and his tomb is in Durham Cathedral,
or so Edna told me ages ago. However the Venerable Bede
Hector is referring to at this moment is not a dead monk but
a live cat. An ancient, fluffy grey cat that lives in winter on
Edna and Hector's bed, coming downstairs only to eat, go
outside for a few minutes to do his business, and then return
to bed. One day every year, either in spring or summer,
depending on the weather, the Venerable Bede (even the
villagers refer to him by his full name), deigns to come outdoors

and if all is to his liking, he then stays either under the garden bench until late autumn, or in the front garden.

I am now filled with foreboding. Hector is hassling me to hurry. Has the Venerable Bede keeled over from too much fresh air and dropped dead? Has he been hit by a car? I know the Humphreys have had him for ever; in cat age he is even older than they are.

Hector is too breathless to answer my questions and I'm now worried that he's the one who will incur sudden death. 'Hector, do slow down. Whatever has happened, I'll deal with it. Do stay calm, please.' Once again I get that look as if I'm the one that's gone loopy.

By now we've made it to the front garden where to my horror I see Edna halfway up a short ladder propped dangerously against the old pear tree that stands near the house. On a fat limb just above the top of the ladder sits the Venerable Bede, his venerable, grey, scruffy tail waving majestically back and forth.

I did ask the Humphreys once why they named a cat after a long dead monk but, as with everything else, they were vague in their answers. 'The Venerable Bede once made a brief visit to Lindisfarne, the Holy Island, in the seventh century,' Hector said by way of explanation. Edna had nodded and added, 'And we were there in the twentieth.' End of story. They both beamed at me as if I had a clue what they were on about. That's what always happened when you asked either one of them a question.

Right now I'm not thinking of how the cat came to be named after a monk but how I'm going to get to Edna before she kills herself. She has climbed up another step and is wobbling precariously. The ladder is as ancient as Edna herself, the cat and the pear tree. The rungs are rotting and even as I watch the one she is on starts to splinter. I rush to catch her but she somehow manages to get down to the rung below, shaking me off as if I were an annoying fly.

'Never mind me, dear, just help poor old Beedy.' Despite her cool I know she's distraught, she hardly ever uses a nickname for the cat. She goes on, 'Hector and I tried but he is just beyond our reach. You're much taller than we are.'

She steps down the last rung. The ladder has only four. They both look at me expectantly. I look at the sad, old ladder. Not even the first rung would take my weight which is quite normal for my medium height. It's a wonder Edna got up two rungs without the whole thing collapsing, even though she's light as a butterfly. She looks like one today too, a Red Admiral perhaps with the blowsy red and black Chinese-style outfit she's wearing. It comes down to her ankles which are shod in plain worn green wellies. I shudder when I think of every health and safety rule she's broken – that long dress, a rotten ladder so unevenly propped that even now as she steps off it topples over and nearly hits Hector over the head. Her owl-like glasses have fallen off and I grabbed them before she can tread on them.

Someone has to take these two in line. It's a wonder they've survived all this time. I grab the ladder before it knocks Hector flying and with the other hand I reach out to steady Edna. The look she gives me is similar to Hector's when I called out to him to stop rushing and calm down.

Edna says, 'I nearly had him. Oh the poor Venerable Bede. Look at him, terrified out of his dear pussycat wits.'

We all look at the cat. His emerald eyes are glaring at us, his grey fur standing all over his head like the ghost of a mad monk. He looks far more cross than frightened.

'Maybe if we leave him alone for a time he'll come down on his own. He's not that high up,' I suggest.

Edna and Hector look at me with exactly the same expression as their cat. Hector says, 'Maid, for a cat as old as the Venerable Bede, it is very high indeed. He is well over twenty years old.'

I agree that's pretty old for a cat. 'How did he get up there in the first place?'

'Oh my dear, that's just what Hector and I have been asking ourselves. He decided to go out today for the first time and before we knew it, he was up the tree. He hasn't done that for years.'

Hector mutters, 'Must have been feeling frisky. Beautiful day like today, spring, sun, rush of hormones, that kind of thing.'

I look up at the cat. Hormones? That skeletal, funny-looking thing with clumps of hair sticking out, his age showing in his white whiskery face, the patches where his once luxurious grey fur has thinned. But I keep quiet. Maybe Cornish tomcats are randy long into advanced old age.

Edna looks at Hector. 'I think we should call the fire department.'

He nods. 'That's what we were about to do when Hector heard you arrive.'

I say, 'Then why were you halfway up that ladder?'

She shrugs that little incident away, 'We decided to try the ladder first. *Then* we were going to call the fire brigade.'

I look up at the cat again. Pear blossom has covered the Venerable Bede with a cloak of white petals. I say, 'Do you have any other ladders?'

'Yes, maid, of course. Many more. But this seemed the right size.'

'It might be, but the rungs won't take my weight.' I point to the broken one. 'It barely took Edna's.'

She says to Hector, 'I told you I was putting on weight.'

I ignore this and say, 'So where are these other ladders? If we can find a decent one, I'm sure I can get Venerable Bede down.'

'*The* Venerable Bede,' Hector corrects me. 'That was always his full title, that's the way he's referred to. Of course we're so familiar with his namesake that sometimes, not often I assure you, we just say Bede, which is fine now and again. But when you use Venerable, you should always put *the* in front as the full title.'

I can't believe I'm having this bizarre conversation. Going around the house, Edna and Hector lead me into an old wooden shed with a door half broken and hanging off. 'This is where the ladders are kept,' Hector says.

I've never seen so many. They're all jumbled, criss-crossing each other like that children's game of Pick Up Sticks. It looks like every ladder used since Hector's father's time has been saved and stored in here.

Edna beams at me, 'Take your pick, my dear.' She says it grandly, as if offering me an Aladdin's cave of treasure, but all of them are extremely old wooden ones, most with broken rungs and rotting frames. I've never seen anything so lethal in my life.

The couple are looking at me hopefully. 'Well, maid, which one suits you best?' Hector says. Then, gallantly, 'I'll carry it for you over to the pear tree.'

'No!' I holler. Then, more quietly, 'Uh, no thank you, Hector. The thing is, you see, these won't do. In fact, they're dangerous. Look at the broken rungs. You really need to get rid of the whole lot.'

Both give me a scornful look. 'Every one of those ladders is made of high-quality wood,' Hector says. 'There is nothing wrong with them. We don't throw things away just because they are old.'

Edna says, 'Never mind, dear. I'll phone the fire brigade.'

I'm about to let her do it when I remember how short staffed the local fire department is this month. Some of the men are my customers and I know one has an ill wife at home, another a broken arm. Of course they would round up enough reinforcements if they were called out, but this is definitely not an emergency.

My voice firm, I say, 'No need for that. I'll get your cat down but first I'll nip home and get my own ladder.'

They start to protest that they have plenty of decent ladders to choose from but I stop them. 'It's best to use a ladder one is used to. Especially when trying to take a cat out of a tree. I'm sure you understand.'

This they do. Thank goodness. I rush home, sling our short, sturdy, aluminium ladder into the car and drive back with it. The Humphreys are under the tree again. 'Oh do come down, Bede, come on old boy,' Hector is saying. He shakes his head when the cat doesn't respond. 'Oh, you be a right ole' bugger, me lover.'

It's the first time I've heard either one of them lapse totally into Cornish dialect, despite the odd word. It sounds as totally natural as it does when he speaks like an old colonial. I'd love to know more of this couple's history but it will for ever be elusive. What I find so incredible is that they've somehow managed to keep their travels and affairs out of the tentacles of that unstoppable rural grapevine, a mystery in itself as I know so well.

Edna and Hector watch me as I prop my ladder carefully against the tree, making sure it is completely safe and stable before I attempt the first rung. I can feel the Humphreys' impatience flitting around me like invisible mites, but I'm determined to teach them a lesson in self-preservation.

I climb slowly up the ladder. Within moments I'm face to face with the cat but now that I'm here, I don't quite know what to do. I don't know this cat very well and from what I've seen so far, he looks mean. He might be old but he's got sharp claws, sharp enough to get up this far. I've taken the precaution of wearing the thick gloves I use for nettle picking and I've thrown on a long-sleeved fleece just before ascending, much to the disgust of Edna and Hector. Neither said anything but I could see it in their faces. Well, it's a lesson they should learn, an ounce of prevention prevents a pound of cure. Or something like that. Goodness they're old enough to have invented that saying, so why don't they follow it?

I take a deep breath and prepare to gently extricate kitty from the tree, shove him under one arm and use the other to get us both down. 'Right, Beedy-boy, here we go,' I mutter in a pussy-friendly whisper. I figure as I'm his rescuer, I've a right to speak to him in a more familiar manner.

But before I can make a move a strange thing happens. The old cat delicately stretches out a skinny front leg, places it on my shoulder then follows with his other limbs and before I know it, he has sedately and with great dignity climbed onto my shoulders.

'Good old boy,' I hear Hector murmur from below.

'Darling old thing,' Edna whispers.

I climb down slowly. The cat remains motionless on my shoulders and when we're down, lets Hector take him and tickle him under his whiskery chin. Hector hands him to Edna who kisses the top of his head. When he's allowed these small celebratory gestures, the Venerable Bede shakes himself in such a way that Edna knows to immediately put him down: he's had enough affection for the moment, thank you very much.

'Dear Bede,' she says as they fondly watch him walk up the garden path and settle in the sun beside the garden bench. Then she turns to me. 'Well, my dear, that was easy, wasn't it. I would have got him down eventually, or Hector would have, but we do appreciate your help. Now let's all go and have a cup of tea.'

This time Edna ladles the tea into our cups from a huge

pot burbling away on the Aga. I peer into it and see that it is full of green things that look like weeds. 'Something I found in the hedgerow, dear, I'm not sure of the name. It's not one of the common plants but it makes a delicious tea.'

I look at it warily. It looks like dirty bath water. I can't refuse so I take a cautious sip but surprisingly the taste is wonderful, sort of tangy and refreshing at the same time.

The Venerable Bede has followed us in and is drinking milk from the lid of some kind of old pot. I try again to ask them how they gave the cat his name and this time I'm lucky. Not only did they travel to Jarrow, where the Venerable Bede lived, but they also stayed at Holy Island where he is supposed to have visited.

'And that's where we found our kitten,' Hector says with a wide smile.

'So sweet,' Edna adds. 'A tiny stray. Wild. So we brought him home and gave him his true name, the one he had before.'

'I beg your pardon?'

Now both of them look cagey. I have the feeling they think Edna said too much. She smiles politely. 'Merely a whim, my dear. He was such a wise kitten and we were studying karma at the time even though we were living temporarily in a Christian community on the island. So we made a little game of it, you see. Now, would you like a top up of my herbal brew?'

Karma? Christian community? I'm buzzing with questions but as I open my mouth Edna says, 'Oh, look at the time. My dear Tessa, I'm afraid we've made such a dent in your afternoon and you've still got your garden to see to.'

They are both standing up, thanking me for my help, making it quite clear that I will not learn another thing from them today. The Venerable Bede looks hard at me with his green eyes as I go. I'm dying to know more. Do the Humphreys really believe that the cat is a reincarnation of a monk that lived up north more than a thousand years ago? Surely it's nothing more than a joke between an old married couple. I catch a rather perceptive look between them and wonder if they've read my thoughts. What an enigma these two are. Fascinating, though.

I go back to the allotment, set out my plants and think about Hector and Edna, how I might help in some way. There are dozens of tiny things I can do or suggest to make their lives easier and not so precarious. Cook a meal now and again, check that they've got plenty of warmth in the winter months. Before I know it, I've finished putting out some cabbage plants. My mind has been so busy organising the Humphreys that I hardly knew what I was doing. I quiet the head noises, breathe in the smell of the warm earth and listen to the birds for a few moments before I go home.

The children are having dinner at Daphne and Joe's place tonight – they're often at the farm, playing with their friends. Ben opens a bottle of red wine some visitors brought us, which we eat with a soup made from chickweeds I picked earlier in one of the Humphreys' wild meadows. It's rather tasty, flavoured with lots of wild garlic, and makes a good starter for the leftover casserole from last night. Nothing is wasted now. We've learned to love leftovers and anything that remains after we've picked over it goes into the compost bucket to be taken to the allotment when it's full. I've got a proper compost bin there now, donated by one of my customers who gave up her vegetable garden when arthritis set in her knees.

'I'll stick to flowers and shrubs,' she told me when I delivered the post to her one day last month. 'The compost bin is nearly new, I've only a year's use of it, so please take it.'

Ben and I talk about our day as we sip the wine. That's a treat too. In London we bought our favourite wines whenever we felt like it, as we love a glass with our meals, but now we only have it if someone brings us a bottle or when we see a decent bottle on sale. It's no hardship, in fact it makes us savour each sip more.

Ben's had a long day, for after his stint in the café he had to rush to the Roswinnick Hotel to give a massage to a client there. Ben is a qualified aromatherapist and sometimes the hotel, which is in St Geraint and terribly exclusive, calls on him when one of their residents desires some therapy. Not long ago the manager phoned him in a complete flap. The chef's wife was suffering with a bad back, the chef couldn't leave her, there was a famous London theatre director coming to dinner that night as well as some minor royalty, and please could Ben help?

He'd treated the woman for back and shoulder pain before, and rushed to the Roswinnick to do it again. This too was successful: the chef was happy because his wife was happy, he went back to work and the evening was saved. For payment the manager offered Ben and me a free meal at the hotel which he accepted gratefully, knowing we'd never in a million years afford to eat there. Now we are saving the treat for a special occasion.

'But how about you?' he asks, after telling me about his latest client at the hotel. 'What kind of a day did you have?'

My day seems so long that I have to think back to the beginning. It started at four when I got up but that happens every day. 'I suppose the first exciting thing that happened came after I'd done my rounds and was at the St Geraint post office.'

Ben grins. 'The *first* thing? You've had more than one exciting event in your day? Fantastic.'

I tell him about Eddie and the life-like snake, and we laugh about it. Next I tell him all about the Humphreys, their cat with the bizarre name, Edna up that rickety ladder, the shed full of broken ones, me running home to get ours to rescue the cat.

When I finish Ben says, 'Snakes and Ladders.'

'What?'

He's starting to laugh again. 'You know, the game we've played with Amy and Will since they were little. You've been playing it all day, by the sound of it.'

I grin. 'So I have. Well, who's the winner then? Eddie with that ridiculous fake snake, or the Humphreys? I suppose it's got to be the cat. The Venerable Bede wins.'

Ben pours us a second glass of wine and clinks my glass with his. 'Not them, you, Tessa. You won by getting through the day unscathed.'

I raise my glass. 'I'll drink to that.'

Chapter 4

A seagull in the attic

The phone rings one evening when I'm on my own. Ben is at Joe and Daphne's farm helping Joe unload some sheep he bought in a market several counties away. Will and Amy have gone too, to help, they said, but really to hang out with their friends.

I pick up the phone and hear a familiar voice, 'Hey, country mouse, at last! We haven't talked for ages. Have you forgotten the big city and all your debauched city friends?'

'Annie, hi, city mouse. Great to hear your wicked London voice. What're you up to?'

Annie is such a Londoner that I'm surprised she didn't send us care packages when we moved to Cornwall. She thought we were totally mad – until she met Pete, the agricultural merchant who lives not far from Treverny. Since then they've had a long-distance romance and Annie has begun to see the positive side of living where we do.

After she's told me all the latest news about our mutual

friends in London, she says, 'Oh, and Pete's coming to London again this weekend.'

'Hey, that's twice in a row. How about you coming here? At least your oldest dearest friend could get a look at you now and again.'

She sighs. 'I'd love to. But I've got a wedding to go to on Saturday, someone from work. Pete's going with me. But I'll be down soon, I promise. Now tell me what's new in Cornwall.'

I tell her about my garden and rhapsodise about the new lettuces. When I take a breath she says, 'What about the old couple who live in the house? They sound so intriguing.'

'They are, but I'm worried about them. They seem to live so chaotically, which is fine when you're young but at their age it could be deadly. Those loose rugs on the floor, the uneven steps and garden path – it's all so deadly, an accident waiting to happen.'

Before we can say any more, I hear the noise again. I hadn't heard it while we were chatting. 'Uh oh,' I say. 'I was hoping it had gone.'

'What?'

'Oh, nothing much. I hope nothing much anyway. There's this noise, up in the attic.'

'What kind of noise?'

'Sort of eerie. Scratching, scrabbling sounds. We've been hearing it off and on all day. It sounds worse this evening. Maybe because I'm alone.' I giggle, trying to make light of it. 'Actually, I think it's a ghost. Oh no, you don't think it's a snake? Could an adder get into the attic?'

'How would I know, I'm a city gal, remember? I shouldn't think so. Don't they just slither on the ground?'

I make a strangled, gurgling sound. 'Don't, Annie. Don't talk about slithering snakes. Anyway, I'm sure it's a ghost. What else could it be?'

'Rats.'

'What?' my voice hollers at her down the phone.

'It's obvious enough. You've got rats up there. You said there was lots of scratching.'

I stare up at the ceiling as if a rat is going to fall through and land on top of me. 'How would you know, Annie? You're a city girl, like you just said. What would you know about rats?'

She snorts. 'That's one form of animal life everyone who lives in a city knows about, Tessa. You know the statistics, everyone in London is never further than a couple of metres from a rat.' There's a pause. 'Or something like that. Statistics never stay in my head unless I need them for the job.'

'Omigod, rats! What'll we do, Annie?'

'Send for a rat catcher. That's what I'd do. Exterminator 2 or whatever they call them down your way.'

'Stop joking.'

'I'm not. I should do it fast too. They breed like rats.'

'They are rats.'

'That's what I mean, you see?'

'Annie, we can't afford a rat catcher. We can't afford anything. Anyway, I'd better go. I hear Ben and the children coming home.'

I put down the phone and roll my eyes at Ben, surreptitiously trying to indicate the ceiling. I certainly don't want to frighten the children with stories about rats in the attic.

Amy says, 'Oh, those noises again. Are they still there?'

Will says eagerly, 'I bet they're rats. Great, maybe I can catch some babies for Elvis.'

I sigh. Rats and snakes, and God knows what else. Sending the children up to bed, I turn to Ben. 'Can you go up and take a look? I think Will is right. There must be rats up there. You'll have to put some poison down. Or a trap, or something.'

Ben assures me he'll take care of it tomorrow when he's

home from work. We go to bed and I lie awake for a long time, first hearing the scratching noises, then not hearing anything. Maybe the rat has died? I'm relieved until I start imagining a dead rat over my head, with only a floorboard and ceiling between it and me. By the time the alarm rings at 4 a.m. I've hardly slept a wink.

On my round the next day I find two of my customers, Emma and Martin Rowland, out in the pasture near their farmhouse with their goats. The Rowlands unwillingly had to give up farming a few years ago, as the struggle against new regulations, larger and larger farms swallowing up smaller ones, the shrinking margin between profit and loss, all combined to make it impossible to carry on. They converted Trelak Farm to a B&B but neither of them is suited to the work, especially Martin. They have slowly been working towards becoming a market garden and plan to go organic as soon as possible. They've also got a small herd of milking goats which they are hoping will make some much needed money.

Unfortunately they can't afford to give up the paying customers. I see by the cars parked around the front that the house must be full. 'Yes, we've got a good week, and it's not even half term,' Emma says, coming out to meet me in the van. We chat for a bit and then I go with her to look at the goats. A tiny newborn is suckling his mum and I want to whisk it home. I love the little kids and spend more time than I should cooing over this one.

My next call is just down a narrow lane, with hedgerows on either side and beneath them, a mass of yellow primroses, crammed together like rows of luscious yellow sweets. They're so perfect, and there are so many of them, that I stop the van to just sit and stare. Once again I'm aware of that special rural silence, the kind that is only interrupted by a robin or thrush, the song of a blackbird, or perhaps the high swish of a soft breeze blowing through trees which are just beginning to come into leaf.

I drive on a short distance and then I spot something else, dandelions in flower in a small clearing. I've got my basket in the van, ready for such finds. Last year Daphne gave us some dandelion flower wine and it was so luscious I'm hoping to make some myself. It'll make great Christmas gifts for next year too. I know it's only springtime but this year I plan to make as many gifts as I can and dandelion flower wine will be a great one.

I feel a twinge of sadness when I deliver to this next house. One of my favourite customers, an old farm worker called Mr Hawker, used to live here and died during my first year. I was fond of the old man. But as I pull up in front of the stone cottage my heart lifts to see his small place, neglected for decades, looking cared for and loved. The front garden, which was a mass of weeds and brambles, has been cleared and there are pansies and marigolds planted along a narrow border. The windows, some broken and papered over when Mr Hawker became a recluse, are mended, cleaned and freshly painted.

'Tessa, hi. All right?' a cheery voice greets me and Dave appears from the back of the house, carrying a ladder.

I'm pleased to see that this is a sensible sturdy one, as safe as ladders can be. The couple moved here from Bristol after a distant relative who inherited Mr Hawker's house said they could live in it and do it up as part of the rent. Dave is Emma and Martin's son. He and Marilyn are Cornish but, like so many young people, had to move away to be able to afford a decent place to live. Now they've been able to move back, as they've been longing to do for ages. They're helping Dave's parents build up the goat-and-garden business but it's an enormous struggle as they are still also working full time as physiotherapists at the hospital in Truro.

Dave asks, 'Have you seen the new young goat at up at Trelak?' I nod as he goes on, 'Marilyn is besotted with it. Besotted with all the goats, actually. Dad and Mum say she can be in charge of the milking later, when she can afford to quit work.'

'Is that where she is now?'

'Yeah. She has a long shift today. They're short staffed as usual. I had a long one yesterday, was called in on my day off, which is why I'm off today.' His normally upbeat manner turns a bit glum. Fitting in overtime at work with helping at Trelak Farm and doing up the wreck of the house they live in is exhausting even for people as young and fit as they are. The dream is that eventually the new project will support all of them but they know the reality is years, even decades into the future. As if reading my mind Dave says, 'We're hoping that at least Marilyn can stop work at the hospital soon, or at least do loads less hours, but we'll see. At least we're back home, back in Cornwall. We're luckier than most and we know it.'

I leave feeling quite cheered. The plight of young people in the county, as in other popular areas of England, is dire. The boom for second homes has put property prices way out of reach for those who were born here or those who live and work here. But Marilyn and Dave have found a way to come back, though it was a rare stroke of good fortune that enabled them to do it.

When I finish my round I go home, have a quick snack, change my clothes and go out to the allotment, but by the time I get there it is beginning to rain so I abandon the garden for today and stop at Poet's Tenement. I still smile when I hear the name and amuse myself wondering who would be the most likely poet, Edna or Hector? Both would fit the role, if I remember my English Lit lessons correctly. Some of those long-ago poets, both male and female, were quite eccentric, and some led spectacularly wild lives. I'm sure both the Humphreys had some bizarre experiences in their youth.

I have to knock hard on their old, swollen, wooden door that hasn't shut properly for years. I've seen Hector nearly topple over backward onto the stony cobbled path as he's pulled on it to get it open. That's another thing I want to do, ask if I can sand the door so it opens and shuts properly.

Where are they? I've been standing out here for nearly five minutes now. It's so much easier when they are outside in the afternoons on their bench, sunning themselves like skinny little lizards. I don't like to intrude, especially on days like today when they don't seem to hear me banging on the front door. There's no bell and not even a knocker. I have to use my fist to make myself heard through the thick wood. Finally I resort to shouting. 'Hello, anyone home? It's Tessa here.'

I know they must be home. They always are. They don't drive any more, they have their food shopping delivered to them from a supermarket and top up with goods from the village shop.

There is still no sound from inside the house. I shout again. Nothing. I don't like to pry but what if one of them is ill or injured? I saw Hector's panic when the cat was in the tree and he wasn't even in danger. Would he completely lose it if Edna was hurt? I've heard of old folk sitting by the bodies of dead husbands and wives, not wanting to let them go and I shudder. I walk around the house trying to peer into the windows but the rain, gathering force, is belting against the panes and there are no lights on inside. Though it's only about five o'clock and the days are long now, the sky is dark and stormy. I go back to the front door and bang on it one more time. When only silence and an increasing wind answer me, I realise I have to go in. I don't really want to, especially as the house is starting to look creepy.

I pull myself together, remembering that the house was named after someone called Pote, or Pottes, or whatever, and it won't be haunted by the ghosts of long-dead demented versifiers. I need to curb my imagination. I also need to get into the house. I know I can't leave without making sure everything is all right. I'd never forgive myself if I left now and then find out tomorrow that a tragedy had occurred that I might have prevented. So I pull on the door, which is so swollen I have to yank it hard. As I do it suddenly flies open and like Hector, I nearly topple over on my back. I'm soaked by now but relieved to be inside. It's odd that neither of them has heard me and I'm convinced something is terribly wrong.

I stand in the cavernous hallway with its piles of books and give one last shout, 'Edna! Hector!' Still no answer.

With trepidation I move through the house, nearly tripping on a stack of what look like ancient texts of some kind, and find my way through the dim semi-darkness to the kitchen. The door is half open and I call again, more softly this time. 'Edna? Hector?' I don't want to frighten them.

Hector's voice says, 'Come in, maid. Since you're in already.'

Edna says, 'Is anything wrong, my dear? You look quite agitated.'

The couple are perfectly fine and calm. They're sitting at the kitchen table, a beautifully carved ivory chess set between them. In front of the Aga sits the Venerable Bede who regards me suspiciously.

I stammer, 'So sorry to interrupt. I knocked, and called out, and no one answered. I was afraid something was wrong.'

They both look genuinely puzzled. Hector says, 'Whatever could be wrong?'

'Are you ill?' Edna asks, suddenly concerned. 'Or is it the garden? The rabbits haven't come back, have they?'

'The hens? A fox hasn't got into their pen, has it?' And now they are both standing up, offering me tea, a chair, fussing over me, sure that whatever it is, it's an emergency they are prepared to deal with.

'I'm fine, my garden is fine. I wouldn't have barged in but when you didn't answer my shouts and knocking I, uh, well I thought I'd better check for myself.'

Hector and Edna look at each other. She says, 'Check what, dear?' Her voice is not as warm as it was moments ago when they thought I was in some kind of trouble. I try to make my voice light, 'Oh, just that everything was OK. And I see it is.' I want desperately to change the subject. 'I see you play chess. I never learned. Must be fascinating.'

Hector says, 'It is, maid. Learned it in Peru, actually.'

Peru? That's a new one. Without thinking I ask, 'Really? When were you there?' But of course they've clammed up again, acting as if they never heard my question.

Hector goes on, 'Yes, it is a very fascinating game. So much so that we get completely engrossed in it. That's no doubt why we didn't hear you knock.'

'We are completely absorbed when we play,' Edna adds.

'Ah. Yes. I see.' *And I interrupted you*, are the words that have not been spoken aloud but are silently flitting around the room.

I'm about to apologise and slink off when I remember why I called in the first place. I look down at the cold, stone kitchen floor with its threadbare rugs and say, 'I wanted to see you as a matter of fact because I brought you these.' I hold out a packet of rug fasteners I'd picked up at a shop in Truro a day or so ago. 'I saw these and, uh, bought some for my rugs at home.' This is a little fib but a necessary one, I feel. 'And I suddenly thought you might find them useful too. I know how easy it is to skid on a loose rug. Will and Amy do it all the time, and so do I, Ben, too, and even our dog Jake, and really it's quite dangerous.' I'm waffling I know, but they are looking at me with totally blank faces. Perhaps they haven't seen anything like this before? I rip the packet open and start putting them on the rusty-coloured rug in front of me. It's thin and slippery, worn with age. 'You see? It works like this. One side sticks to the rug and the other to the floor. It prevents the rug from slipping out from under you.'

I work feverishly then demonstrate how much more secure the rug is now. Neither Edna nor Hector has said a word. I've bought enough of the things to do all the rugs they could possibly have in the house and now I lay them on the table next to the chess set.

Finally Edna says, 'Thank you, dear.' Her voice is polite but not enthusiastic. Hector still has that blank look on his face. I remind myself that they're old, set in their ways, and that they will need time to adjust to even something as simple as rug fasteners. But they'll come around.

I say, 'I'd be happy to do all your rugs, next time I'm here. I'd do it now but you're in the middle of your game.'

Hector finally speaks, 'That's kind of you, but it won't be necessary. Now how much do we owe you for these?' His voice is distant.

Neither of them have made a move to even look at the rug fasteners and I realise, far too late and to my extreme mortification, that far from being helpful, I've offended them by implying that they need help, need an outsider like me to come in with my health and safety rules, my busybody attempt to organise their lives. Oh dear, I think, what do I do now? Finally I manage to stutter something about the items being merely a few extra we had left over that we have no need for.

Edna says, 'We really don't need them either, to be honest. Our rugs have never given us trouble.' She pauses then adds politely, 'Though it's kind of you to think of us.' The way she says it, I can tell she is fibbing too.

Hector is nodding in agreement. I say, as nonchalantly as possible, 'That's fine, if you don't need them. Just thought I'd ask.' I pick up the rug fasteners that are on the table and put them in my pocket. 'I'm sorry I interrupted your chess game.'

And now they are themselves again, that awful distance between us gone. Walking me to the door they talk in unison, offer to lend me an umbrella for the rain and see me out.

Despite the storm I walk home slowly, getting drenched but not noticing. I think wryly that my efficient, organised, managerial ways that stood me in such good stead in London, are not just useless here but sometimes positively detrimental. Well, live and learn, I think as I put on dry clothes and make tea. I'm on my own in the house again and suddenly I hear that same scrabbling rat-like sound in the attic. Ben is going to go upstairs and look tonight when he gets home from work. I'll be glad when he does as that constant scratching is unnerving. And then I remember – I've got a box in the attic of some family photographs, old ones left to me by my parents before they died, and I don't want any horrid rat chewing on them. The photographs are special, precious. How could I have forgotten they were there?

I sit with my tea and listen to the noise coming from the attic. Am I imagining it or does it sound louder? Perhaps there are dozens of rats up there, all having a romping great feast on my family photos. The thought upsets me so much that before I know what I'm doing, I grab the stepladder, position it below the attic opening, and get myself up there before I can think.

I've not been here since we moved. There's the usual stuff, a couple of crates of things we brought from London that we didn't quite know what to do with but were reluctant to throw away. They are still there, looking untouched. Next to the crates is a small cardboard box with a few albums, including the one from my parents. I make my way to it noisily, thinking that any self-respecting rat will hide when it hears me coming. All I want to do is grab the irreplaceable album and get out of the attic.

Luckily it looks untouched. I'm tempted to take the whole box downstairs but I remember Edna on her ladder against the pear tree. I'm more or less half her age, and my ladder is in excellent shape, but I don't fancy coming down on my own carrying an entire box. Sensibly, I decide to wait until Ben gets home before doing anything more than rescuing the album. I'm halfway down the ladder again when I hear the scratching noise. I yelp, thinking a rat is about to land on my head which is now on a level with the opening. Then there are more scrabbling sounds and I'm petrified, frozen to the ladder for a second or two until I hear another sound, more like the caw of a bird than the squeak of a rat.

The noise comes again. It's definitely a bird. Slowly I poke my head back into the attic's opening and look around, noticing for the first time, some feathers near the crates. I scramble down the ladder with the album and go up again, no longer afraid. I like birds, and I don't like the thought of one trapped in my attic. Slowly, so as not to frighten it, I creep over to the crates and peer behind one of them. There, looking up at me, is a baby seagull. I haven't a clue how old it is but it still has fluff instead of feathers. And it can't fly either, because as I approach it starts flapping about in a panic but doesn't seem to be getting anywhere.

I'm not quite sure what to do. Making soothing noises, I try to get a better look to see if it's injured. It seems only to be frightened. I back off down the ladder, grab some bits of bread and cheese from the kitchen and go back to the attic. I make myself comfortable, sitting on the floor behind the crate, and try to pop some food around to the bird as unobtrusively as possible. The gull looks up at me and opens its mouth, whether in shock or in an instinctive gesture, I'm not sure, but I take the opportunity to pop a tiny piece of crumbled cheddar in its beak which he swallows ravenously. Then he opens it again and this time I try some bread. I know from experience that seagulls eat anything – Cornish ice cream, pasties, fish and chips – so I'm not worried about feeding it correctly.

When the bread and cheese is gone, I go down for a bowl of water which I place not far from the bird. I'm not sure about their drinking habits so this will have to do. Its beak is still wide open but I decide it's had enough, for now. 'Go to sleep, little thing, have a rest,' I say softly. 'We'll figure out what to do with you later.'

For the next hour or so I listen for more sounds but all is quiet in the attic. I vacillate between feeling good that the baby is now having a peaceful slumber and being terrified that I killed it off with the wrong kind of cheese or something. I remind myself how the seagulls are thriving in St Geraint, Morranport and all the other seaside places, living on the rubbish from restaurants and food dropped by tourists, so they must have cast-iron stomachs.

Ben and the children arrive home at the same time and I tell them about the seagull. Ben goes up straightaway to investigate. When he gets down he says, 'It obviously got through from the attic next door. There are seagulls nesting there and one of the babies must somehow have scuttled into our attic.'

That makes sense. Our cottage is a semi and the one next door has been a rented for years. It's now up for sale and the owners haven't bothered to do a thing to it despite a hole in the roof and other problems. I say, 'Oh Ben, we'll have to put the baby back into the nest, at once.'

The children are all for this idea, identifying with the poor baby bird separated from its mum, dad and siblings. But by now it's not only raining hard, a gale has started to blow. Though the nights are pulling back and the days getting longer, it's like late autumn this evening with the black storm clouds and lashing rain.

'Tomorrow,' Ben says firmly. 'We'll do it tomorrow morning.'

And so I soak some more bread in water and take it to the gull which devours it hungrily. Then we leave it for the night, and when I'm woken by scrabbling noises I'm reassured rather than frightened, knowing that the sound is not a rat noise and knowing, too, that our baby bird is still alive.

Ben wakes early to see to the gull before he goes off to work. Luckily, I have a day off. I'm not about to let him climb up a ladder with a baby gull in one hand without me to steady it. He takes our tallest ladder from the shed and marches with it to the next-door chimney, doing a recce before trying to restore the bird to its home.

When he comes down he says, 'It's no use. There's no way we can get to the nest. I can't just drop the little thing down the hole, the nest must be quite a way down. I can't even see it. I've checked if there are any places I can get into the attic but there aren't. And the house is well locked up.'

I know the owner lives in London and there's no way he'd drop everything and come down to open up the house for a baby seagull. I say, 'Ben, we'll have to look after it. First we must get him out of our attic. He'll die up there.'

I find a box and put an old, soft cushion in it, as Ben brings down the gull. It flaps about in panic but seems to settle when placed in the box, standing there calmly looking at us as if to say, 'Well, here I am. So what're you going to do about me?'

What indeed. Ben leaves for work and the children, after making a fuss of the bird and insisting on feeding it, go off to school, leaving me alone with the seagull. We stare at each other. It looks about a week old, the size of a chick, maybe a bit bigger, and covered with soft grey down. It has a few black spots on its head and looks gawky and pitiable. I feel a fool, but my maternal instincts are coming to the fore. I need to take care of this baby.

First of all, I need advice. I try to phone the RSPB but can't get through for some reason. So I think; what do gulls eat when they are in the wild? I mean, really wild, not along the seafront at Morranport or St Geraint. I recall seeing them swooping out over the water, plucking things from the sea. *Fish*. Of course. But I haven't any fish in the house and I also know that none of us will have time to buy fish regularly or cut it into tiny pieces to feed to the seagull. Somehow I see that this is going to be a long-term project. I decide to go to the village shop and see what ready-made foods I can find that contain fish but that would be easy to feed a baby bird. I might also be able to glean some information about the habits of seagulls from the locals.

Last night's wind has died and there's now a bright sun, drying the tree branches that were blown down in the night. The church-yard and woodland are alive with colour, the vivid pale green of early spring leaves and foliage, the white of the garlic flowers now beginning to be taken over by the deep colour of the blue-bells which are everywhere, looking fresh and bright after the storm, the scent divine. I cut through the path between the church and churchyard, noting the fresh lilies on a couple of the grave-stones. It's an ancient church and used to be part of a much wider parish so some of the old plots are still carefully attended to by new generations. The church warden has forbidden plastic flowers so that there are always masses of freshly cut flowers here, but as always they seem pale and insipid next to the living growing ones. The rhododendrons are everywhere and, have been for a while, their colour spectacular. The neglected garden at Poet's Tenement is a mass of purple and red as the huge rhododendron bushes that have been there for years flower at once. Azaleas abound too, their colours adding to the glow. There are times that I feel I've moved to a Technicolor world after living in a black and white film for years. Up above me in the trees the rooks have built their nests and are feeding their young. In the mornings and evenings their noise and chattering fill the whole village with caws and cries. There's been a rookery in Treverny for four hundred years, apparently.

Our one and only local shop is tiny but well stocked. There are five people in there and it's crowded. The sun is so lovely and warm on my face that I decide to wait outside until one or two people leave. The first to come out is Doug, the farm worker. Jake, who is with me, yaps at him gleefully. To Jake, every person he meets is a possible candidate for a doggie game. 'Oh Doug, hello, great day, isn't it?' I call to him.

He peers around him then at the sky before saying noncommittally, 'Might be.'

'I was wondering, Doug, what you might know about seagulls.'

He snorts. 'They should all be shot, that's what I know, me lover. Why d'ya ask?'

'Oh, uh, no reason.' He's looking at me suspiciously so I add, 'Many about, that's all.'

'You telling me? Should be blasted outa the sky, every last one of them,' he shakes his head, glowers, then makes another snorting sound. Doug has the largest repertoire of snorts of anyone I know.

The shop is almost empty now. I look around at the shelves for fishy things. There's tuna, sardines, pilchards. All of them will do but will they be a bit messy to feed? And how much do young gulls eat? Maybe I should just stick to bread. The gull seemed to like the softened bread we've been feeding it. While I'm thinking I decide to get a treat for Jake so I look at

the pet food section. And there it is, right in front of me –
dried cat food with salmon in it. What could be better? I don't
have to waste a whole tin if the bird eats only a little and if
it's soaked in warm water it'll have the texture of bread, plus
it's got fish in it. What more could a baby gull want?

I buy a packet just as Daphne comes into the shop. 'Oh hi,
Tessa. When did you get a cat?'

I smile. 'Not a cat. A baby seagull. We found it in our attic
and this is to feed it.'

More people have come into the store and are listening
unashamedly to our conversation. I found this unnerving when
we first moved here, the way everyone openly eavesdrops, but
I've not only got used to it, I like it. Well, mostly I do. When
Ben was ill last year it was a great thing that the village soon
knew, for they came around with offers to help, with food and
comfort. I couldn't have carried on without them. Just sometimes, like now, I find myself longing for a secret or two.
Daphne is looking concerned but the man and woman behind
her have expressions on their faces I can't quite read.

Daphne says, 'Feed it? Look Tessa, I know your intentions
are good but wouldn't it be kinder not to? It'll die anyway, they
always do, when they drop out of their nest.'

Before I can answer the man behind her says, 'She's right,
y'know. It'll be kinder to all of us, not just that bird.'

The woman is nodding. They're both locals, usually easy-
going folk I've spoken to once or twice in the shop, but now
she says, 'You need to knock it on the head right now, maid.
We can't be doing with more seagulls about.'

The two say a few more things along the same lines. Daphne
to my surprise seems to agree with them though she says it in
a gentler manner. I mumble something that I hope sounds
neutral and slink away home.

The baby bird is awake and gives a little chirruping sound

when it sees me. He's already recognising me as the bearer of food. I soak the dry cat pellets in hot water, talking to the gull as I do so, telling it not to be impatient, food is on its way. It cocks its head to one side as if it understands, or at least is trying to. When the cat food cools down, I hold a soft pellet over the gull's beak and like before, it opens and I pop in the food. He loves it, I can tell by the way he nearly snaps my fingers off along with the cat food. As I continue with the feeding, I realise I'm referring to the bird as 'he' more and more, rather than 'it'. How do I know it's a he? I don't, of course, but 'he' he is, until we know for sure. Which we probably never will, I muse as I continue popping pellets into the wide open beak. But this seagull is definitely acting like a boy baby, I decide, with the greedy way he's demanding more food. I'm realising something else. I am acting as if this bird will stay in our family for ever, like Jake or Elvis, but I know, even without Daphne telling me, that baby birds don't live long in captivity. I know, too, that even if we could get him back into the nest, the parents probably would not accept him. Oh dear, I think, what do we do now?

I ask Nell this question the next day, when I'm back at work. The warm sun has held and she's shed her fuzzy jumpers to put on a thin, vivid turquoise long-sleeved T-shirt with a scoop neck, showing off her massive cleavage to perfection.

'A *what*? What you be telling me exactly?' her voice is incredulous as she turns to stare at me. Her extravagantly frizzy white hair looks as if it's standing on end.

'A baby seagull, Nell. Found it in our attic. Not sure what's to become of it.'

Nell grunts, 'I be telling you what's to become of it, maid. The nasty bird will grow up to drive us all mad like the rest of 'em, screeching and quarrelling amongst themselves over a bit of pasty someone dropped in the bin, pecking open our rubbish bags, stealing food outa the mouths of babes and pensioners.' She stops to take a breath. Luckily a customer comes in before she could say anything else.

It will be the same no matter who I talk to, I realise as I walk along the seafront. Seagulls are the most unpopular birds in Cornwall and it's understandable, I have to admit. Nell wasn't just quoting clichés, the gulls have often snatched sandwiches from children on the harbour, or ice cream from someone sitting on a sea wall. In a crowded seaside town they can be a real health hazard with their aggressive behaviour.

Some of the offending creatures are perched on the rocks at the edge of the water and I stop to look at them before continuing my round. Two of them fly off, graceful and elegant as they swoop through the sky, the sun making their white feathers dazzle. To me, the gulls don't look predatory at all, but beautiful and even majestic as they fly around the shallows and sand or sun themselves on rocks. They belong here and they were here first. Maybe it's us who are the predators, I think as I finally tear myself away from the birds and carry on delivering the post. Maybe we're the intruders, not them.

I go home with some trepidation, knowing there's a good chance I'll find our little bird dead, but to everyone's surprise, our seagull lives. And grows stronger over the next few days, more noisy and demanding too.

'He's getting bossy,' I say to the children.

Now that it looks as if our gull will survive, we need to find a name for him. I've been calling him Google Gull, as I've been on Google nearly every day trying to find out how to raise a baby seagull. I was quite chuffed to discover my dried cat-food theory was a good one, that information on the search engine confirmed it was a decent food for gulls. We have a heated family discussion on names but since no one can agree on another name, Google he is, officially now.

'You've got a *what?*' Annie asks on the phone.

'A pet seagull. He's adorable.'

'But I thought seagulls were the most hated bird in Cornwall.'

'Um, yes. They are.'

There is a pause on the other end of the line, 'Let me get this straight. You can't stand snakes yet one lives in your house. Seagulls are considered a menace by all the locals you're trying to fit in with but somehow you've managed to adopt one.'

'Actually, Annie, I think it was Google who adopted us.'

A long drawn out sigh comes down the phone from London, 'Ah well, maybe you're still a Londoner at heart.'

'What do you mean?'

'Always at the cutting edge,' she giggles. So do I.

Suddenly Google, no doubt thinking our laughter has something to do with him, starts cawing to be noticed, and Jake, unsure of this new creature in the household, starts barking madly at the tall, sturdy box we keep the gull in. I say goodbye and begin to embark on a training session with Jake, on how to live with a seagull. It looks like Google is going to be around for a while.

Chapter 5

The mole whisperer

I'm surprised to find Pete, Annie's Cornish boyfriend, home on this Tuesday morning as he's usually at work, but he comes to do the door feverish and coughing. 'It's only a cold,' he tells me. 'Not the flu, but I'm feeling rough and sorry for myself so I've taken the day off. C'mon in for a coffee unless you're afraid of catching something.'

I'm being plagued by moles in my allotment digging under the ground and tunnelling under my vegetables. No one quite seems to know what to do with them, so I accept Pete's offer, hoping he'll know of a solution, having been in the agriculture business all his working life. It's also good to see him. I like Pete and think he's perfect for Annie. He's a solid dependable guy but also intelligent and fun.

I follow Pete into the neat kitchen in his tiny bungalow.

'Annie's coming down this weekend, as you probably know,' Pete says. 'I hope this cold is gone by then.'

I nod. 'We're getting together for a meal, right? The four of us?'

'That's the plan,' Pete says. 'We're both looking forward to it.'

'So am I.' When Annie visits now she doesn't stay with me like she used to do but with Pete, which is understandable. They only have weekends after all. At least now I don't have to spend hours hoovering up every last dog hair and keep Jake off the furniture for a whole weekend. Although Annie loves dogs, she is allergic not just to them but to animal hairs, tree pollen, grass seeds, plants and feathers – you name it and Annie sneezes. She lives on antihistamines when she visits.

We talk mostly about Annie, as Pete is besotted with her. Before I go, though, I bring him back to earth by asking his professional advice. 'Pete, I've got moles digging tunnels under my garden. What's the best way to get rid of them?'

Pete blows his nose before he answers. He's really full of cold, red-eyed, red-nosed and washed out. 'You need to get back to bed,' I say. 'I'll ask you another time.'

'No, it's fine. Moles are tricky things, hard to dislodge. We've got various things I could sell you, but none of it is very nice. For instance, smoke bombs.'

'How do they work?'

'You put them in the tunnels, smoke the moles out.'

'Does it work?'

'Not really. I've not had anyone rave about how they got rid of their moles that way.'

'So what does work?'

Pete sighs, 'Frankly, nothing much. We've got some newish product, some kind of solar thing that emits high-frequency sounds that apparently freak out the moles and they leave fast. It's expensive, though, and the few I've sold haven't had spectacular results.'

'So that's no help.'

'Well, there are products that kill them. If you want to go down that road.'

'Kill them? But they're so little, so cute. I could murder them for tunnelling under my garden but not kill them.'

He laughs. 'Try talking to them. People talk to bees and horses. Why not talk to the moles and ask them nicely to leave your garden alone?'

He sees my face and turns serious again, 'Sorry, Tessa, I shouldn't tease you. I know what a pest moles can be, believe me.'

Next day on my round I park the van at a tiny beach where I sometimes stop to eat my lunch. It's another fine day so I get out to stretch my legs and take a short walk on the sand. The changing nature of the shore never fails to fill me with wonder; it's never the same two days in a row. Though the beach is sandy today and the tide out, I came here once after a storm and found to my astonishment that there was no sand only an expanse of pebbles. For a few moments I thought I'd gone to the wrong beach, but there was the same old harbour wall at the end with the rotting fishing boat moored to it. Bemused, I went back a few days later and there was the sand again.

One of the locals told me it wasn't a rare occurrence. 'It's the power of the sea, maid. When a storm's that fierce, combined with the spring or autumn tides, the sand gets sucked back into the sea, only to be brought back on another tide.'

Today there is a mass of interesting seaweed washed up on the shore. The shape, texture and colour – deep greens, rich browns, purple-blacks – are fascinating. A strand of copper-coloured seaweed, washed over a rock, looks like an exquisite fine stone necklace. Impulsively I pick it up and drape it around my neck over my red postie polo shirt. It smells divine, faintly fishy but mostly that wonderful ozone scent that I can't get enough of.

An hour or so later, delivering post to the Yellands, I'm waylaid by both of them to see the magnificent blooms of the Old Garden Rose, which have outdone themselves this year. The great white roses are truly exquisite and Mr Yelland actually takes his pipe from his mouth to inhale deeply.

'The scent,' he explains. 'Just smell.'

I take a deep breath and the perfume is truly heavenly, or it would be if a slight fishy smell wasn't mingling with it. I glance down and see my fat seaweed necklace hanging down my chest, the sun having dried away the salty sea scent leaving only an odour of decaying sea creatures.

The Yellands must have noticed my unusual drapery, as we have been discussing roses for some time, but being so formal and polite they, of course, would not mention it. And, of course, I can't begin to explain now to them just why I decided to adorn myself with seaweed jewellery. And so we all pretend that nothing is amiss, that I'm still their spruce uniformed postie and not some crazy woman pretending to be a mermaid.

When I go, Mrs Yelland pays me for the week's newspapers while Mr Yelland hands me a paper bag full of garlic mustard. 'To thank you, Mrs Hainsworth,' they say politely.

Mrs Yelland sheepishly hands me another bag, this one full of Swiss chard and says, 'I wonder if you could please do us a favour and deliver these to Mr Perkins on your round? He loves Swiss chard, his wife used to grow it year after year before she died.'

'It's just that we don't see him that often these days, not since we moved,' Mr Yelland adds.

I take the bag, assure them that I'll deliver the vegetable which I do shortly. There's no post for Perkins (the Yellands are the only ones I've heard refer to him as Mr) but I drive out to his semi-isolated cottage anyway. He takes the chard with great pleasure and asks me to wait while he hobbles back into his house on his painful hips, coming back with an armful of magazines.

'For the Yellands,' he says with a huge smile that shows numerous gaps in his teeth. 'He do love farming magazines, since he left Falmouth and moved to the country to grow his roses.'

I put the magazines in the van with all the other stuff I've collected during the day. It's full of a huge variety of vegetables, newspapers and magazines, jars of homemade jam, rabbit food and an assortment of other items. The barter system is still going strong. In exchange for a plastic bag of chicken scraps from one of my customers which I take to another, I get half a dozen eggs to take back. Another buys dog food in huge fifty-pound sacks and every week gives me a small bag to take to a pensioner for her tiny terrier. In return, I take homemade scones to the dog food buyer.

I've somehow joined the bartering myself, exchanging eggs from my hens, which are laying prolifically, for purple sprouting broccoli, elderflower wine, and, last autumn, box loads of eating apples. I've even exchanged Ben's special vegetarian lasagne, which everyone loves, with Harry and Charlie for fresh fish from Charlie's father's boat. I still fantasise about getting rid of money altogether and living purely on the barter system.

Meanwhile, as the produce in my garden grows, so does Elvis. The snake has grown several inches in the short time he's been with us. Every month his shiny skin grows dull, opaque, and within a couple of days he sheds his old one and has a spurt of growth. With great delight Will shows us his first discarded skin, not long after we first have him, to compare his size. He grows that much in a month? This is not good, I think to myself as I smile and try to show Will some motherly enthusiasm.

Google Gull is also growing. He's now got feathers so he must be at least four weeks old. I've been frantically Googling baby seagulls and have found that by four weeks, they have their flight feathers. We've moved his box outside, something that had to be done when he started hopping out of his box and around the kitchen. Unfortunately Google is not house-trained, so out he had to go. He's not flying yet, though he flaps as if he'd like to. I'm worried about what will happen when he does. I've been told he won't survive in the wild, after he's been hand-reared. But does Google Gull know this? Will he go off and be pecked to death by other birds, or starve because he didn't have parents to teach him how to forage for himself?

In the meantime, he seems happy enough outside. We've put him in the old chicken run, which is perfect for a non-flying bird. He seems contented enough there, though if I forget to shut the little gate he follows me right back into the house where he and Jake usually confront each other with yelps, barks, squawks and caws loud enough for the whole village to hear. I have to intervene, admonish them both, and gently carry Google back into the fenced run where Jake, frustrated, can't get at him.

On Saturday I have a rare rota's day off. Ben is working at the café, Will and Amy are playing with friends in the village, and I'm off to work on the allotment. As I pass Poet's Tenement, I see Edna and Hector walking up and down taking their 'constitutional' as I've heard Hector call it.

'Beautiful day,' I comment as they stop to say hello.

The Venerable Bede looks at me disdainfully. The more I make a fuss of him, the more he looks at me as if I were a ragamuffin of a mouse that he can't be bothered to acknowledge, let alone chase. You'd think he'd be a little more affectionate after I rescued him and I tell him so as I tickle the top of his head. I know he loves this, but won't admit it, rewarding me with another condescending glance.

I go see my hens and decide it's time to clean them out which I try to do once a week, though I think it's been ten days this time as so much has been happening. The lamb has arrived, the one we are going to raise for food. Joe found him at a neighbouring farm where it was one of a pair of twins being bottle-fed. The mother died and the farmer is rearing one of the lambs for his own freezer but was selling the other. Luckily it's a couple of weeks old so doesn't have to be bottle-fed more than three times a day, but it's enough. All four of us take turns going out to the farm, Ben in the morning, me usually right after work, and Amy and Will in the evenings. That's the general idea anyway. In another couple of weeks he can be down to just a couple of bottles, Joe tells us.

It's a cute thing, mostly white but with a black circle of wool around one eye. Already it follows us around whenever we go to feed it. The children have decided to name the lamb Patch, though I told them that maybe it wasn't such a good idea to name something we're going to eat one day.

'Remember, this creature is not our pet. It's an animal we are raising for meat. That was the deal, remember. We want to feed you children wholesome food on prices we can afford and this is part of that scheme.'

'We know all that,' Amy said after this little speech. 'But everything has to have a name.'

Right now I'm not thinking about meat production but focusing on my egg producers. I find the hens enormously comforting, there's something about their clucking and scratching in the earth that I could watch for hours. Today I've brought a flask of tea from home and I pull out an ancient lawn chair I salvaged from one of the Humphreys' sheds which

I sit on in the overgrown orchard. As the hens peck around my feet I feel perfectly content, perfectly at peace.

I'm nearly asleep in the sun when I hear a familiar voice calling my name. I look up to see Annie of all people running towards me, Pete following closely behind. She grabs me in a huge bear hug and in between laughs and embraces, she gasps, 'I knew we'd find you here. Goodness look how things are growing!' She's looking over at the allotment. 'When you showed it to me last, it was just a mound of dirt.'

As Pete hugs me, Annie starts to sneeze. The hens are flapping about with the intrusion and making indignant noises, so the three of us go out of the tiny gate in the enclosure to stand at the edge of the allotment. 'Oh wow, those rhododendrons, how fabulous,' Annie cries. 'I've never seen so many in one place.'

We're all talking at once. Annie admires the view – you can see the sea from the allotment – and Pete commiserates over the mounds of dirt the moles have made under some of my vegetables.

'They've made quite a mess,' he says.

'Maybe I should talk to them like you said,' I joke.

'Just the sort of thing you'd do,' Annie grins.

Finally there's a pause in all our gabbling. I look at Annie and as usual she looks fabulous. Her dark hair is a bit longer than usual, just below her ears, and it's a stunning cut, suits her tall frame, her luscious figure. She's wearing a deep sea-colour summer skirt with funky wellie boots, ice blue with little cows all over them, and a long silky cardigan over a close-fitting tee shirt. She looks London through and through. Annie's sophisticated elegance used to make me feel dowdy every time she visited, but now that I've got used to living in my rural skin, and learned how to buy great clothes in charity shops and at discount stores, it doesn't bother me.

I say, 'Well, it's terrific to see you both, but what a surprise. I knew you were arriving last night, Annie, but I didn't think we'd see you till dinner at your place tonight. Or isn't it on now?'

Pete says, 'Of course it's still on. But Annie couldn't wait.'

'Wait for what?'

'For tonight,' Annie cries, her face radiant. 'I couldn't wait for tonight to tell you.' She looks at Pete who puts his arm around her tenderly then she turns back to me. 'We're getting married.'

'Omigod. Oh. My. God,' I'm so dumbfounded I'm virtually speechless.

For the next few minutes the air is filled with shrieks of joy and amazement and the three of us are once again hugging each other, breaking apart, and hugging again. When we calm down a bit I say, 'Let's go back to the house. I'll make coffee and we can celebrate.'

'We'll do that tonight, when Ben's there,' Annie says. 'Pete and I have loads to do before then. We're on our way to see Pete's parents to tell them the news.'

'We've been invited to lunch there anyway,' Pete adds.

'We're on our way now, but I had to tell you before we told anyone else.'

'When did you decide?'

Annie smiles. 'Last night, not long after I arrived. It's been so awful, these snatched weekends. Neither of us could bear it any longer.'

We indulge in another round of gabble and excitement. Then Pete picks up a carrier bag he'd put on the ground and pulls out a bottle of champagne, cold and just right to drink. Annie says, 'We have to have a mini celebration together, Tessa, before we tell Pete's parents.'

Pete opens the champagne and Annie gets out a packet of

plastic flute glasses which she rips open. This is crazy, it's only eleven o'clock in the morning and we're sitting on stones and fallen logs in a ramshackle old garden drinking a toast to my sophisticated London friend who is marrying a Cornish agriculturalist.

To add to the bizarre atmosphere, Edna and Hector have come to the gate and are watching us with open curiosity. I wave to them, and Edna calls, 'Sorry to intrude, dear, but we thought something was the matter. We'll leave now.'

Annie whispers, 'Oh, do call them over. You've told me so much about them, I'm dying to meet them.'

'We need someone to help us finish the champagne,' Pete adds. 'I'm driving so I can't have any more.'

Annie giggles, 'And I've got to be a bit sensible when we tell your parents.'

I manage not only to persuade Edna and Hector to join us, but to have a glass of the superb champagne. Annie can't help staring surreptitiously at the old couple, dressed today in something a bit frayed and vaguely Chairman Mao-looking. They are wearing identical straw hats which seem to shed a bit of straw every time they shake their heads. I can see Annie's mind clicking, thinking what a wonderful BBC documentary could be made about them if only they could be made to talk about their lives.

We drink another toast to the engaged couple then they say they must leave, they'll be late if they don't. I hug Annie again and off they go in a flurry of waves.

Hector says, taking another sip of his champagne, 'Very enjoyable. Reminds me of that wedding we went to in St Petersburg.'

Edna nods but says, 'I think that was vodka we were drinking.'

'No, the vodka came later. After the Soviet soldier made such a peculiar speech.'

I open my mouth for the inevitable questions but before a word has time to exit my lips, Hector says, 'We must be off. Goodbye, dear maid, and many thanks for letting us join in your celebration.'

Edna thanks me too, adding, 'I'm sure your friends will be as happily married as we have been.' She smiles at Hector. 'There's nothing like a good Cornishman to see you right.'

As they walk off he takes her hand and keeps holding it until he has to drop it to open the gate.

There's no time now to clean the hen house, I'll do it later. I'm zizzing with crazy joy for Annie and Pete and also from the glass of fizz. But I really must calm down and do some work, so I turn to the allotment. The earth around the plants is no longer smooth but is in rough mounds, all ploughed up in places. The moles must have brought all their aunts, uncles and cousins into my patch.

'Tis moles, my lover,' the voice comes from the gate to the road and sure enough, leaning over it and shaking his head mournfully is Doug. 'Bad year for them. Moles done dug tunnels all under Joe's best fields, this year.'

I sigh. 'I know. So what can I do about it?'

He purses his lips, makes that whistling noise again as if he's sucking in air. I wait for the usual head shake that accompanies it, and yes, here it comes. I stifle a giggle. It's a noise, a gesture that says so many things: how hopeless it all is, and how I could have told you so anyway. When he speaks at last he says, 'Not much can be done for doing in moles, me handsome.'

I look at him and shrug. 'That's what I thought. Oh well, I'll just have to learn to live with them.'

'They'll be ruining your garden. They got to go. Shame you can't do nothing about them.' A cunning look comes into his eyes. 'Unless . . .' His voice trails off.

'Unless what, Doug?'

'Unless you be willing to go out to the crossroads at midnight, under a full moon, and do the mole curse.'

I narrow my eyes at him. 'What's the mole curse?'

'Why you say whatever words you like, as long as you be cursing them moles.'

I stare at him. He's trying hard to look sombre but he's got a sly grin just itching to start on his face. He really does want me to believe him, so he can tell all his mates at the pub another tale about the daft Londoners who have moved into Treverny.

'Is that so, Doug?'

'Tis true, my lover. Folk been cursing moles at the crossroads at midnight during the nights of full moon, for as long as my granddaddy can remember. And y'know, there be a full moon tonight. How about trying it?'

He leans over to me, deepens his voice as if he's telling me some ancient secret. 'It do work,' he coaxes. 'I done seen it meself. Just one night, one curse, and you be rid of moles for ever. Them buggers won't go near your garden.'

He's so convincing that I'm beginning to wonder if he's serious or just pulling my leg again. It wouldn't be the daftest thing I've heard since I moved here. There are folk around who are said to be wart charmers, making the pesky things disappear with a magic word or two. Still, I'll never know, as Doug would never admit anything. So I just smile, tell him I'll think about it. He seems satisfied with this and we part on good terms, though I'm hiding a smile as I wonder if he'll come out tonight under that full moon and hide behind the beech tree at the crossroads, to see if that gullible postie shows up. I almost feel like doing it, to give him something more to talk about but I need my sleep and anyway, we have our cele-bration dinner with Annie and Pete tonight.

Back I go to my garden, painstakingly trying to repair the

extensive damage the moles have done. When I finish, I plonk myself on the flat rock at the edge of the garden and think about moles. Actually, I like them. They have this beautiful rich brown fur, almost no eyes but adorable little pink paws. I want them to live and thrive, just not under my garden.

I realise that I've said the last sentence out loud. Probably it was the champagne talking: Although I only had one glass, it went straight to my head at this hour of the day. I crouch down and whisper again. 'Not in my garden. Please, moles. I do recognise that you need to make your little tunnel homes, but please can you do it somewhere else, in some big field somewhere? I'd appreciate it.'

I should be feeling like a complete fool but in fact I'm getting into my stride. Pete might have been joking, but he's right about people talking to bees and to horses. And to plants too. Why can't there be some kind of communication between other living things and ourselves? Here in the country, the connection is especially strong. I bend my head lower so that I'm actually talking into the new molehill. I croon in what I hope is a mole-friendly voice, saying the same thing over and over, asking them nicely to leave. I try to be as polite as possible. I want to show them I respect their right to live. But not under my garden.

Finally I lean back, feeling that I'm about to get a crick in my spine. This gardening lark is not good for backs and knees, I've discovered. I stretch up and find myself looking straight at Doug who for some reason has come back and is standing yet again at the garden gate. Cursing silently to myself, I try a bright cheery wave of my hand at him in greeting.

'Back again, Doug? Are you working at the Humphreys' today or over at the farm?' I smile, a mad smile no doubt. 'Loads of work to do here.' I indicate with a sweep of my hand the whole expanse of my allotment. I am not going over there to the gate; I am not getting involved in another conversation with that man.

I turn back to my plot but Doug's voice carries across it loud and clear. 'Well, my lover, so you be talking to your plants now, are ye?' He roars with laughter then goes on, 'So, you city lot think talking to plants can make 'em grow?'

'Uh, yes. Yes, why not?' I straighten up and look at him. I've made a rapid damage-control assessment in my head and have decided that being known as a weirdo who talks to her plants is a whole lot better than a complete nutter who talks to moles. 'In fact,' I go on. 'My vegetables are going to be so big that I'm entering something in the Treverny autumn show this year.'

Now he really starts falling about with more wild guffaws. Honestly, that man laughs with his whole body: his legs tremble, his shoulders shake, his belly quivers and his jowls are rock 'n' rollin' with a life of their own. 'Oh, my lover, you won't stand a chance. 'Tis my very own parsnips that won the first prize for the biggest last year. As for my cabbages, this last three years in a row they took first prize as well. Try and beat that, my handsome.'

I know from Joe and Daphne that Doug has had a small allotment on their farm for years. He's a bachelor, and at fifty-odd years, still lives with his mother in a tiny cottage at the edge of the village. He's passionate about his garden, as are so many folk in our village. The annual harvest show is the big event of the year. The competition is fierce. There are prizes for every kind of vegetable, for various flowers and plants, and nearly everyone in the village strives all year for one of those awards. It never would have occurred to me to enter the fray if Doug hadn't goaded me. Now, faced with his laughter, I've committed myself to something I'm not ready for.

But it's too late now. I say merrily, 'Well then, perhaps it's time someone else won for a change. Now if you'll excuse me, I've got work to do.' And turn to my garden, first giving him a jolly wave as he leans on the gate, chuckling to himself before he finally goes off, calling a huge 'Cheerio then, my lover', as if we were the best friends in Cornwall.

Chapter 6

Feathered friends

It's not till late that afternoon that I get back to my hens. First I take Jake for a walk along Penwarren Beach, near to our home. The tide is in and there's only a small expanse of sand where I throw a ball to Jake. When we've had enough of that game, we explore the bottom of the cliffs, Jake looking for interesting dead sea creatures and me for treasure. Not that I've ever found anything of value but the sea does wash up some odd things. I've found a tin box, rusted through, which when pried open at home revealed what could have once been a letter. I've also found a few lovely green and blue bottles, quite old, which I've cleaned and put on the bathroom windowsill.

As I wander I stare up at the cliffs. Here they are not granite but a kind of chestnut-coloured earth, quite crumbly, as once this was the bed of a great prehistoric river. They collapse frequently, which is a good thing to be aware of. When parts of the cliff fall they change the landscape yet again so that it's never static but a changing organic entity.

Walking along I watch tiny crabs make holes in the wet sand as they dive beneath it. The beach is alive with life, not only in the water but on land and in the sky, with small sandpipers running along the water's edge and the seagulls calling to each other above my head. A half dozen grebes are poking about in the shallows, their plump white breasts dazzling in the sunlight.

With reluctance I realise it's time to go back to clean out the hens. I will leave Jake with Will and Amy as I can't risk him chasing the Venerable Bede. I'm afraid the old cat would have a heart attack if he even saw our bouncy dog. Cleaning is not my favourite chicken job, in fact it's horrid, but needs to be done. I take the side off their coop and muck out the straw, trying not to gag at the rather nasty, sweetish smell. It's hard, back-breaking work. When the hen house is finally clean, I lay newspapers on the bottom and then straw. The hens gather around me when I finish as if thanking me, though I know they're really after another handful of bread crusts. I'm so pleased that the job is done that I throw them an extra scoop of corn.

Something is missing, though. It's not the first time I've thought of it. It's a cockerel. Of course the hens don't need one to lay regularly, but I'm sure they'd enjoy a male companion. I've already asked Edna and Hector if they'd mind a cockerel waking them up every morning and they'd replied that they'd love it.

'It will remind us of that time when we stayed with those Buddhist monks,' Edna had said to Hector, a gleam in her eye. 'There was a little bantam cockerel outside our tiny wooden hut that crowed every morning at four o'clock. We loved it.'

'But whatever kind you get for your hens, maid, it will be a joy to have at the Tenement.'

It's time I got around to finding a cockerel, so next week will start checking the local newspaper as well as putting word out on my post round.

Dinner at Pete's house that evening is a celebration, with more champagne, happy tears and wedding plans. To our surprise, Annie not only wants to get married in Cornwall, but intends to live here with Pete.

I'm flabbergasted. 'Annie, that's brilliant! My dearest friend permanently in Cornwall, I can't believe it. But – what about your job?'

'You know that I've not been wildly happy at the BBC for some months. I've wanted to move on from researching but nothing has come up. I have felt for a while that it's time to move on. And what better move than this?' she beams at Pete, her face luminous with joy.

'But – Annie, you're allergic to Cornwall.'

As soon as I realise what I've said we both burst out laughing. Annie had made that remark herself, ages ago when she first started visiting us here. She giggles, 'Antihistamines are much more powerful these days.' She takes Pete's hand, 'Anyway, I seem to be getting immune to things that used to set me off. I'm not nearly as bad as I used to be.'

We've just finished a scrumptious seafood risotto that Pete cooked for us and are lingering around the table in his small kitchen. I try to imagine Annie here, and somehow, seeing her go to his freezer, bring out some Cornish ice creams, get some dishes and spoons, I see how at ease she is with him. Seeing me watching her she says, 'Don't worry, I'll find something to do down here. Didn't you say there might be a vacancy for a postwoman?'

I do a double take until I see her grin and I realise she's pulling my leg. She says, 'You know, there are loads of authors living in Cornwall, some quite well known, and I thought I could maybe hire myself out as a researcher for them. Do freelance work, and not just for authors. There're loads of jobs I can do from home, including the odd contract for freelance work in London. I'll find something.'

I know she will. When Annie is determined, she's formidable.

Next day, Sunday, we leave our men and take a walk together on the beach, for some proper girlie talk. She tells me she wants to get married in the church at Creek, a beautiful old place at the mouth of the estuary looking out over the sea. Luckily Pete lives in a village nearby so he lives in the parish and it shouldn't be a problem.

'Just think,' Annie sighs. 'I'll have this every day.'

We're walking barefoot, making footprints in the wet sand. The tide is out and the sand stretches for miles. We amble along, picking up shells, examining pebbles and stones of all colours. I find a shiny brown one that looks exactly like one of my hen's eggs and Annie pockets a delicate flat, pink, pearly stone which she says she'll take home to remind her of this weekend.

With May and the Bank Holiday approaching the towns along the coast gear themselves up for the onslaught of the holiday-makers. St Geraint is buzzing as shops and cafés which have been either partly or completely shut suddenly throw open their doors and spruce themselves up. Windows are washed, faded paintwork touched up and the ferry that crosses everyday into Falmouth is clean and sparkling, ready for the crowds. Geoff and Millie buy a couple of new tables and a few chairs to put outside their tea house and bakery and the local Spar starts getting in the more exotic produce they know the second-homers will be wanting: tasty fresh olives from Greece, Spain and Italy, fancy confectionery, loaves made of organic spelt wheat.

From early May the harbour comes alive as the boats go back into the water. With the sounds of the masts and stays clinking and clattering, the buoyant chattering of the boat owners, the sea birds gathering around with their young for titbits, the place is living and vital after the long dormant winter months.

Though the Treverny autumn show is still ages away, I find people are already talking about it. On my rounds I find myself telling everyone that I'm entering at least one of my vegetables in the show, after my rash statement to Doug. My reasoning is that if everyone knows, I can't back out. I didn't realise, though, just how competitive it is. I hear remarks like, 'Oh, I heard tell that old Doug sat up all night for forty-eight hours before the last show, keeping an eye on his cabbage,' and 'Old Doug, he not be the only one keen to win. Half the village do live the whole year for that blue ribbon and if they don't be getting it, well Lord help their families the rest of the year.' Goodness, I hope I don't get as competitive as some. I had enough of that working in the city.

Back at work, there's been a change in our routine at the post office with one of our posties leaving and I've temporarily taken over a different round while things are being shifted about. I've done the round a few days now and I've become increasingly dissatisfied. It's a long one and ends at a very steep hill which is a killer at the end of a postie's day. It's been done this way for years, and no one seems to remember what the reasoning was behind this pattern. I'm going to be doing it for a week and then a new postie will take over, so I figure maybe I should help the poor soul out before he or she gets here. So the next day, I do what should have been done in the first place – start with the hilly bit when I'm feeling fresh and fit and leave the easier stretch of route for last. In other words, I do it the other way around, beginning at the end and ending at the usual beginning.

This works fine and not only do I have loads more energy, I've also made the round more efficient as it takes far less time. I'm feeling quite pleased with myself and am humming a little tune as I meet Susie going into the St Geraint post office.

'What's up, bird?' Susie asks. 'You look like my cat when she's caught a mole.'

I wince at the mention of moles. As a matter of fact, I haven't been bothered with them since the day Doug caught me talking to them. A coincidence or did they really listen? It's something I'll never know, for I'll never be able to tell anyone, it's far too embarrassing.

I say, 'I've just rearranged today's round. Much easier and much more efficient.'

Susie rolls her eyes, 'Steady on, my bird. Folk around here don't like changes much.'

I smile, thinking she's teasing me. I'm feeling the old energy surge through me, my mind thinking up ways to be more organised. It must be spring, the sap rising and all that. I'm used to taking a problem and gnawing at it like a bone until I can find a solution. It's what I did in London, not only what I got paid to do but what I had to, juggling job and family. I'm good at it I know, you have to be, to survive in the world I used to live in. I'm happier out of that world now, but still it has given me a buzz today, making this postal route much more efficient and energy-saving.

Margaret at the post office hardly waits until I'm through the door before she's accosting me, 'Tessa, thank goodness you're back. You can sort out this mess.'

'What mess?'

'The phone hasn't stopped ringing all morning, complaining about the post. The customers on your round today.'

'I don't understand. What's the matter?'

Susie is looking sagely at me then exchanges a knowing look with Margaret. 'Told you,' Susie says under her breath. 'Bet I know what the complaints were.'

Margaret is looking thoroughly fed up. 'I've got no time for this, Tessa. Bad enough running the shop and post office single-handedly with the cutbacks and all, but having to answer the phone every five minutes to an irate or bemused customer is just too much.'

Out of the corner of my eye I see Harry come into the shop. He's listening to this with an amused expression on his face.

I say, 'Margaret, please just explain what the problem is. I still don't know.'

It takes a while to get the picture of what has happened. All the people whose post usually was delivered early in the morning had called to ask why it wasn't there. All of a sudden everyone seemed to be waiting in for some important missive or something, and wanted to know why the post hadn't come yet. 'Always here by this time,' was the most common refrain, 'but not a sign of any postie yet.'

'What about those on the hill that got their post early?' I finally ask. 'At least they must have been satisfied.'

Margaret shakes her head impatiently. 'You must be joking. I got complaints that the post came before they had time to put their dogs in, or open the latch of the front porch where the post usually goes. Or they had a letter they wanted to give you but you came and went too early.'

I look over at Harry who winks at me. Deflated, I say to Margaret, 'Well, they'll get used to it, won't they? It's so much easier not just for me but for any of us, doing the round this way.'

Susie chimes in before Margaret can answer, 'No, m'bird, they won't get used to it. Best carry on the way it's been done for years. Feels more comfortable that way for everyone.'

Margaret agrees. I throw my hands up in the air with an exaggerated gesture of defeat. 'I give up.'

'You'll learn,' Susie says as I go out the door, patting me on the shoulder as if I were a child being taught a gentle lesson. 'Don't fret about it.'

Harry whisks me off for a coffee, this time to the Sunflower Café as the sky is threatening rain and we need to be indoors. Ben is in there, serving coffee and food, but he's too busy to sit with us and say more than hello. We find a small table in the corner by the big picture window, looking out at the sea. It's a deep navy blue-black today and the surface is pocked with raindrops as the threatened deluge begins, the boats in the harbour securely moored but bobbing about in the swell. The café is soon filled with people sheltering from the storm.

Over coffee Harry says. 'I couldn't help overhearing. You know, about changing the postie round.'

'Harry, this is me you're talking to. Your ears were flapping away, taking in every word. You loved it.'

He grins, 'OK, I admit it, I was openly eavesdropping. And yes I love it – I love your naivety sometimes. It's very endearing.'

'What do you mean, naïve?'

'Oh, about rural life. You've done a brilliant job adjusting to it, fitting in, and everyone loves you for it. But now and again you haven't a clue.'

'Well, what did I do wrong this time? I was only trying to help out.'

'That kind of help is neither wanted nor needed here. People get used to their routines, they live their lives by the simple, ordinary rhythms of life. The time the post is delivered, the hour for walking the dog, those sort of things. It's the frame around which they live their lives. Changing the framework makes them jumpy, as if the picture inside has turned crooked.'

I grimace at him, 'You're getting poetic all of a sudden. Anyway, how do you know all these things?'

He laughs. 'I made the same mistakes you did. Tried to organise the sleepy little firm of accountants I work for, make it more efficient like the one I worked for in London. Did the whole managerial bit. No one wanted to know.'

'Like no one wants an easier, more efficient postal service.'

'Not if it interferes with life as it's been lived for ages.'

Before we say anything else, Ben has a chance to come by for a few minutes between customers. He says hi to Harry and then, to me, 'I think Google Gull has learned to fly. He was gone from the chicken run this morning.'

Before I can reply, a half dozen wet soggy customers come through the door and he has to leap up and sort out the rush for tables and service.

Harry looks at me quizzically. I've not told him about Google. 'So *what* has just learned to fly? You're not breeding canaries to feed to Elvis, are you?'

'Elvis eats baby mice, not birds. I'm sure I told you that.'

Harry says, 'C'mon, confess. What or who is Google? And what's the relationship to the Internet?'

Honestly, you're really not allowed to have secrets here. 'Google Gull is a seagull.'

'A seagull?'

I tell Harry how we found him, how we've managed to keep him alive in spite of all the odds. 'In fact Google is quite sweet. He's getting very tame and follows me around the hen compound.'

Harry doesn't say anything but rolls his eyes and shakes his head. I can read body language all right and what he's saying is, oh no, here she goes again, the whacky postie. I'm starting to feel quite defensive.

'Google is a very sweet seagull and it's a miracle he didn't die. Most baby birds do when they fall out of their nests. He's very affectionate and we're all very fond of him. Besides, Ben has just said he's learned to fly. So no doubt he'll be off soon and we'll never see him again.'

I lapse into a brooding silence, thinking that I'm going to miss our little bird when he flies away. Not that he's particularly little anymore. He's grown enormously, with glossy grey feathers, a long yellowish beak and pink legs.

Harry says, 'Well, good luck to you. Just don't tell any of the shopkeepers around St Geraint and the other seaside villages that you're rearing another seagull to join the others driving them berserk in the summer months.'

'Don't *you* tell them,' I say as we get up. 'Anyway, Google's not like that. He's a very civilised seagull.'

Before I go I try to catch a few words with Ben but he's too busy to talk so I only whisper, 'See you at home.'

I'm eager to get back now, to see for myself if Google is flying. But when I get there, the old chicken pen is still empty. Has he flown away already? I thought he'd at least have had the decency to hang around and say goodbye. I walk deject-edly to the back door of the house. I'm about to go inside the kitchen door when a loud cawing makes me jump a mile. I whirl around and find myself eyeball to eyeball with Google. He's perched on the old picnic table in the lean-to outside the kitchen, looking perky and pleased with himself. 'Google,' I shout. I go inside to find a bit of food for him and when I turn around, there he is right at my feet. Jake sees him and hares over, barking wildly, and I pull him away, shutting him in the living room for a minute while I sort out the bird.

'Hey Google, you can't come in. You know that.' He flaps

his wings and makes argumentative seagull noises. It's like having a teenager in the house. 'C'mon, I've got some leftover tuna fish for you but you have to have it outside.'

I put the food on the outdoor table and he flies onto it then devours the tuna ravenously. I'm so impressed by his newly acquired flying skills that I watch him rapturously.

When the others come home, we all go outside to watch him fly, but our seagull has a stubborn streak and won't perform on demand. Instead, he stands on one leg, tucks his head under his wing and stands there immobile on the outdoor table, waiting for us all to go away so that he can have a little snooze in peace. Despite this stubbornness we're immensely proud of him. Our baby has grown out of the nest, but he's still happy to come back to us. How satisfying life is.

Well, perhaps not all the time. A few days later when it's time to muck out the hen house again, I start to feel itchy and when I lift the roof off their perches I see a rash of bright red everywhere. There seem to be some horrid tiny insect lurking in the hen house, thousands of them. They're on my chickens too, which I notice are also scratching themselves and acting restless and unhappy.

A consultation with Edna and Hector informs me that I've got red mites, or rather the hens do. This is a particularly nasty parasite that gets onto a chicken's skin and sucks their blood. In haste I phone Pete who brings me a supply of anti-red-mite powder which I have to put on all the hens, rubbing it onto their feathers and underneath them as best I can. I'm itching myself the whole time I do it and, of course, the hen house has to be cleaned thoroughly and powdered everywhere. It's a huge job and I've got to do it on my own. It's half term, Ben is working triple time at the café and the children have gone away for a few days with some friends and their parents.

When the work is done I feel as bedraggled as my sweet

hens, who are scratching indignantly after being covered with the powder. They didn't like it one bit. That's the trouble with creatures whose language we don't speak, I think as I finish clearing up after the awful job – you can't explain that what you're doing to them is for their own good.

When the mites have gone and the hens are clean again, I tell them they have a wonderful surprise in store. I've at last found them a cockerel, through an advert in the local weekly gazette. He's a little strutting Ancona cockerel, black with white spots, and he makes himself at home quickly amongst the other chickens. We've called him Pavarotti because he's like a little Italian opera singer. Already he's bossing the hens about the place and I love the way they let him, although you can see they're merely humouring him and that they are the ones who truly rule the roost.

I'm spending more time than I should sitting on my lawn chair watching the antics in the chicken orchard and communicating with the birds. It's marvellous to watch how they follow the sun around their enclosure, grouping together on one side to get the morning beams and then gravitating like the earth itself to bask in the afternoon light. In fact I'm so mesmerised by the chickens that one evening at the end of the month when Ben is working, the children are still away and I've had a satisfying afternoon in the allotment, I take a half bottle of chilled white wine left in the fridge, and a glass, and drink it in the garden to enjoy every moment of this long day, this fantastic light. The sky is cloudless and the blue is deepening as I take my first sip, though the sun is still far from setting. There's something about the quality of the light that tells you night is approaching, though it's coming slow and lazily, as befits this warm, perfect day. The hens and the cockerel are still out but you can sense, by the way their busy scratching has slightly slowed, that they'll be thinking of going in soon and hunkering down for the short night. In the distance the sea changes colour with each passing moment. Until we moved here I never knew that there could be so many shades of green and blue.

I sit for ages, drinking wine, watching the hens, the lowering sun and the sea in the distance. I'm thinking, as I often do these days, that life really can't get any better than this.

Chapter 7

An Englishman's (second) home is his castle

I'm out on my rounds on an early June morning when I'm confronted by a customer I hardly know, not only talking to himself but punching his fist into his hand so hard that I'm afraid he's going to break a finger or two. As my van pulls up a short distance from him, he turns and sees me. Now he looks embarrassed rather than raving mad and I smile and wave at him in relief.

I grab my bag of post and we walk towards each other. Mr Armstrong is one of the newcomers who have taken over Trescatho. When I first began delivering here, this isolated village, set in a cul-de-sac at the end of a rickety narrow road a couple of miles from the nearest amenities, was a sleepy Cornish village, tiny and rural. I used to fantasise that Trescatho was another Brigadoon, a hidden place frozen in time that only appeared every hundred years. But sadly not any more. In the last year nearly the entire village has been taken over by holiday homes and the old stone houses have been repaired, renovated and painted up like an illustration for country living in a stylish Sunday supplement. The result is disquieting. I can't help remembering the lovely old village as it was.

Now the place is bustling back to life again, after the early months of the year when it looked not sleepy but completely dead. Even at this early hour, I can see people at windows, or outside staring over their back gardens across a lush field to the sea beyond. But Mr Armstrong, normally a happy sort of man, does not seem to be enjoying either the beautiful morning or the view.

He and his wife, both retired civil servants, are one of the few people in Trescatho who actually live here all year long. Most of the local inhabitants have succumbed to the temptation of the ludicrously high prices being paid for property in Cornwall and have sold up and moved away to less salubrious towns and villages inland, though even these now are beyond the reach of most of the Cornish. It's good to see permanent residents like the Armstrongs settling here, making Cornwall their first home not their second.

Mr Armstrong looks deeply troubled. 'Are you all right?' I ask.

He shakes his head. 'Sorry, I don't usually talk to myself. But I was so furious I had to get out of the house, as I didn't want to worry my wife unduly. She's been so happy here; it's been a dream we've had all our married lives, moving to Cornwall. And now—' This normally placid man suddenly makes a fist with his right hand and plunges it again into his left.

'Has something happened?' It's a daft question.

He unclenches his fist and sighs. 'It's our neighbours again. The Carsons. At 7.30 a.m. this man is phoning me from London, ranting on about his wall.' Mr Armstrong points to a low stone wall next to the driveway that goes to his garage. On the other side is the Carson's drive.

This wall, causing so much rage, looks like an ordinary Cornish dry stone wall that has been patched up here and there over the past few years with bits of concrete to stop total erosion. A few stones are still falling out as I can see by the holes in the wall but other than that it looks no different from thousands of other such constructions in Cornwall.

Both of us stand staring at the wall. Above us the morning sky is radiating warmth and the promise of another perfect day, and a hawk is circling, looking for prey in the fields on edge of the cliff. In a beech tree nearby several birds are singing all at once. In the distance the sea is frisky with little white-caps under a slight breeze. The sky is such a clear blue it hurts to look at it for too long.

I hate to break the silence of birdsong but Mr Armstrong is looking so glum I have to speak. I don't like to be in the middle of a neighbourhood war but since I'd already been told about the phone call, I know he wants to tell me more. 'So, what is Mr Carson upset about?'

'The fact that I tried to mend his wall. Well, I had to do something. As you can see it's practically falling down, and the way it's built, it's leaning towards my drive. I've already had a tyre ruined by driving my car over a sharp stone that fell out as I drove in,' his face darkens.

'I don't understand why he doesn't want you to mend it. Surely he doesn't want a tumbledown wall separating the two driveways any more than you do.'

Now we both turn our heads simultaneously to stare at the neighbouring house. This is a second home for the Carsons, who are in early middle age, prosperous, and whose Cornish house has been painted an expensive but lurid pinkish colour. Mr Carson is a banker in the City and Mrs Carson's profession is anyone's guess. She tells everyone, on her visits, that she is a professional woman but never gives a hint of what she does.

Mr Armstrong looks away as if he can't bear the sight of the Carson house. 'I can't repair the wall because he says that I can then try to claim it as my own. The deeds are a bit hazy on where the boundary is but Carson insists the wall is inside his property. I'm quite happy about that: I've got my dream house, what do I care about a wall, for God's sake? But that man won't believe me, though I tried to tell him when he was here at Easter.'

Mr Armstrong is getting so agitated that he's practically jumping up and down in front of the postal van where we're standing. A few more villagers come out of their houses and are looking at their gardens or the sea, or taking deep breaths and listening to the birdsong. You can tell this is a village of holidaymakers and retired people; in other places still inhabited by locals, everyone is rushing to work or getting children to school and beginning their day.

This reminds me that I'd better get on with mine, but I can tell the poor man still wants to talk. 'What are you going to do?' I ask.

He sighs. 'Every time a stone falls out of his wretched wall, I have been putting it carefully on his side of the wall. Right against it, I will add. I have no desire to rip his tyres out as well, though he deserves it.'

I think this is a sensible solution and say so. Mr Armstrong shakes his head. 'Carson didn't. That's what the phone call was about. His wife saw the stones when she was here on her own last weekend and told him. He phoned and shouted at me to leave his property alone and not to touch one stone of it.'

I don't like taking sides but this to me sounds totally

unreasonable. I make sympathetic noises which seem to calm him down. Before we part he says, 'Don't mention any of this to my wife. She is easily upset.'

As I do my rounds in this idyllic little village, I think how sad it is that even here, where most people have been fortunate enough to acquire their perfect homes whether first or second, there is still bickering and pettiness.

From there I go to my next round, a village much larger than Trescatho which still has a shop, a couple of pubs and even a small garage. There's a thirteenth-century church here which has not been kept up as most of the others in the area have been but I see there is some scaffolding about so perhaps it is being restored. The locals greet me warmly and we talk mostly about gardening, this being the time of year when nearly everyone is at it. We compare the size of our runner bean plants and the state of our lettuce. We rejoice that the month looks to be a fine one, according to the long-range forecast, forgetting how often it is wrong.

As everywhere, there are second-homers in this village too, and one of my stops is at the home of Marmalade. I still call it Marmalade's place in my mind even though that is the name of a cat I accidentally killed when it jumped out in front of me on a dreary winter's day when I was still new on the job. The cat belonged to a London couple called Adam and Elizabeth who have a twin boy and girl around seven or eight. I can't help liking the parents, despite the fact that I had to dispose of the dead cat after they had asked me to hold the corpse in my freezer so that the terrible twins could give it a proper burial. By the time the family had come back for spring break they'd lost interest in Marmalade, having replaced him with a new feline pet. But that was last year's adventure. Since then I'd seen them a few times. They are always friendly but rather vague, as if they don't quite know how to treat a rural postal deliverer. Sometimes they are overly friendly, sometimes they are intolerably rude, without meaning to be.

Today Elizabeth greets me with a cry of delight, as if I were a treasured friend long lost to her. 'Tessa, how lovely to see you. We missed you at Easter, but we just couldn't get away. The children had so many activities they couldn't get out of. And then there was that wonderful children's play at the National Theatre; of course we had tickets for that. Such amazing acting.'

Once, during our first winter here when we were going through a particularly hard patch, I used to be consumed with envy when I was around this couple. They are so confident, so stylish, so sure of their place in life. It reminds me of what Ben and I were like years ago, before we began to yearn for something more than a lucrative job and an exciting life in the city. Going to the theatre now is a luxury we can no longer afford; we can barely take the children to the cinema except for the special two for one tickets that are sometime available, but we've got so much else that I truly feel richer than I ever used to.

While Elizabeth tells me in detail about her children's activities, Adam comes out and asks if I want a cold drink. Elizabeth cries, 'I was just about to offer Tessa an elderberry cordial. Darling, could you get us one? We'll sit here in the front garden; it's far too splendid to be indoors.'

I'm longing to get home to my garden on a day like today but they have both assumed I'll say yes and Adam was already gone to fetch the drink. We sit on brand-new striped lawn chairs, the expensive retro wooden kind, and I have a private little chuckle when I think of the real one I found in the Humphreys' shed which I use every day. Adam comes out with tall iced glasses filled with ice cubes and a bottle of fancy Waitrose Elderflower cordial. It tastes delicious; but I don't tell them that I'm now making my own and it's ten times as good.

In moments Anna and Jamie, the twins, come squabbling out. They are cross because they can't take Bronco, their soppy Bassett hound, on most of the beaches in Cornwall after Easter. Bronco has replaced Marmalade as the main creature in their young lives and now the twins are insisting that he goes with them on their outing to the seashore later today.

Elizabeth and Adam, modern parents that they are, explain patiently why they cannot. They talk about hygiene, dog mess on beaches where children play, the dangers inherent on a crowded summer's beach filled with dogs. The more reasonable they are, the more the twins whine. Elizabeth and Adam dither, try to find solutions and fail. The few, tiny, secluded beaches that do permit dogs during the season are not acceptable ones for the twins.

Elizabeth says to me in despair, 'Do they really enforce that law? Bronco is such a sweet thing and we're responsible dog owners.'

Adam nods, 'We always clean up after him.'

The twins, sensing victory, become even shriller, as if raising their voices can ensure a total surrender from their parents. Maybe it can, as they are looking quite at a loss. I have to tell them gently that yes, the rule is enforced, and the twins glare at me malignantly. Now Adam and Elizabeth are starting to dither aloud about what to do and at once they are disagreeing, but in an oh-so-civilised manner, doing it with a bright look my way every now and again as if assuring me that it's all in playful fun. As the twins now begin to take sides I decide it's time to go, especially as Bronco, who has wandered onto this minefield, is drooling all over my Royal Mail baggy shorts trying to get at one of the dog biscuits I keep in my pocket for the canines on my round. I give him one and wave a hasty goodbye as he starts jumping up and barking madly for another, outdoing the twins with his raucous antics. Adam and Elizabeth wave me off as if they've forgotten who I am.

'God, I wish I were back in London,' I hear Adam say as I hop into my van.

'You're not the only one who wishes you were there!' cries Elizabeth.

Oh dear, I think, it's home away from home, even with second-homers.

It's another weekend and Annie and Pete are coming to dinner at our house tonight. Luckily Ben is cooking the meal and Pete's helping him in the kitchen, so Annie and I get a chance to talk wedding plans together.

She says, 'The wedding will definitely be in Creek church, but I need to find the perfect place for a reception. Loads of my London friends and colleagues will come down, so it needs to be fairly big.'

I tell her I'll have a look around. The wedding is planned for October, less than six months away.

She goes on, 'Tessa, you'll help, won't you? It's so hard, me being in London and the wedding here. Pete's parents are darling but it's not up to them and anyway I said they wouldn't have to worry about a thing. Pete will help at this end but I need a woman's hand.'

I assure her I'd love to. We spend a wonderful half hour discussing wedding invitations, food, flowers, church decoration and of course wedding dresses before Ben and Pete join us.

'Dinner's almost ready,' Ben says.

'Oh great. Did you make a salad? I brought in the first lettuce from our allotment for tonight.'

The men admit they forgot the salad so Annie and I take

our turn in the kitchen. She's at the sink washing the lettuce when suddenly she shrieks and drops it on the kitchen floor.

'Annie, what is it, is it your allergy? Has something bitten you?' I remember the time we had to rush her to the hospital in Truro after she had a severe allergic reaction to some grasses. I'm sure now that she's in some state of anaphylactic shock, the way she looks.

She shakes her head. 'It's *that*,' she says, her voice weak. 'I was washing the lettuce and put my finger on *that*.' She points to my beautiful lettuce now sitting forlornly on the kitchen floor. I pick it up gingerly, look closely and then it's my turn to gasp. Curled amongst its outer leaves is the biggest, ugliest slug I've ever seen.

'Oh dear.' I pick up the lettuce again and examine it closely. There are so many slugs crawling around it that there seems to be more holes than green stuff. So much for my lettuce being the crowning glory I'd imagined it to be at my dinner table tonight. We'll have to make do with rocket.

Annie says ruefully, 'Guess I'll have to get used to that sort of thing when I embrace the rural life. That and the tree pollen.' She dosed herself up on anti-allergy tablets before she came so Jake wouldn't set her off but she still sneezed a few times when she first came in. She is pleased, though, that the more she visits Cornwall, the more her allergies are tolerated. Certainly she isn't as bad as she was when she first began to visit. Now she says, 'Shouldn't we get rid of that compost bucket? What if the nasty slimy thing crawls out at night and into your bed when you're asleep?' The thought makes her shudder. Even pale and shuddering she looks great. She's wearing comfortable jeans and a light summer cardigan buttoned tightly at her waist, showing off her fantastic figure.

'Annie, that's ridiculous, the slug is probably more frightened than you are. And yes, city girl, you'll have to get used to all sorts of creepy crawly things lurking outside in the Cornish dark.'

She's peering into the compost bin where I threw the lettuce. 'It's a bit full. Where do you dump it?'

'I'll take it outside. I need a breath of fresh air anyway, the kitchen's stuffy with all this cooking. Are you coming out? It's a balmy evening, just perfect.'

Annie follows me out of the kitchen door. As I'm putting the compost into the big bin at the end of the garden, I hear a tremendous screeching and another shriek from Annie. Oh hell, I think, I've forgotten about Google. He's fluttering his wings in an angry manner and making the most horrendous gull noises at Annie while she stands there with her hands in front of her face. I extricate her as quickly as I can and bring her back into the safety of the kitchen and set her down at the table with a glass of white wine.

'So sorry, Annie,' I say. 'Google must have been asleep and you must have frightened him when you sat down on the picnic table bench.'

'Me frighten that thing? All I wanted was to sit outside for a few minutes and admire the sunset and that bird attacked me.'

'I'm so sorry, I wanted you and Google to meet properly. He's the baby seagull we rescued from the attic. Annie hasn't been to our house for the last couple of months as we've mostly met at Pete's or on the beach when she's been down, so she hasn't seen our baby bird.

'Baby? That thing is huge.'

'They grow quickly. He's flying already.'

'So why doesn't he fly away home with his mates? Or annoy the tourists at St Geraint with the rest of the seagulls?'

I shake my head at her. 'Goodness, you're as bad as everyone else. I know they're a nuisance, and I know they do damage, but really you can't blame them. The way we humans throw rubbish out and leave so much waste lying about, no wonder the gulls see it as easy pickings. And they're beautiful birds too, if you stop and look closely.'

'And that one I suppose is exceptionally beautiful?'.

'Well, he's still in that awkward, grey, adolescent stage, but he has wonderful feathers, and . . .' I break off as I see her giggling and realising that I'm acting like a proud boastful mother.

We both end up forgetting dinner for the moment, drinking wine and laughing as we so often do when we're together. Finally Annie says, 'What next? You're going to tell me that you've adopted a couple of orphan slugs?' This sets us off on another bout of giggles until finally she starts to sneeze, then says her eyes are itching again, so I hand her a glass of water and some tissues while she tries to figure out when she took her last antihistamine.

When the sneezing and itching are under control I say, 'Not slugs, but there's Will's snake. Would you like to be introduced to Elvis?'

She declines, saying that she's had enough of the animal kingdom for one day and she'd be happy to meet Elvis another time. Just as she says this, Will joins us with Elvis draped on his arm. The snake seems to be growing out of all proportion and he's well over two feet long already.

Will says to Annie, 'You can hold Elvis if you like.'

Annie declines with a grimace which she tries to hide from Will. She's not phobic like I am about them but that doesn't mean she'd like to touch one. When Will is gone she says, 'All of a sudden I'm very glad I'm not sleeping here tonight, what with wild predatory birds pecking at the window, slugs crawling between the sheets and only some thin glass or plastic separating me from a monster snake.'

'You're exaggerating as usual,' I say, smiling at her. But part of me wonders if she has a point. Only the other night Google perched on the windowsill outside our bedroom window and pecked it as if he wanted to get in. The window was slightly open and I wonder if he'd have come hopping in if it had been open wider. I still keep expecting him to fly away for ever, but though he sometimes goes off to unknown places, he always comes back to sleep on the table in the lean-to, no doubt dreaming of the big breakfast I will give him in the morning. I've become quite attached to Google, if not to Elvis.

A few days later I find Edna and Hector walking up and down the garden path in their slow silent meditative manner. For the summer, they have both donned their Gandhi-type robes but now they seem to have dug out some thin floppy trousers of various bright colours that they wear under the white tunics. When I commented on these outfits once, saying how cool they must be, Hector replied, 'Perfect for the heat. We picked them up in Goa. That was way before the hippies got there, of course.'

When I reach them now they stop their walking and thank me for the lettuce I left for them the other day. 'I'm sorry it was so full of slug holes,' I say.

'Why? It was a fine lettuce, my dear, very tasty.'

Hector agrees, 'Edna made an exquisite supper, salad from your lettuce and a hard-boiled egg from your hens. What could be tastier?'

I say, 'But the lettuce was practically inedible. Holey. Full of slugs. We had to throw ours away in the end, it was so riddled there were hardly any leaves left.'

Hector says, 'Slugs, my dear maid, are part of life. Where there are lettuces, there are slugs.'

'Quite easy to pluck them off if you soak them in a sink of water. Sometimes merely shaking the lettuce dislodges them.'

A vision of my kitchen sink swimming with dead or dying slugs does not exactly fill me with delight. 'Uh, isn't there any way to stop them from getting onto the lettuces in the first place? I know there are slug pellets but I've heard birds eat them and I don't want to use them.' I think of Google keeling over after scoffing poisoned pellets; I'd be devastated. 'And I've also heard that if you put saucers of beer around, they'll crawl in and drown, but I tried it and it doesn't work.'

Edna draws herself up to her full four foot nine inches. 'My dear, you must just learn to live with slugs.'

There's no answering her back.

Later, as I walk home, I think of Edna patiently ridding the lettuce of all the slugs, trying to find edible leaves in between the slug holes. I remember what Hector said, that their supper last night was that lettuce, which probably amounted to no more than a full leaf each, and one hard-boiled egg. Tiny as they are, how can anyone live on that? Perhaps I could make them a healthy quiche with all the eggs I'm getting now? Or even give them a pot of Ben's special lamb casserole?

Whoa, Tessa! I stop myself before I go further down that road, remembering the incident with the rug fasteners. The Humphreys have lived their lives their own way for nearly ninety years, and the best thing I or anyone can do for them is to let them live it the way they please for as long a time as they have left.

Ben is home from work when I return from the allotment and he's got news. He's been offered a job acting with a small but excellent rep company, with the chance to do a number of roles, one of them a main role he's always dreamed of performing, that of Petruchio in *The Taming of the Shrew.*

His old agent had phoned him to tell him about the audition a few days ago. An actor in the company had suddenly become ill and they needed someone to take his place quickly. Ben had gone up at once, mostly just to keep his hand in, rather than thinking he would seriously either be offered the job, or if he were, that he'd accept it. But the offer has come through and it's a good one. The pay is not great but at least it will be better than the odd jobs he's doing now. The best thing, the most important part, is that he'll be back doing the work he loves, the work he was trained for. *And* getting a crack at his dream role.

Before he can accept, though, we need to talk it through. 'You realise I'll be away for several weeks, touring,' he says now as we sit down with a cold glass of homemade lemonade and try to get our heads together. 'It'll be hard on you.'

'Will and Amy will miss you and so will I,' I don't even like to think about how much I'll miss him but he's got to take the opportunity. Giving up acting to move to Cornwall was a hard thing for Ben, but he's done it wholeheartedly and unselfishly, never once moaning about his lost career. I can feel his exhilaration over this chance to get back into the theatrical world, even as I can see his apprehension at the separation it will entail.

'I'll miss all of you. It's a huge thing to do, Tessa.'

'I know. But a chance like this might not come up again. You've got to take it.'

His face lights up as if he's been given the biggest birthday present ever. 'I'll come home whenever I can. We'll have days off and we'll manage somehow to see each other in between bookings.'

I know how strenuous reparatory theatre can be with all that travelling from place to place, often with two or even three plays to perform. Staying in spartan B&Bs and guest houses, trying to make a home away from home, tough enough when you have no family but dreary when you've got roots else-where. But it's Ben's life, or his working life, and he's got to go for it.

He leaves a week later. It's all a rush, but he needs to get to London to rehearsals before the tour starts a couple of weeks after that. The night before he leaves we go to the Roswinnick Hotel in St Geraint, to have the free meal we were given by the manager when Ben attended to the chef's wife.

It's a lovely evening, though poignant because we're not sure when Ben will get his first few days off to come home. The sun is only just beginning to sink in a deep blue sky as we arrive. The hotel entrance is modest for such a posh place and you could miss it entirely if you didn't know where it was. It's a simple stone arch that leads to a winding stone stairway to the terrace. This exquisite simplicity extends to the inside, all white, pale greens and blues, with a tessellated floor and beautiful low lighting. It's got a kind of New England feel to it. What it does so tastefully is to make sure nothing interferes with what it's there for − to give you a place to sit and eat while looking at the most stunning view of any restaurant in Britain. You face the western shore of the peninsula with the lighthouse, the harbour in front and the open sea beyond. It's magnificent, with the ancient woods coming right down to the water's edge and the lighthouse beam flicking on and off.

Our meal is discreet and delicious, as the food always is. To the chef's amusement, when it comes time for pudding I order another starter, this time a kind of salad with fresh crab and avocado. I haven't much of a sweet tooth and I love savouries, so why not?

I look around at the clientele, wondering if I'll see someone famous enough to be recognised. There's no one familiar, but there are faces I feel I should know, as if I've seen them on telly or met them in my other life when I got to know many celebrities through my work with Anita and Gordon Roddick at The Body Shop. Because it's nearly summer, the place is buzzing with the usual chatter of people who are rich and confident and want everyone to know it. I once peeked into the restaurant in winter, though, and it was completely different, not as crowded and almost subdued, the people there having come for a special occasion and feeling slightly awed by it.

I smile as I think of that time and say to Ben, 'Remember when Jake came with me in the postal van that time and jumped out in St Geraint?'

'The time he found a gorgeous, fluffy auburn chow on heat and got her pregnant? I remember it well,' he grins back at me.

The chow's owner, Mrs Cunningham, a stout woman with steel grey hair and a steel grey voice, was livid; she was hoping to mate her with another pedigree dog in Surrey and now Jake had spoiled it all. I offered to try to find homes for the puppies when they came but the woman wanted nothing more to do with me, Jake or our entire delinquent family, until the day the pups were about seven or eight weeks old and I had a hysterical phone call from Mrs Cunningham.

'My puppies have disappeared,' she announced without any preliminaries. 'I have finally managed to find a good home for all of them and they've gone. Scarpered, scuttled away no doubt by a doggie thief. You wouldn't happen to know anything about them, would you?' The inference was that the kidnapper could only be me.

I assured her I had nothing to do with it and that the puppies must have wandered away again as they had done in the past. There were three of them, a lively inquisitive bunch, and had been seen several times frolicking around St Geraint, having escaped from their kennel in Mrs Cunningham's garden. I was sure they'd be found again. But as soon as I put the phone down it rang a second time. It was the manager of the Roswinnick Hotel saying the puppies were there in the courtyard, having been entertaining the guests with their winsome ways for over an hour.

'They belong to Mrs Cunningham,' I told him as we giggled about it.

'I know, I know. I've just phoned her but she's out.'

'Looking for the little rascals no doubt. She just phoned here.'

'Look, they've been adorable, but they're starting to be a nuisance, messing everywhere, chewing things. Could you do something about them?'

Of course he knew I was family, knew Jake had sired those pups – everyone in St Geraint knew. Being a responsible person, I drove down, gathered the puppies and returned them to their rightful owner.

'You can tell these animals have exquisite taste,' I said to Mrs Cunningham as I deposited them back in her garden. 'Nothing but the most exclusive hotel in the county for them.'

She didn't think it was amusing. Her look let me know that anything Jake sired could not possibly have taste.

Ben and I have a quiet laugh remembering the incident. I had wanted one of the puppies but two dogs would have been a bit much in our house. 'They were gorgeous, though,' I say now. 'So cuddly and cute.'

Before we go I give Ben a small, heart-shaped box tied with a bright red ribbon. 'This is your home away from home. Your second home, until you come back to us.'

Ben undoes the ribbon and opens the box. Inside I've put photos of Will and Amy and one of Ben and me laughing together in front of our house. There are also snaps of Jake, Elvis and Patch the lamb, and of course Google.

'I'll look at it every night,' Ben says, as we get up to leave.

'My second home away from home.' He picks up the box carefully, puts his arm around my shoulder and we take a last look at the sea, the lighthouse and the old harbour sparkling in the moonlight. Though sad at the prospect of parting, we know that it will only be temporary, and that before long we'll be reunited in this magical place where we now belong.

Chapter 8

Billy Goat Gruff

Adjusting to Ben's absence is not easy. Apart from missing him, it's more of a struggle than ever coping with children, a full-time job, the hens and the allotment. We'd never be able to do it without Daphne and Joe. Since the children are at their farm so much of the time these days as there's so much more room to play than at our place, Daphne suggested that Amy and Will bed down there for the nights when I have to get to work early.

'It's just as easy to get four of them off to school as it is two,' Daphne said.

When I started to protest she shushed me with a smile. 'I have an ulterior motive as well. Joe and I have a chance to meet some old dear friends in Scotland in November; a kind of reunion someone has organised. If we had someone to look after our kids for a few days we could do it.'

And so it's arranged and working out fine. Will and Amy love it, playing with the three sock lambs on the farm along with our lamb Patch, who like the others should have been off the bottle ages ago. But the children can't resist giving him an extra treat now and again, even though he's mingling with Joe's sheep, eating grass and growing bigger every day. In fact most of Joe's lambs have grown so much that we always feel sorry for the poor ewes, standing patiently while their babies, some as big as they are, head butt their bellies to get another drop of milk.

It was quite a lot of work at first, those early bottle-feeds, but everyone helped, and it was great fun watching Patch race towards us, his little bottom wagging furiously as he sucked on the bottle. Every time we check on him now, Patch leaves the flock and runs towards us, pushing up against us as if still hoping there's something for him. We always bring titbits of food, scraps of lettuce or cabbage leaves, and Patch nibbles them politely, though I'm sure he prefers the fresh green grass of the lush pasture he's kept in.

It's hard too trying to get to the allotment after being up at dawn for work. The exhilaration at the beginning has turned into anguish as my back aches from the endless hoeing and weeding, my knees have crumbled and my hands feel gnarled and ugly despite wearing gloves. And even with all the hard work, the vegetables aren't doing that great. Slugs, cabbage butterflies and rabbits again – sometimes it seems a losing battle with all the little creatures determined to eat everything I produce. Still, the feeling of euphoria that envelops me after a good day's digging and planting makes up for every ache and pain.

I pick up the postal van behind the boatyard at St Geraint. It's June and there's a drizzling chill rain. At least it is better than the storms we had during part of half-term, though that didn't stop the holidaymakers from coming down, much to the relief of everyone involved in all the businesses that rely on tourists. The seafront was filled with bedraggled visitors filling the cafés, trying to soothe irritable children and spouses. Today is still grey but at least the gales and torrential rain have stopped, but we're all longing for some sun.

I usually take a few moments before starting the van to look over at the sea, watch the gulls and terns, the changing blues of the sky. Today the horizon is a solid grey, impossible to tell where the sea ends and the sky begins. I'm missing Ben, fretting about my vegetables, fed up with the long spell of bad weather and worrying about the increasingly noisy and demanding adolescent seagull we've adopted, and the snake living in our house. Elvis seems to shed his skin and grow inches every day, although of course I know that this happens only once a month. Still, it's incredible how he's grown. I can't get over my nervousness of him. Will walks around with Elvis draped all over him and my insides shrivel. Try as I may, I just can't learn to love a snake.

Then there's Google. The seagull tries to come into the house at every opportunity and it's difficult keeping him out when the weather is good as we often leave windows and doors open. During one of the storms this past week he managed to get inside the kitchen door when I was holding it open trying to herd the children out. By the time I'd got them sorted and into the car before they got saturated, Google had demolished a fresh loaf of bread I'd baked, attacking it with his strong beak and plucking great holes all around it. Frustration and fury all fought a battle inside me. I only learned how to bake bread a few months ago, thinking I could supply the family with good wholesome organic loaves at half the price of bought bread. Since we don't have a bread maker, I had to learn from scratch. My first few loaves were disastrous but this one was perfect. And now it was demolished by our tame seagull. If Ben had been around, we'd have ended up laughing about it, but all I can think of now is the chore of having to bake again when I get home.

My mood is as gloomy as the weather, which is unlike me. Shaking my head to snap out of it, I try to start the van. As usual on damp days, it splutters and mutters and won't start. It's been looked at by a mechanic who can find nothing wrong. This is totally maddening as I know there must be something wrong when it keeps doing this to me. I get out of the van, sighing over the phone calls Margaret will get if the post is late. Some will be complaints, most merely queries. It's inevitable the post is delayed sometimes, with new relief posties or van breakdowns such as today, but you can't tell that to some customers. As Harry had said to me, many rural folk time their chores by the arrival of the post and any variation in the routine is upsetting for them.

Standing out in the rain, stomping about wondering if I should give up and walk back to the post office to try to arrange for a replacement van, I have one of those 'what am I doing here?' moments. As I'm thinking this, there is a shift in the light. The sun, hidden for days, is at last nearly visible behind a sheen of thin clouds. This causes a kind of iridescent effect on the water, as if thousands of tiny jewels have been scattered all over it. It's magical, and so mesmerising that I stand there for a good five minutes watching the changing patterns of light and colour. This is why we're here, I think as I finally get back into the van. This is why it is all worth it. My mood shifts back into its normal optimistic mode again.

I've forgotten the van wouldn't start. I only remember when I jump in, give it a go and it splutters into action first try. This day is getting better and better. Even the weather is beginning to clear up at last and I'm not only smiling but humming as I drive out of the town.

By the time I've gone a mile or so my smile is gone. There's a terrible clunking sound under the van and my heartbeat quickens. Has something important fallen off? The engine perhaps? No, I'm still chugging along, but the sound seems to be getting worse so I immediately pull over in a layby. What now?

I get out, wondering what I'll find dropping off the underside of the vehicle, but I don't have to look far. There's a forty-foot fishing net trailing along behind. I can't believe it. Somehow it must have hooked on to the car as I drove out of the boatyard. I don't remember even seeing it, no doubt because I was too busy being blissfully spaced out with the light on the ocean. Sighing, I get down under the car as far as I can, seeing if I can unhook it, but it's no use. The net is totally wound up and fastened tightly. I have to call for help and by the time I'm on the road again, I'm an hour late on my round. Oh well, can't be helped, and it'll be a great story to tell Annie and my other old London friends.

At least the sun is now fully out and it looks like the weather has turned at last. When the sun appears after days of cloud and rain, people rush outside, and sure enough, there are Emma and Martin, sitting in their front garden enjoying a cup of coffee. They ask me to join them and for once I do, as I'm so far behind that another twenty minutes won't hurt. When the coffee is poured, I ask them about their week, and I'm regaled with horror stories of the visitors they've had at the B&B.

'Most are pleasant and no problem,' Emma says. 'But this week the complainers and troublemakers seemed to come all at once. It must have been the weather, which they seemed to blame on us. One couple actually accused us of false advertising on our website because we didn't mention how wet and miserable it could be in Cornwall.'

'Surely they must have been joking.'

As Emma shakes her head Martin says, 'It wasn't a joke.

They actually said they were going to report us, God knows to whom, not that it matters it's so ridiculous. They got really obnoxious at breakfast and while the room was full, too. I had to walk out in the middle of their tirade as I'd have thrown them out there and then. Poor Emma had to go deal with them.'

His wife reaches over, takes his hand comfortingly as he's getting agitated again, remembering the incident. He loathes having to run a B&B, misses his farm with a passion and now longs for the day when their market garden and goat herd will pay enough so that he and Emma can shut it down for good.

Emma says soothingly, 'It was bad luck, having so many awful people in one week. It's not usually like that. Most weeks pass with no problems at all.'

'I know. It's hard, though, even with the nicest of folk. People in our house, the house I grew up in, the house we married in, raised our son – I can't get used to it.'

I feel I'm intruding now and finish my coffee quickly, start to rise. But Martin stops me. 'I'm sorry, Tessa, I'm a miserable old sod I know. Come have a look at the goats before you go.'

I tell him truthfully that he certainly is not miserable and that I'd have problems too with people who treated me so rudely in my own house. 'Forget them,' Martin says. 'That's why I loved my cows when we were in farming, they never talked back, never made nasty comments. Like the goats. Can't beat animals, a lot less complicated than humans.'

He's in a much better humour as we wander over to the goat paddock. The kid I'd seen when still practically a newborn is nowhere around and I ask Martin about it. I've been watching it grow, feeling it was one of my own animals somehow, having been there not long after the birth.

Martin says, 'It's weaned now and down at Dave and

Marilyn's, just took it there earlier today. It's been sold to a man I know who keeps a few goats outside Truro. Dave's going into work later and will drop it off in the van.'

I'm sorry that the kid is being sold but I don't say anything. I'm trying to be sensible about animals on farms and not get sentimental over them. After all, I eat meat as does everyone in my family. I do wonder why Martin is selling it when he wants to build up his herd but I'm sure he has valid reasons.

I've got a few letters for Dave and Marilyn so I go there next. I'm pleased to see that the young kid is still there, in the fenced-in front patch where eventually Marilyn wants to create a proper English flower garden. 'But that's in the ten-year plan,' she'd said to me, shrugging her shoulders. 'There's so much clearing up to do first.'

She's there now, painting the downstairs window frames, her ginger hair shining in the sunlight. She's wearing a sunhat as usual to prevent more freckles on her fair face, as she's told me before. Plump and pert, she has round cheeks and wide expressive blue eyes. She makes a nice contrast to Dave who is tall, skinny and dark-haired.

Marilyn stops work to say hello and we rejoice together about the change in the weather. I tell her how they've made such a difference to old Mr Hawker's house in the few months they've been here.

'Still so much more,' she sighs. 'But we'll get there in the end. I feel so lucky to be here I don't mind the work.'

I remember that's how I felt this morning, when I stood looking out over the sea and watching the light break through the clouds. I nod. Refusing a cold drink I say goodbye and get into the van. I have to back up and turn around to get away and as usual I check in my rear-view mirror that nothing has come up behind me, not that anything could as the cottage is at the end of a disused dirt track. I know that they haven't a cat or dog, or hens, or geese, all the animals that might be wandering around a house in the country, so when my mirror indicates all is clear I slowly reverse. Before I go more than a few inches I hear Marilyn screaming for me to stop. I brake, jump out of the car, and look in dismay as she falls to her knees next to the young goat.

I'm devastated. 'Did I hit it? Is it OK? I thought it was fenced in?'

'It's supposed to be. It was, but somehow it must have got out, I don't know how.'

The goat is lying on its side, panting. There don't seem to be any outward injuries, nor is there blood. I was going extremely slow and hadn't moved far, so perhaps it is only stunned. As we watch, unsure of what to do, the goat struggles to its feet. I'm filled with relief until I see it try to walk; it can hardly put its back right leg down.

At that point Dave comes driving down the track. The goat has now collected itself and is munching foliage at the side of the road, but he's still not using that one leg.

Dave says to Marilyn, 'I'll have to ring the man who was having it. He won't want it now, even if the injury turns out to be nothing much. He's very particular about his goats.'

By now I'm wracked with guilt. I can see Marilyn and Dave are in a quandary. Marilyn says, 'We'd better take it up to your parents, let them keep an eye on it. We're both on a shift later this afternoon and I don't think we should leave it on its own.'

I'm remembering how tired both Emma and Martin looked, about all the work they have to do with the animals and market garden now that most of the paying guests have left. They surely don't need a maimed goat on their hands. Besides, Martin wanted to get rid of it.

This is all my fault so I say, 'Look, leave it with me. I know someone who'll check the goat over, a retired vet living not far from me. I'll take the kid and bring it back to you tomorrow if you'll be around.'

They look relieved. 'Are you sure?' Dave says. 'If you are, that'll be great. I've got a day off tomorrow and Marilyn's on a late shift.'

'Perfect. I'll bring the goat back in the morning and let you know what the vet says.'

'OK. But if you run into any problems just take it back to Trelak.'

Dave puts straw in the van and gently lays the injured kid on top of it. My round finished, I head towards home, planning to return the van and pick up Minger later. But first I need to get this goat to the vet so I turn down the lane where he lives. Ben and I knew the man quite well in our old city days, before we all moved here, and I know he'll help. Quite honestly, I can't afford to go to a vet's practice; I know the price of a visit is out of my league. I'm sure one of the Rowlands would have offered to pay for it but seeing it was me who ran it over, I could never accept.

My vet friend is just about to go out but kindly dons some overalls, comes out to the van and has a quick but thorough feel for broken bones or other injuries.

'No need to do anything, that leg's not broken. A good night's rest is all that's needed.'

He's in a rush so I hardly have time to thank him properly as he waves goodbye and jumps into his car, overalls and all. The goat bleats all the way back and I wonder if it's homesick, or hungry. Dave threw some kind of feed in the van so at least it'll be OK for tonight.

By the time I get home, Will and Amy are there to help me unload the goat and move it to the fenced-in patch of our back garden, transferring the straw from the van into the old chicken house. It's clean and dry and should be fine for now.

The children are hopping with excitement, asking if we can keep it, and I must say I'm tempted, thinking of fresh milk, creamy goat cheese, rich goat yogurt. *Why not?* So what if I don't know how to milk a nanny goat; I can learn, can't I? I go up to the darling little thing, stroke its head as it lies quietly, resting after its harrowing day. It really is adorable. If the Rowlands can't sell it because of the bad leg, why don't we keep it? The old chicken house could be a perfect home for it. I'm getting more excited by the minute.

I've just about decided that a goat of my own to milk is an absolute necessity for this self-sufficient life when Daphne comes over with a batch of scones she's made. I love her scones; they're the lightest, fluffiest and tastiest I've ever eaten. Every week she bakes a batch for her family and an extra dozen for me, and in exchange I supply her with eggs as they no longer keep hens themselves. Often she throws in a pot of the rich thick clotted cream she actually makes herself, from their own milk. Daphne comes from a long line of Cornish farmers and has maintained a number of the old ways of doing things.

The goat is putting weight on her back leg now, though it still has a bad limp. It bleats at us both and wobbles over to investigate. I tell Daphne about my plans to keep it. 'Isn't it gorgeous?' I say. 'Look at that tuft of fluff on top of its head. Oh, I'm in love with this creature already.'

Daphne doesn't answer. She's gone into the enclosure with the goat. I say anxiously, 'Do you think the pen is all right? Plenty of room? It's quite a good grassy area; the hens were happy here.'

'It's fine,' Daphne bends down to examine the animal. 'And the goat looks fine too; it's obviously got over its shock. What I don't quite understand is what you want with a goat. Don't you have enough on your plate, with Ben away, your job, the allotment? Not to mention this fellow here.' We both look at Google who is perched on top of the hen house, or rather the goat house now, squawking for food. I have to give him a titbit to get him to pipe down.

'I've always wanted a goat, Daphne, ever since last year when Emma and Martin Rowland started to get some in. This one is obviously meant for me, the way it happened, it getting out and me accidentally bumping it with the van. Besides, I was there when it was born, so I felt a connection with it from the start.'

Daphne doesn't say that this is the dumbest thing she's heard but her face betrays her. I try to explain further, 'It's not only that, it's the practical side of it. I'm sure I can learn to milk a goat and Will and Amy should be able to as well. Think what a saving, never to have to buy dairy produce.'

She's looking at me with a very odd look. I suppose it's a bit ambitious, all my plans, so I say, 'Oh I know it'll take time, learning to make cheese and butter. I'm not silly enough to think it'll be easy. But there's plenty of time to learn.'

Now Daphne is shaking her head, 'Tessa, hold on. Didn't Martin tell you?'

'Tell me what?'

'This kid isn't a female, it's a male.'

I stare at her in shock, 'But – it can't be.'

'Didn't you look?'

'No, I didn't think to look. I've hardly had time. I, oh dear, I guess I just assumed it was female.'

'Didn't anyone tell you?'

I think back over the day. I didn't give anyone a chance to tell me anything; I was so upset about accidentally hitting it. I shake my head. 'Whoops, goofed again. It just never once occurred to me that it wasn't a female, I suppose because all the goats at Trelak are milkers.' I ponder my mistake for a moment. 'Hm, so that's why they were selling it, huh?' Daphne nods. I go on, feeling dafter by the minute. 'Well, I guess I won't be making goat's cheese and yogurt in the near future.'

Daphne is grinning like mad. 'No, I suppose you won't.' She starts to laugh. So do I. 'Anyway, Tessa, it was a crazy idea, believe me. I've kept goats before and they can be a right pain. It's not that easy to learn to milk them either; it takes ages to learn to do it quickly and efficiently.'

I sigh. 'You're right. I'll take it back tomorrow morning as planned.'

We go inside to have a scone and a cup of tea. Google wants to come in and we have to scuttle past him. After we've settled at the kitchen table I say, 'It's all for the best, anyway. I don't have time right now to learn how to milk a goat, let alone make anything from the milk. I got carried away.' I shake my head ruefully. 'As I always do.'

She grins, 'Don't stop, getting carried away. We all think it's delightful.'

I roll my eyes. 'You mean the whole village likes a good laugh at my expense.'

'Of course I don't mean that,' she laughs but I'm not so sure. Ah well, I think, it's better to make the neighbours laugh than offend them.

When I take the goat back next morning, Marilyn and Dave are working, cutting back masses of overrun brambles at the side of their house. 'What's going to happen to the poor little thing then?' I ask as Dave carries him into their front garden. 'Is he still going to be sold?'

'No, not now. Because he's injured, the buyer doesn't want him.'

'But the vet says he'll be fine in a day or two.'

Marilyn, who has been making a huge fuss over the kid, looks up. 'I'm having him. We talked it over last night and decided. We've got all sorts of overgrown places he can graze in, and a shed out back that will make a great house. I love goats, and have always wanted one, but we just don't have time to start milking and all that.' The goat bleats, demanding Marilyn's attention again and she goes back to stroking him.

Dave says, 'We never had a pet in Bristol and we can't have a dog here yet, our working hours are too erratic, so this little billy goat will be perfect. Marilyn's wanted some kind of a pet since we moved back to Cornwall, so she's over the moon.'

I can see that. Marilyn finally gets up and comes over to thank me for taking the kid to the vet and adds, 'That was the best thing you did, Tessa, knocking down that little billy goat. Do come visit him often, okay?'

I promise I will, and go over and scratch his head before I leave. He rubs his face against my hand endearingly. I can see why Marilyn was so keen to keep him.

That evening Annie says on the phone, 'I can't believe that you couldn't tell the difference between a male and female goat.'

'Could you?'

'Probably not but then I don't need to. Besides, I'd never be able to get near enough, I'd be sneezing, itching and swelling up like a balloon.'

'Anyway of course I can tell the difference. As soon as Daphne mentioned it I could tell. I know it sounds bizarre but I just didn't look. It all happened so quickly. I would have noticed once things calmed down. But that's enough of goats, I've given up the idea of having one here. When are you coming down to Cornwall again? We've got loads of wedding plans to discuss.'

'As if we've not been talking about it every minute we're on the phone or together! Pete's coming to London this weekend but I'll be down the next. Oh I can't wait until I'm there for good. I still have to pinch myself to believe it's all happening. Who'd have thought it?'

'Listen, I think I've got a place for the reception, next time you're down here we'll have a look. It's a small, elegant boutique hotel but with quite a large room. I know they sometimes rent it out for weddings and other big events. It's central to the church and everything, and it's not in a village or town but on a cliff top overlooking the sea. Spectacular.'

'Sounds bliss. How did you find it?'

'How else?'

'One of your customers.'

'Right. Someone who works there put me on to it.'

I give her the details so she can look it up online but I know she'll love it; and I look forward to taking her to the charming hotel restaurant for lunch when she comes down so we can both have a nose around. But apparently that's going to be sooner than I thought as she says, 'Fantastic. Can we go Friday?'

'But you're working Friday. And Pete's up in London this weekend, isn't he? Aren't you seeing some old friend who's in town?'

'That's Saturday. I'll come down on the train Friday morning and Pete and I will drive back the next day. And the hell with work – I've got loads of holiday due me and what better reason to take one than to see this hotel of yours?'

And so after delivering my round on Friday morning I rush home, change clothes, grab Jake, pick up Annie at the Truro train station, and we jump into Minger and head for the hotel. The weather is still overcast but it's breaking up as we park in the gardens which are well maintained but not overly formal. The grass is sweet smelling after the rain and I wonder if it's a camomile lawn. There's a beech hedge edging the garden which will look lovely in October, the leaves beginning to turn yellow and gold. There are wrought-iron benches discreetly placed near mature shrubbery and everywhere you walk, there is that stunning view of the sea. Today it's churning but in a benign manner, as if tired of all its frantic stormy activity and is settling down for a time. There's quite a breeze, and grey and white clouds scurry across the sky but the patches of blue in between are intense. 'Like it so far?' I ask Annie.

'Fantastic. If the inside is as stunning as this, let's book it here and now.'

It is. Exquisite Italian tiles on the corridor as you come in with a couple of elegant pots on the floor which each contain a young, healthy lemon tree. The furniture in the reception area is a mixture of comfortable antique and stylish contemporary. The manager who shows us around is charming without being smarmy, he's obviously handled many weddings and understands exactly what we want. After showing us into the room where the reception will be held he tactfully leaves us alone to discuss it.

Annie is dancing around with excitement. 'It's perfect. Great size, and look at the view, that whole wall of windows facing the sea. Oh I can see us all here, all my friends, everyone, dancing and celebrating,' in her enthusiasm she grabs me around the waist, begins to sing loudly, 'Oh, how we danced, on the night we were wed . . .' She draws out the 'wed' on a long melodic note as again we dance around the room. 'Remember that song?' she says as she sings it again. 'My grandmother used to sing it to me when I was tiny, God knows why. I haven't thought of it since then.'

We whirl and twirl around the room, bumping into tables and chairs, me joining in the song, humming and making up words. On one of the twirls I see the sophisticated manager peering through the door at us and I give him a little wave as Annie tries to end the dance with an intricate flourish and we both tumble onto the floor. The manager rushes over, tries to help extract us from the heap of arms and legs while we're breathless with the exertion and laughter.

Still on the floor Annie beams up at the manager, 'I love this place. We'll have it.'

Still suave, as if there was nothing out of the ordinary, he smiles and invites us to his office. No doubt he's seen it all before.

Later, I ask Annie what Pete thinks of it. I know he had a look yesterday as he was doing a soil test for a farmer nearby and was able to pop into the hotel. 'Surely you've talked to Pete before booking it?'

She nods, 'Last night, on the phone. He said it was fine, if that's what I wanted.'

'But what does he want?'

'He opted for a good old-fashioned pub at first but he knows how much this means to me. And he agreed the location is fantastic. We're coming to have a look together when he finishes work.'

I leave Annie at Pete's house after a quick walk along the cliff path with Jake, who waited patiently in the car while we explored the hotel. She can't wait for Pete to get home, shortly, to take him back to the hotel.

'Tessa, thanks so much for finding this,' she enthuses. 'You're a star.' We kiss goodbye and plan a longer time together when she is next in Cornwall.

That evening I take Jake into the front garden for his last outing before bed. It's a working day tomorrow and I need an early night as usual. It's still quite light, and Google hasn't bedded down yet. He hears Jake and me and flies out to join us, perching on top of the open door frame. Jake leaps up and tries to catch him but the seagull flaps his wing and makes excruciating noises at him. Google knows full well he's a match for Jake any day. I'm sure the gull teases the dog deliberately.

As Google grows, I'm becoming more and more aware of our neighbours. We're only a mile from the sea here and gulls have been a plague on this village for years. Though the problem is not as bad as it is for the seaside towns, the villagers here have had trouble with seagulls nesting in their roofs, tearing rubbish bins and even trying to get into compost bins. It wouldn't be so bad if Google wasn't so incredibly noisy. All seagulls are, but he seems to be more vocal than most, attracting attention to himself. The children think it's because he wants to talk to us and is trying hard to make us understand what he's saying.

I'm still surprised that he hasn't flown away for good. He goes off for a few hours every day but then returns and seems content to hang around the house. Lately he's taken to following me around the village, flying ahead of me and then hopping down in front, causing the rooks in the trees above to kick up a noisy fuss. They do this every time they see Google almost as if they're wondering what this strange bird is doing in their village.

The other day when he was following me, Old Yeller, the ancient Labrador who walks himself around the village, tried in his lumbering way to take a look and sniff at Google but the gull squawked so loudly at the poor dog that Old Yeller went yelping away. I had to admonish my bird, tell him not be so bossy.

'You know you're really a pussy cat underneath all that screeching and flapping of wings,' I told him, hoping Doug wasn't around to see me talking to a seagull.

'Shush, Google,' I say now, trying to shush him, and shush Jake who is barking madly at the bird. 'Both of you, stop making so much noise.' But they ignore me so I rush into the kitchen to find some treats for the bird and the dog. Finally when they're both munching the village is quiet once more.

A few days later when I'm delivering some post to Dave and Marilyn I ask about the little goat, for he's nowhere in sight.

'Oh he's fine,' Marilyn says. 'C'mon around the back and say hello.'

We skirt around the house onto the back patch which one day the couple hope there will be a lawn and a garden. The old man who used to live here never went out of his house so right now it's a semi-cleared wasteland, full of weeds and all sorts of foliage growing out of control. In the midst of this, though, is a nifty new wooden shed which Marilyn says is full of straw for her new pet.

'He's tethered for now, but Dave is getting fencing material. Then Gruff will have all this to walk around in.'

'Gruff?'

She smiles sheepishly. 'Yeah, as in "Billy Goat Gruff". My favourite story when I was a kid.'

I give Gruff a nuzzle and feed him some lettuce leaves I've brought with me. He bleats loudly. Marilyn says, 'That's his thank-you bleat.'

'You can tell?'

'Oh yes,' she's quite serious. 'I can already distinguish his sounds. He's got a *I'm lonely and no one wants to play with me* bleat. There's his *I'm hungry why doesn't anyone feed me?* bleat, and his *it's raining and I'm getting wet* bleat which is weak and pathetic; he used it yesterday afternoon during that sudden heavy shower. He's got a dry stall with straw but when he's feeling sorry for himself, and knows I'm around, he'd rather stand in the rain so that I take pity and fuss over him.'

Goodness, I think, Marilyn is as dotty about animals as I am.

From then on, every time I deliver there, I bring a titbit for Gruff. Today I pass a hedge trimmer at work so I stop, pick up the trimmings scattered on the road and gather them for the goat. Even if Dave and Marilyn aren't home, like today, I go around the back to say hello to Gruff which is fine by them. He's no longer tethered and as I go into his enclosure, he gives me his play signal, pushing his nose into my hand. I gently push his nose back and he leaps into the air, gambolling like a young lamb in springtime. I spend a good ten minutes playing with him, admiring his grace as he jumps up onto his wooden shed in a ballet leap, kicks up his legs and jumps down again.

Before I go I scratch his head again in his favourite spot, deciding that the next best thing to having a milking nanny goat in my garden, is to have unlimited playtime with a Billy Goat Gruff.

Chapter 9

Let it be, city postie, let it be

Though my allotment is still not the perfect specimen of vegetable growing I'd hoped for in my overexcited naïve way, the food foraging is a huge success, although I have made a mistake or two. I was thrilled to find cow parsley growing wild and picked a batch of it, having read that the tender young leaves are similar to chervil and can be used in all sorts of stews and soups. Before I used it Daphne asked if I was sure I had the right plant, as cow parsley is similar to all sorts of poisonous plants including hemlock. I did know this but when confronted with the actual plant, rather than a photo in a book, I had some doubts. Daphne did too, so I asked Edna who peered at it through her huge owl-eye spectacles and said it was probably cow parsley but the only way to be sure was to make a tea of it.

'But – what if it *is* poison? And you drink the tea?' I stammered.

'You *sip* the tea, dear. Don't drink it. If it tastes fine, then no doubt the plant is perfectly edible.'

The look on my face must have been one of horror, for she went on placidly, 'If you like, I could try it out for you.' She reached out to take my bag of either cow parsley, hemlock, or some other toxic foliage, but I held on tightly and muttered something about trying to get a positive identification. Edna said, 'Just as you like, my dear. If you try the tea method, remember to take only a sip or two.'

I left her and deposited my haul in the compost bin. If no one could identify it positively without a shadow of a doubt, it wasn't worth the risk, but all my anxieties about the Humphreys flooded back. What an outrageous, totally crazy way of trying to find out if a plant or herb is edible or poisonous, by trying it out! Did Edna do this all the time, is this how she made all her herbal tisanes? Hit and miss? Then I remembered her age, her fitness, and thought not for the first time that if she's survived this long, she's probably immune to many things that would kill off the rest of us.

I've found all sorts of other goodies though, so I didn't mind about the cow parsley. I've been gathering elderflowers to try my hand at making champagne out of them and I've found edible ground ivy, wild thyme and comfrey. I take long walks on the cliffs with Jake, rucksack on my back, eyes roaming from the stunning sea views across to the fields and meadows where I'm always on the lookout for plants.

The light is so fantastic these early summer days as I head for work that I feel sizzling with energy. It's as if the sun's rays reflecting on the glassy blue sea and bouncing onto me fill me with purpose and vitality. This is going to be another great day, I know it. I breathe great gulps of sea air as I park Minger in the boatyard and do a few deep breathing exercises. Since becoming a postwoman I've become amazingly fit, and it's happened without trying. All the years I used to go to the gym, struggling to keep trim and healthy, never came near to achieving the fitness I have now. It's the kind of health that only comes with plenty of fresh air, loads of walking for hours a day, and eating as much home grown, or at least local, food as possible.

In fact I feel so high today with the ozone, the enchanting sunlight, with life in general, that before I leave the boatyard I skip a few steps and dance a couple of jumps, yelping glee-fully as I twirl and land face to face with Mickey, the man who works now and again on the boats.

'Oh, Mickey, what're you doing here?' I manage to stammer, slightly out of breath by now.

He's looking at me as if I were a lunatic. 'I work here, remember?'

'I know. It's just that it's so early. Didn't think anyone was around.'

He gives me a cheeky look, 'So I see.' He's waiting for me to explain why I was gyrating about like a Native American, but what can I say? I decide a dignified silence is the best policy. Finally he says, 'I got me loads of work. Boats with engine trouble which need fixing. All them emmetts keen to be out there, weather like this.'

'Don't blame them. Well, you've got work to do and so have I. See you later, Mickey.'

When I get to the St Geraint post office I see Susie and Eddie taking ages as usual stretching red elastic bands around the mail they are going to deliver, as they do every day. All the posties need to put the mail in the order of delivery for the day and most of them also use red elastic bands about each and every delivery. This not only amounts to around three hundred red elastic bands a round by my calculations but it takes longer to prepare, although when you're out delivering the reasoning is that you can be quicker if the post for each individual address has been banded together. I've devised a different way of doing it by getting the mail ordered and bundled up just a section at a time. This gets me out of the post office quicker and it still speeds up delivery as all I have to do is quickly glance at the individual mail to double check before delivering and it takes only fifty red rubber bands, rather than three hundred.

I total in my head how much Royal Mail could save in both time and money by doing it my way and decide it's enough to mention it. After all, we're always hearing about what dire straits the post office is in financially, and also hearing about ways in which it must learn to be more efficient. I want to share my time-saving idea with the others, so when I see Susie and Eddie later, I tell them about it.

'You must try it,' I enthuse. 'You'll be out of here loads quicker if you do it this way.'

I wait for their response but they are both staring at me, not saying anything. After another moment of silence Susie says, 'Why?'

'Why what?'

'Why, my bird, do we want to be out of here quicker? 'Tis warmer here than out in the vans in the winter and friendlier too, gives us a chance to chat before we get out delivering.'

'Yes, but – it's loads more efficient this way. And we don't waste rubber bands, you see? It's such a waste, the amount we use.'

Susie shrugs, waves in her nonchalant way and goes off, saying she's late starting on her round.

I turn to Eddie. 'What d'you think, Eddie? Why don't you at least try it the other way? I bet you find it works better.' He turns from his post and glares at me. Eddie is so easygoing and relaxed most of the time that his fierce look takes me by surprise. I say, 'Is something wrong?'

''Tis you, Tessa. All of a sudden, lately, you've been trying to organise us. Susie just laughs but some of the rest of us, including me, are getting fed up with it. Mebbe that's what you used to do in London, telling folk how to do their jobs, but here we been doing it this way for years and don't need no city person interfering.'

I'm stunned and hurt. I try to mumble something, say I was only trying to help save them all some time, but he's finished banding his mail and is out of the door before I can formulate the words. It's true that lately I've tried to suggest some changes over things that seemed so time-wasting and cost-consuming but I didn't think anyone minded. It used to be part of my job in London, trying to make the team at The Body Shop as efficient as possible, so in that respect Eddie is probably right, but why not use the skills I learned if they would help out in my new job?

I'm subdued during my round this morning, which is so unlike me that some of my customers remark on it. I keep thinking about what Eddie said. When I finish work I go home, get Jake, and take him for a long walk along the cliffs. After I've dropped him home again, I go to Poet's Tenement to take some food scraps to the hens. They greet me with noisy enthusiasm and even Pavarotti, my cocky cockerel, struts up to say hello. The pushy way he walks around, shoving the other hens out of the way to get at the scraps of food I throw them, used to make me feel he was a bit of a bully. After watching this manoeuvre a few times, I've realised that what he is actually doing is selecting a particularly tasty grub and laying it at the feet of one of the hens, as a kind of tribute. This amazes me every time I see it, and I've had to completely revise my opinion of Pavarotti. He's not a pushy chicken with a sense of entitlement after all, but on the contrary a wonderful gentleman.

I squat on the ground, holding out both hands palms up with some stale breadcrumbs, and they gather around me

clucking their delight. At least my hens like me, I think patheti-
cally as I remember Eddie's words this morning.

I have to go to Morranport later to buy some organic bread
flour at Baxter's, the wonderful shop there that sells everything
under the sun. It's beloved by locals and visitors alike as it
stocks such a variety of goods that everyone is satisfied. At
the shop I run into Harry who lives in a nearby village. We
seem to encounter each other often at Baxter's and this time,
once again we end up at the tiny café opposite.

Harry is full of the new art gallery which will be opening
soon and I listen with interest about Charlie's plans, the artists
involved, and Charlie's own new innovative work. When he
winds down Harry says, 'So, Tessa, what about you? How's life
in the Royal Mail?'

Harry and I are such good friends now that I find myself
telling him all about my attempts to make the post office a tad
more efficient, and then Eddie's comments. 'And it's not just
Eddie. I could tell Susie felt the same, though she's too sweet
to ever say anything. Eddie was speaking for all of them.'

Harry understands totally, as he always does, since both of
us are in more or less the same boat, both ex-Londoners
making a permanent home here, we understand each other
and share our experiences. 'It's like when you did that post
round back to front, remember? The customers hated it, even
though you were only trying to help. Eddie's right, we can't
bring our big-business schemes and try to force them on people
here.'

I sigh. 'It's a continuous learning curve, isn't it? What's done,
what isn't done. How and when to join in, and when to stand
back.'

'What I've learned is that ideas, changes, have to grow organ-
ically in rural places like this. They've got to grow from inside,
not be thrust on people from outside.'

'Especially from us highly organised, ultra efficient London city types,' I say with a smile.

'Absolutely right, we're the worst kind,' Harry returns my smile with a dazzling one of his own. Every time I forget how good-looking and charismatic Harry is, he gives me one of those smiles. The lovely thing about him is that they're sincere too. He's a genuinely nice guy.

He's going on, 'But the great thing is that we're changing too, Tessa, shedding our London skin bit by bit and becoming more Cornish.'

'Like Elvis, right?'

'Exactly. Now tell me how that snake is, and that seagull of yours, and your chickens, and allotment, and that magical old house and garden with that intriguing old couple . . .'

And so I do. I'm slowly learning to let go and let things be.

Of course there are some things I learned in my London job that are valuable in my new life in Cornwall, and one of these is something I learned from Anita Roddick who founded The Body Shop where I worked for so long. She instilled in all her employees and colleagues the importance of putting something back into the community. On all her printed material was her personal mantra: 'Do something, do anything. Just do *something.*'

The something I've been doing in Cornwall is volunteering for ShelterBox, and today on my day off I drop the kids at school and go straight to the headquarters in Helston. ShelterBox is the international disaster relief charity which specialises in emergency shelter provision all over the world for people struck by earthquakes, floods, hurricanes, tsunamis and other disasters. Founded in Cornwall, ShelterBox has helped people in more than fifty countries, providing them with food, warmth, shelter and dignity. Tom Henderson, the Cornish man who founded the scheme in 2000, said he was moved to start ShelterBox when he watched a TV report in which loaves of bread were being thrown on the ground from a relief truck for refugees to pick up. 'That image of people having all their dignity stripped away really upset me,' Tom said. 'I couldn't understand why they were throwing the bread on the floor and why they didn't just hand it to them.'

The warehouse where the boxes are packed is bustling, with perhaps twenty to thirty volunteers at work filling the boxes. Each box is filled with enough survival equipment, including a tent, for an extended family of up to ten people. Volunteers turn up for as many or as few hours as they can manage and the only qualification for volunteering is that you have to be sixteen or over for insurance purposes.

The first time I came I expected I'd have to undergo some kind of training programme, but the warehouse manager told me briskly what to do and expected me to get on and do it; I had a feeling he wouldn't repeat it twice. I knew we had to wear warm clothing in the winter under our yellow protective jackets, for health and safety, as the warehouse wasn't heated. Sturdy boots and shoes were, I was told, also a necessity.

It didn't take long to get the hang of it, once I got used to the activity in the warehouse, especially the great fork lifts whizzing around getting in the new stock. Normally we don't know where the boxes are going but when there is a major disaster, like the earthquake and tsunami in Indonesia, there is a frenzy of activity. Two days after that quake we filled two hundred boxes, as ShelterBox was sending out a thousand boxes by the end of the week. My job was to put in the blankets before the ten-man tent went in.

The boxes themselves are amazing. As well as the tent there is survival equipment such as water purifiers, an insulated ground sheet, tools to help survivors cope with the environment – basically everything needed to enable people to start coping after a trauma. A key piece in every box is either a wood burning or multi-fuel stove, so that each family or extended family can have something to cook on, keep warm and gather around for safety and consolation. The boxes themselves are strong and durable, and can be used over and over for storage or as tables. ShelterBox keeps a mass of equipment on hand so that the boxes can be varied if necessary.

Today as I begin to work I recognise a soft-spoken older woman who doesn't say much but from the fine clothes she wears under her protective jacket, her well-coiffed hair, and the discreet but expensive-looking jewellery she wears, you can tell she's not on the poverty line. I've noticed she's here often and we've exchanged a few words despite her reticence. She's an extremely hard worker and never seems to tire or require a break. Her name is Sandra and she lives alone in Helston. Someone told me that her husband died many years ago, when they were both still in their twenties, and she's never remarried.

As a contrast to Sandra there's Ralph, whose physical appearance reflects the homeless state he lives in. Ralph appeared for the first time during the tsunami disaster, unshaven, dressed in tattered clothes and looking rough, the usual condition for someone forced to sleep on the streets. Ralph told reception that he had no money to give to any charity but that he wanted to help somehow.

'I don't got much,' he said, 'but I got sheds more than the poor sods in other places. At least I get a bed in the hostel some nights, and a hot meal now and again. Them poor souls are fighting for their lives and I got to do something.'

That day Ralph worked all day filling boxes, and every so often he appears again, working the odd half day. He's still homeless, still lives rough, but he's stubbornly determined to help others worse off than he is.

I felt quite emotional, my first day at ShelterBox, putting in the purifying tablets and the flat plastic water container amongst other things. As the lids closed down over the completed boxes I was imagining them being opened, probably somewhere on the other side of the world, the family taking out the things we packed, items that would hopefully enable them to survive.

Next time I went I found they had changed the contents of the boxes. Instead of sleeping bags, they were packing blankets.

'Why is that?' I asked the manager.

The reply stunned me. 'We've just had some feedback about the sleeping bags. Apparently they're being used as body bags as there's nothing else, so people are afraid to sleep in them, in case they're taken for dead and carted away.'

As I placed the blankets in the boxes I thought of all those tragic, suffering people, too frightened to even curl up in a sleeping bag because so many were dead or dying around them.

Today I have a less sombre job. I'm filling the children's bags which go in each box. These are bright yellow, drawstring bags with a blackboard, chalk, maths set, ruler, shorthand pad, pens, rubber, sharpener, colouring book and crayons. For children who have lost all their possessions this can be a real treat. I can imagine their beaming faces as they open the bags and it makes me smile as I work.

When I finish my stint I get up, stretch, and prepare to leave, but out of the corner of my eye I see Sandra, hunched up unnaturally over one of the children's bags. I wonder if she's ill and go over to her, tap her on the shoulder. She doesn't reply but shakes her head slightly and I see tears on her face. This is so unlike the composed woman I've seen here for several months that I sit down next to her and say, 'Sandra, has something happened? Can I help?'

She shakes her head again groping for a handkerchief. I say, 'Can I get you a drink of water? Or do you want to be alone?'

'No, it's all right. I'm sorry. I was just so . . . overwhelmed. By these,' she points to the children's bag she'd been holding.

'Oh, I know what you mean. I felt the same, worrying about those poor mites who will get them, wondering what conditions they'll be living in.'

Sandra's pale face is drawn, her large eyes still full of tears. 'It's not just that. It reminds me of other things. Other . . . more personal disasters.'

She starts to talk, slowly, haltingly. She tells me of a time over thirty years ago when she and her young husband, both fresh from university, got teaching jobs in the Argentine for a year. 'Many of our friends were also going abroad, but most to India. Following the hippies, the Beatles.' She smiles slightly which makes her look years younger. 'Damien and I wanted to be different. We'd both got our degrees in Spanish so the Argentine was perfect. It was even better when I got pregnant. We were both absolutely delighted.'

She stops, doesn't say anything for so long that I wonder if she's going to start again, but she's somewhere else, in another time, another place. It takes ages for her story to come out. It's a sad and tragic one. Shortly before the baby was born a civil war broke out and they tried desperately to get home to England. However, they lived in a remote area and travelling was dangerous, with warring factions everywhere and guerrillas of both sides behind every rock and hillock. Sandra went into labour and was taken to a makeshift hospital with untrained staff; their son was stillborn. A few weeks later, heading for Buenos Aires and the airport, they were caught in a local skirmish in which Damien was shot and killed. 'An accident,' she tells me now. 'So they kept telling me. This man who killed him, a young man the same age as Damien. "We thought you were the enemy," he kept saying over and over. As if it mattered. As if anything mattered, with my baby and husband dead.'

We're both silent when she finishes her story. All I can do is commiserate with her in my heart, and I hope she knows I am doing this. There are times when words are totally inadequate.

'Thank you for listening,' she says as we say goodbye. 'I've not talked about it for a long time. It's just that today is the anniversary of my son's birth and death, and seeing those little bags, thinking of the grandchildren I might have had . . .' she breaks off, determined not to cry again. 'It was just too much,' she finishes.

As I drive away I think about how disaster and tragedy are not only in those remote places where the boxes are sent.

When I get home I call to Jake and set off for a quick walk. Google decides to come part of the way with us, half flying, half hopping alongside me. By now Jake totally ignores him. He's got so used to Google that now he pretends the gull isn't there, as if by doing that the bird will go away. When Old Yeller joins us he greets the Labrador with enthusiasm, obviously relieved that he can walk with another canine instead of a pesky bird.

As we trot along, who should turn up but Doug who no doubt was lurking somewhere, hoping for another laugh. The jowls on his face are dancing with curiosity. Looking at Google who is perched next to me on a low wall at the edge of the road, he says, 'Well, well, what have we here, my lover?'

'As you can see, Doug, we have a seagull,' I say brightly.

'So what be the matter with it? Why ain't he flying off?'

'He's perfectly OK. Just friendly, that's all.'

'Friendly? I ain't met a friendly seagull yet.' He makes a sudden aggressive swooping movement, trying to shoo Google off his perch. The seagull is so stunned that instead of flying off, as Doug had thought, Google starts flapping his wings and making the most horrendous noises. 'Yikes,' Doug shouts, flapping his own arms at Google. 'The bloody thing's attacking me.'

'He's only trying to hold onto his perch. You're scaring him.' I try to pull Doug away as now he's really lashing out at poor Google and shouting at the top of his lungs while the seagull screeches back at him. Jake is barking his head off at both of them and even placid Old Yeller decides to join in the fun with his deep, mournful howling. They're all making such a racket that people have come out of their houses to see what's going on.

Finally Google has enough of the whole scene and flies off, much to my relief. Doug is swearing and saying nasty things about seagulls in general and Google in particular, while I try to calm him down. 'You've got to admit, Doug, there's never a dull moment in Treverny,' I say in my jolliest voice.

'Too right,' he mutters as he brushes some seagull feathers from his shirt. 'Not since you moved here anyway.'

Google is home on his perch when I return from our walk. He looks at me expectantly, waiting for a treat. 'Oh Google, you don't have a good reputation around here anyway,' I mutter. 'Now it's completely shot.'

I know it's not Google's fault – Doug shoved him quite hard, trying to get him off his perch, but flapping those great wings furiously in his face is not a way to win friends and influence people, especially in a seaside area where gulls do not have a good reputation. I give him a treat anyway. For better or for worse, this bird is part of our family.

Chapter 10

A rural oracle

These bright, sunny, early summer days have changed the landscape again. In the city so much remained the same for me, whatever month of the year. Though the changes were there, of course, they were peripheral to the main thread of my life, that incessant juggling of family and career. Here, it's like moving around on different planets, the landscape alters so dramatically as the light shifts. On days when the fog and mist swirl over sea and land, the little villages with the old stone churches, the patchwork fields, the cliffs and rocks, look not only mysterious but out of time, out of place. There's a sense of wonder on those days, as if everything is an illusion and reality is not really what we see at all.

Today, though, the sun is out again, and many of my customers are up early, either pottering in their gardens, walking dogs or just enjoying the perfect morning. I spend time admiring Mr Yelland's roses which are in full and glorious bloom, his front garden a mass of crimson reds, misty pinks and blazing oranges. Some are scented and it would be idyllic except that he's lit his pipe today and I'm getting a nose full of the smoke instead of the heady aroma of roses. Never mind, he doesn't seem to notice and neither does his wife. They beam and fuss over their flowers like proud parents in love with their newborn.

Before I go Mr Yelland asks me how his friend Mr Perkins is. 'I heard he was poorly, Mrs Hainsworth,' he tells me.

I saw Perkins yesterday so I was able to tell them that he'd quite recovered from the influenza he'd caught by spending the day in the garden without his hat on that morning when the weather turned into a chilly drizzle.

'Oh, good,' Mrs Yelland cries. 'We were so worried about poor Mr Perkins. Do tell him we're happy he's fit again.'

I promise to pass on the message. It's not the only one I had today. Several folk in Morranport asked me about Perkins as he used to live there before moving out into his rural cottage. Though Perkins has a phone, he's too stubborn to use it, according to those who know him, so I've been relaying messages from a score of his old friends. Not only do I take the local newspaper to the Yellands but now also to a few others, mainly pensioners who are stranded in rural areas where there are no deliveries or any local transport. Many coped quite happily when there was a village shop or two nearby, but now so many shops have closed along with the post offices. We're in constant fear that ours will too and Nell, predictably, is always warning me that dire changes are on the way. So far though, the St Geraint and Morranport post offices are safe.

And so I find myself delivering milk, fresh vegetables, bread and other items as I go about my rounds. I'm somewhat of a local oracle as well, I often feel, as I'm forever being asked about the weather, houses for sale in other villages, about incomers moving into the area and, of course, about people's health. I like this aspect of my job enormously, it means it's never dull, and it gives me intimate contact with a whole range of people I'd never have met if I wasn't a postie.

At Poldowe I'm hoping that Ginger will be in, as I've got a lettuce for her from my garden. I've not forgotten her kindness in giving me that packet of lettuce seeds when she heard my initial crop had been eaten. She's in most of the time these days, unfortunately, as she's been made redundant after the private dentist she worked for moved away. She had no luck finding another job either. She's in her early fifties, with little education and no particular skills though I've heard from others that she's a hard worker, honest and reliable.

I find her sitting on her front doorstep, smoking a roll-up and staring out into space. She looks dejected, not the usual feisty Ginger I've got to know lately. I'm sorry to interrupt her reverie but I've got post for her as well as the lettuce which she accepts with a quick nod of the head and a mumbled thanks, obviously touched by the gift and that I remembered the lettuce seeds.

'Have a seat,' she says, indicating the stone step. 'Want a rolly?'

I decline the cigarette but can't resist the little suntrap that is her front doorstep. Even the stones are warm and I feel the heat through my shorts as I sit down. 'Any luck with a job?' I ask.

'Nah, not a thing. Every one I've tried, you can tell they're looking for someone younger, or someone with more experience than I have. Seems even receptionists need a degree these days. Don't know what the world's coming to.'

I commiserate. Before I got my job with the Royal Mail, Ben and I were in the same position, applying for all sorts of jobs and never getting a look-in. For many we were considered over- rather than under-qualified, which was just as frustrating. I can only wish Ginger good luck as I start to get up.

Unusually for her she's in a talking mood. Ginger usually keeps herself to herself not just with me but with the locals that she's known all her life. She's well liked though. The villagers know she's been flat out raising the three boys on her own and having to earn a living besides, and she's never complained.

Now she says, 'I suppose there's nothing for it except to sell up.'

'You mean your house? This house?'

'Yep. Don't like to, mind, but what's the choice? It's worth a pretty packet, y'know. I was gobsmacked when I heard what the house just down the road went for, and it weren't half as big as mine.' The thought doesn't make her happy and she sighs, puts the end of the roll-up in the lid of a clean mayonnaise jar she digs out of her pocket.

She's right about the house here in Poldowe, a short walk down the side of the cliff to the sea, close to Morranport and only a few short miles from St Geraint. She could get a fortune for it from either an incomer desperate to move down here or, more likely a second-homer.

'What would you do?' I ask.

She doesn't answer for a moment as a young mother is walking past, her newborn in a pram. She stops, obviously wanting her baby to be admired, which we take time out to do. The mother seems to know Ginger quite well and they exchange a few pleasantries.

When she's gone Ginger says, 'She lives with her mum, just up the road, and the babe's dad, a nice enough guy. Known them all my life, good people. House a bit crowded though these days. It's telling on them.'

For a moment I think how, if Ginger sells up, the young couple can buy her house and everyone will live happily ever after. Until I remember they'd never in a million years be able to afford it. Bringing myself back to earth I say to Ginger, 'Where will you go, if you sell this place?'

She waves to an elderly man and woman walking by, the man with a severe limp. I wave too. They're both customers and ones I take a bagful of fresh-baked saffron cakes once a week from Baxter's shop as they can't get in there themselves.

Ginger shrugs. 'I'll probably have to move to Truro, get a flat there, something small. Put the rest of the money in the post office and make sure it sees me out.'

'Do you really want to live in a flat? And in town?'

She's been looking out over the village and towards the sea in the distance, but now she turns to face me, 'Course not. I've lived in Poldowe all me life, came here when we were married. Buried my husband here down there in the churchyard.' We both look over to the old church that stands sentinel in the middle of the village. She goes on, 'I know all the folk around here, the locals that is, though there not be many of us around these days. But the ones that are, well, they're family, y'know? I might not see them loads but I know they're there. Just like they know I'm here. That's enough.'

I tell her that I hope it doesn't come to that, but she's resigned. She's thinking of going to the estate agent in the next week or so to get things rolling.

As I leave she says, 'Look, you couldn't do me a favour, could you? Sort of keep a lookout for one-bedroom flats, either in Truro or anywhere for that matter. You might hear of someone wanting to sell.'

I assure her I'll keep my ears open and let her know. I go, looking back once to wave and seeing her still sitting on the front step, arms wrapped around her knees, face pensive, looking out over the village that she'll soon have to leave.

One of my last deliveries is to the village of Creek and after I've finished my round there I wander around the gardens of the thirteenth-century church, thinking about Annie and Pete getting married here in just a few months. The church is built on a tidal creek and when the tide is in, the church perches practically right on the edge of the water. When it's out, though, there's just a vast expanse of estuary mud. I make a mental note to make sure the tide is full before they decide the time of the wedding.

It's such a perfect day that I decide to wander around the church gardens. There are wonderful little paths meandering around small streams and tiny ponds and through the most magnificent display of plants and flowers. The vegetation is quite tropical, with exotic shrubs as well as more familiar ones. Over the past few months the gardens have been bursting with camellias, azaleas, wild garlic and bluebells, lilies, fuchsias and hydrangeas. There are also clusters of bamboo and giant gunnera plants dotted about. It must be one of the most enchanting gardens in Cornwall.

Sitting on one of the wooden benches, I think about the coming wedding. Annie has made another flying visit and we had a hilarious time checking out all the guest houses, B&Bs and hotels within a reasonable radius of both church and reception. I knew of some good ones through my customers, but because my round didn't extend as far as the hotel, I had the addresses of some unknown places. Some were brilliant, as well run as Trelak Farm which is on the list, but others were definitely not on. There was the elderly couple from Up Country who had run a guest house in Brighton before moving to Cornwall some years ago.

'We had to leave,' the woman confided to us in a whispery hiss as she showed us the bedrooms. 'You wouldn't believe the unnatural sort that Brighton attracts these days. The people we had to turn away.'

Her husband, joining us, added, 'In our day, only decent

married folk stayed at our guest house. Now it's hard to tell who's who sometimes.'

The wife nodded her head at Annie, 'But you look the respectable sort. I'm sure the friends who come to your wedding will be too.'

Annie and I tried to keep straight faces as we looked at the rooms which though clean and decently furnished, were definitely *not* going on the list to be sent with the wedding invitations.

We finally compiled a list of decent places, their various prices, email addresses and phone numbers. There were a couple of other definite nos though and I'm glad we checked them out before recommending them. One was straight out of a much earlier generation of B&Bs, with nylon sheets and scratchy-looking blankets; the other had a couple of vicious-looking mongrel dogs fenced in that didn't stop barking the entire time we were looking around.

On the way home from Creek I drive through Poldowe and my thoughts turn from wedding plans to my customers, especially Ginger. She seemed so defeated; I've never seen her like that before. I'll ask all my customers if they know of anyone with a small property to sell; perhaps with the money she gets for her well-situated house, she could find not just a flat but a tiny house in a less sought after area. But then she needs a job, so maybe Truro would be best and there's no way she'd be able to afford a house there.

At home a raucous noise pulls me from my reverie. Google is crying for attention outside the kitchen door. I go outside with some bread crusts which he grabs from my fingers.

'Steady on, you, watch that beak,' I say warningly. 'Learn some manners, you daft seagull.' He looks me straight in the eye, screeches loudly then flies off, no doubt to annoy the neighbours.

Someone mentioned the other day that having a seagull hanging around frightened away all the thrushes, 'Which is most unfortunate, don't you agree?'

Of course I did agree that it was unfortunate. Owning a pet seagull is not conducive to fitting in with community life here in Cornwall. The good relations I've had with the locals is being threatened. Google also has been stealing the cat food that a neighbour puts outside for his three cats. Another neighbour had her black rubbish bag torn open.

It's a worry, but what can I do? I'm very fond of our seagull, we all are, and I can't just turf him out. Knowing there's absolutely nothing I can do about the problem, I decide to let it go. Google has come to live with us, shows no sign of moving on, so somehow the village will adapt to having a seagull resident here. I'm sure it'll all work out. Things have a habit of doing so, if we're patient and wait long enough.

Perkins is laid up again. Having got over his influenza, he's now suffering badly with arthritis and when I deliver to him I have loads of messages as well as baked goods, homemade bread and a tureen of soup from my other customers. Though he's not as old as many on my round who live alone (his wife died years ago), Perkins has always been in poor health, enduring a bad hip which he refuses to have replaced, a shoulder frozen with arthritis and various pains in his knees and other joints. He's always seemed happy and active enough despite this, pottering in his garden, occasionally being visited by the Yellands on their once-a-week jaunt in their immaculate, ancient car. Not a driver, Perkins gets lifts with neighbours to do his weekly shop. The retired headmistress who lives in the cottage next to Perkins drove him about, but a long-standing feud over a beech tree on the boundary of their two properties finally escalated into total warfare and they no longer speak to each other. I'd love to encourage them to make amends but I learned long ago that getting involved in any rural feud is a huge no-go area. It's a shame, as the two cottages are on their own and the next neighbour is quite some distance away.

Perkins has been confined to an armchair in his large kitchen, beside what must be one of the very first creamy Aga cookers, which is pumping out heat despite the warm weather. He can hobble about but you can tell he's in agony. Before I go down his short drive, I put the post in Eleanor Gibland's plastic container at the head of her property. She's the neighbouring headmistress, now retired, the same one who fell out with Susie. Susie was quite rightly trying to stop Eleanor from destroying the beech tree on Perkins' property, which she was determined to do because the branches overhung her green-house and kept away the sun.

Fortunately the beech tree is still standing. I admire it for a few moments, those pale coppery new leaves shimmering in the sunlight and I'm bowled over by the beautiful blue agapanthus flowers that grow wild around here. I have to tear myself away from standing there doing nothing but stare and make my way to the kitchen door where, as arranged, I let myself in. Since Perkins has been poorly I usually leave all the offerings of food on the table, give him the verbal messages for a speedy recovery, and take time for a little chat before I go.

This time there's no answer as I call out from the door, something I always do to warn him I'm coming in. At first I'm heartened by this, thinking it means he's better, up and about somewhere, and doesn't hear me, but then I get a shock. Perkins is slumped on the floor not far from his chair, not moving, not talking.

Terrified, I rush to him, and thank God he's alive, but barely conscious. He tries to speak but the effort is too much and he closes his eyes again. Cursing that I have no mobile signal in this area, I grab Perkins' phone from the kitchen dresser but that seems to be totally useless and I can't even get a dialling tone. Rushing out of the house I jump over the low fence that separates Perkins' house from Eleanor Gibland's, finding her in her garden.

'Your phone, quick, dial 999. It's Perkins.'

To her credit she asks no questions, doesn't hesitate, but runs straight into her house. I go back to Perkins, who is still breathing but in a bad way. I hold on to him, willing him to stay alive, praying that the ambulance will get here soon. Within minutes Eleanor is with us, taking his pulse, wrapping a blanket she'd brought with her loosely around his chest and legs. We don't say anything as we stay there with him until rescue comes.

The paramedics are gentle, efficient and get him away quickly, taking him to the hospital in Truro. Perkins is awake but in considerable pain and each breath he takes seems to make the agony worse.

When they've gone, Eleanor and I look at each other for the first time. I've not seen her for ages, ever since she put up that ridiculous plastic box in the tree at the end of her drive for the post. She looks older now, drawn and unhappy. It can't be nice, battling with your only close neighbour, falling out with old friends.

She says now, 'Come over to my place. We need a cup of tea.'

We hardly speak as she makes tea in her pristine kitchen. We're both still stunned. Only after we've drunk some of the tea does she say, 'I'll let the Yellands know. They'll have the numbers of Perkins' kinfolk, though I don't think he's got many. They had no children, he and his wife.'

It's only when I'm about to leave that she says, suddenly, 'I knew he was poorly. People up the road told me.'

I don't know what to say. She goes on, 'I should have looked in on him. I regret not doing so.'

Still I'm wordless but she's not expecting a reply. As I head towards the van she says, almost to herself, 'He's been as stubborn as I have, but that's no excuse.' The look she gives me is sad and forlorn. I leave feeling not only terribly sorry for Perkins but for Eleanor Gibland as well.

News of Perkins travels quickly and next day I have to make numerous pronouncements on his condition. Luckily I'm able to say that it wasn't a stroke or heart attack as everyone feared at first, but a fall, hitting the side of the low table near his chair and breaking a couple of ribs. It must have happened a couple of hours before I arrived and the poor man was lying there all that time, the pain too great for him to call out for help, though it's doubtful Eleanor would have heard him. He's now recovering well.

And on the rural grapevine I hear that Eleanor Gibland has actually gone to the hospital to visit him. Not only that, she stayed a half hour and told him in her usual brisk manner that she'd keep an eye on his house and garden until he returned, and, as she put it to him, 'If you're not too stubborn as usual, Perkins, I would be happy to keep an eye on you, too, until you've fully recovered.'

'The wonder of it, Mrs Hainsworth,' says Mr Yelland to me a few days later, 'is that Mr Perkins seems happy to let her do it.' He shakes his head, plunges his nose into a magnificent orange rose nearly dislodging his unlit pipe. 'Wonders will never cease.'

Chapter 11

A snake in the duvet

Summer storms have hit our area. Delivering the post is more hazardous than on some winter days, especially when the wind blows and I can hardly walk against the south-easterly gales.

'It's been going on for days,' I tell Ben during one of our daily phone calls, after we've talked about all the other things we want to share. 'My Royal Mail wet weather gear is useless in this, the rain gets into all the zipped-up crevices you never thought it could. The door of the postal van is nearly ripped off every time I open it and there's flooding too.'

He's immediately concerned, warning me to be careful. Not wanting to worry him I say lightly, 'It can't carry on like this. I'm sure tomorrow will see the sun out again.'

There are a few near-disasters at sea. Archie's godson, Wayne, is called out twice, once with the all-weather lifeboat when a big Spanish fishing trawler is in difficulty and not long ago with the inshore boat.

'Last one was frightening,' Archie is telling me now as we talk outside his house.

We look out over the sea which today seems blissfully unaware of any trouble it might have caused, it is so innocently tranquil. The storms have at last stopped. The tide is far out, as if it's distancing itself from the fury of the high tide a few days ago. The sand and shingle which was churned up so ferociously is now back in place and the seabirds are placidly patrolling the shores and peeking in the calm rock pools.

Archie goes on, 'A yacht, 'twas taken out when it shouldn't have been, the storm was already brewing. Went down but luckily the two men on it radioed for help. They were in the water with their life jackets on by the time my godson and the crew got there and it was dead lucky they found them. The waves were enormous.' He shakes his head. 'Y'know, I hate that, when folk disregard gale warnings, think they know better, or that they're such good sailors they can weather any storm. Puts the whole lifeboat crew in danger.'

Archie tells me more about the crew, their bravery and dedication. 'Cornwall has a long history of heroic rescues from the wrath of the sea,' he says with pride, the teacher he once was coming out in his speech. 'And for every massive lifeboat rescue, there are hundreds of stories of individual courage. I've been hearing them all my life. Wayne told me how one of the men battled tremendous waves to be roped and winched onto the trawler, so that the crew of the ship in trouble could be pulled to safety.'

I go away thinking about the brave lifeboat crews over the years but as I go on my round, I'm reminded, too, of all the other kinds of bravery especially in the face of personal misfortune. So many people have confided in me of their troubles, yet afterwards they brush the problem away, on the outside anyway, and chide themselves for self-pity, or for not 'getting on with it'.

My thoughts stop abruptly as I approach Trehallow, or my doggie hamlet as I call it. There are loads of dogs in all the villages but Trehallow seems to have double the amount of most. When I first started delivering here it was a nightmare to remember which dog liked a particular kind of biscuit.

The largest, fiercest dog in the hamlet is one called Batman, a huge black and brown German Shepherd that terrorised me when I first delivered here. I've since then found that he's a cuddly puppy if he hears the word *ham,* stopping his ferocious barking and lying down, his tongue out and salivating, waiting for a morsel. So now I have to make sure I bring a slice of ham with me every time I go to the hamlet. This irritates the other dogs, which get upset when they're only offered a biscuit after smelling the ham. I can't afford to give all the dogs ham, so it's yet another problem for a rural postie, one they don't tell you about in the Rules and Regulations of a Postal Deliverer.

Batman's owner is a young lad I've never seen, the great-grandson of a cherubic rolypoly woman who is as old as the hills apparently, looks decades younger and is spry as a young lamb. The lad seems always to be off surfing somewhere. There is a fisherman father but for some reason he can't keep Batman, so this tiny, ancient, round, old woman lives alone with the biggest German Shepherd I've ever come across.

Her name, I've discovered, is Belle. She comes out to greet me as a docile Batman scoffs a thick slice of ham from my fingers. His teeth, which could maim an elephant, gently pick up the ham before that great mouth devours it. Even a Gruffalo would quake if it came face to face with Batman. But now he's wagging his tail, looking for more.

'That's your lot, Batman,' I tell him.

'Go sit in your place,' Belle orders. The dog meekly trots over to the mat outside the front door and lies down.

I ask her how she is and we talk of the damage the recent storms have wrought. I tell her how it was so bad one day as I was delivering that I found myself having to seek shelter in a customer's garage, there were so many objects flying about including dustbins, tree branches and gravel. Finally I decided enough was enough and rang the Truro manager to ask when it was considered too dangerous for us posties to go out, only to get the textbook reply: 'Your safety is of the utmost importance but you do need to complete your round so the decision is up to you.'

We shake our heads and smile ruefully at this. Then Belle tells me about her grandson Blake who is also a volunteer on the lifeboat crew, at the same station as Wayne. He was at both rescues over the last month and she tells me more or less the same story as Archie did. She too is cross with the yachtsmen who insisted on taking their boat out after being warned.

"Tis me grandson's very life them folk be trifling with when they go out in dangerous seas. They've got no right, no right at all.'

Her sweet face looks so concerned and anxious that I remind her that the weather has changed now and the forecast for the next few days is good. She brightens up, offers me tea but I need to get on. My last stop today is Trescatho, the once sleepy village which is now a showpiece for Farrow and Ball paint as it's been restored and tarted up by incomers and second-homers. I've not seen Mr Armstrong since the day he told me about the row with his neighbour over the wall between their two drives.

'How's it going?' I ask him now, seeing him working in his front garden. 'I see the wall has finally been mended.'

He beams. He looks a changed man, serene and calm. 'Yes,

all sorted, thank the good Lord. My wife nearly had a nervous breakdown over it.'

'So Mr Carson next door relented? Let you patch up his wall?'

'Oh, far from it. I had several more nasty phone calls, but then he discovered how house prices have shot up this year so he quickly put it on the market.'

Mrs Armstrong comes out to join us, smiling and placid, looking the least likely candidate for a nervous breakdown. It makes me realise how horrid life can be when neighbours don't get on. For months this couple have lived in a state of constant anxiety.

She says, 'We met the couple who have made an offer. Apparently it's been accepted. Incomers like us but they've been coming to Cornwall for the last thirty years, looking forward to taking early retirement and moving down just like us.'

That's a happy ending, then. I thought it would be the Armstrongs who would end up moving, which would have been a pity. There's another happy ending too, for the foul weather has ended in time for the Falmouth Tall Ships weekend. The Russian Tall Ship *Mir* is moored in the harbour. She's magnificent, the second-largest sail training vessel in the world, with three tall wonderful masts and a length of 364 feet. It takes a crew of 198 to man her and to see her sail is a breath-taking sight. Other tall ships have joined her in port for the festival and it's a fantastic experience, seeing all those ships in full mast sailing into harbour.

I catch my first glimpse of the *Mir* sailing out of Falmouth at the end of my round. I've got my camera with me as I often have, and try to get a shot but it's too far away. Then I have a eureka moment and rush back to St Geraint to the harbour office where there is a CCTV camera. I know the harbour master and he's happy to zoom in on the ship and we can see it clearly on the screen. Best of all it's near a yacht, so we get a brilliant perspective of how big the ship is next to the yacht which looks like a dinky bath toy beside the splendid *Mir.*

I love this time of the Falmouth festival when the tall ships arrive. As I go on my round I'm invited in to customers' balconies, patios and hilly gardens where the views of the ships are fantastic. I'm introduced to guests who are staying and treated to a variety of drinks and nibbles. It's a wonderful party atmosphere everywhere I go. I can get used to this, I think as I finish my round. Sun, sea, breathtaking views of some of the world's most magnificent tall ships, and happy people everywhere. What a life.

Today I've come down to earth, for after my round I'm off to Truro, to browse around the summer sales, especially the surfer shops end-of-season lines. I've found some amazing vintage clothes in charity shops so they are my next stop. Although Christmas is still a long way away, I'm always on the lookout for presents, as this year we're either going to make our own or find them in second-hand shops, having set a limit of five pounds for each present. I find a lovely bracelet with green stones in it that is unusual and just right for Annie. There's also a fairly new hardback in the book section that Ben would love, a memoir of one of his favourite actors who has had a long life in the theatre.

Happy with my finds, I go on to the next charity shop to find some shirts for Ben. I'm lucky here too as there are several his size that I know he'd like. He's managed to get home a few times since he started the tour, although only for a couple of days and a night, but he'll be back in August for good. Luckily it's working out fine with the children. On days I have to be up early for work I take them over to the farm after dinner and homework, where they have some quiet time either reading or watching television with Daphne and Joe's children, then go to bed in the spare room. Daphne gets all four to school and I'm home when they get back. Daphne is so delighted with the arrangement that she's planning all sorts of mini-breaks for her and Joe in the near future, as I keep telling her how much I owe her, much more than just one weekend away.

I check the chickens on the way home and throw them some of the stale bread one of my customers always gives me. I squat down, letting them eat from my hand. They cluster around and as usual Pavarotti thrusts out his feisty little chest and struts about importantly. Then I get a shock when I realise there are only five hens. I rush up to the nest boxes, to see if one is in there laying an egg but it's empty. It's one of the brown Rhode Islands that's missing. I rush about the orchard, afraid that she's ill or that a fox has got her. I doubt that she could have got out as their area is well fenced with chicken wire, but if she were all right, she'd be bustling around me like the others.

The hens and rooster follow me as I go searching under and around the tufts of long grass growing about the trunks of the gnarled, old apple trees. I'm clucking all the time, calling to her. The hens join in, like some feathered Greek chorus. Before I know it, Edna and Hector, hearing the commotion, have joined me as well, and the three of us, plus five hens and one cockerel, are all madly scrabbling about the place making ridiculous chicken noises.

'No sign of her,' Hector says finally.

'She must have got out,' I wail. 'But where?'

We circle the perimeter of the fence, trying to find where she could have got out but there's nowhere we can see. I cry, 'A fox must have got in somehow and dragged her away.'

'There'd be feathers everywhere. Sign of a struggle. Let's have a look outside the compound.'

So off we go, searching and calling throughout the overgrown old garden but after twenty minutes, we give up. I'm still convinced a fox got her, or even a stoat – I saw one not far from my allotment a few weeks ago – but the Humphreys are adamant that if something had got her, there would be some sign of a struggle with feathers everywhere.

Despondently, I return to the henhouse to collect the eggs while the Humphreys, as they often do, chat to the chickens, calling them 'gorgeous girls' and 'you handsome old cock, you'. It soothes me, picking up the eggs from the clean straw, feeling the warm roundness in my hand. I put them in a basket and join the Humphreys, still upset about my hen but resigned to my loss.

Edna says mildly, 'Look at your chickens, my dear.'

I do and can't believe my eyes. There's the prodigal hen, scratching away at the ground with the others, feathers intact, looking as if she hasn't moved an inch. 'But where was she?'

Edna shrugs as Hector says, 'It's a mystery. Life's one continuous mystery, even with chickens.'

With this sage pronouncement we drop the subject, though I do check the fence once more. There is no way that hen could have got out but somehow she did. And got back in, too. I decide not to worry about it, to let it go, to accept Hector's philosophy.

Before I go I take a quick look at my allotment. I'm pleased to see that the vegetables survived the recent storms and though the earth was soggy for days, the hot sun has efficiently dried everything out. My beetroot are getting bigger; I thought they'd never grow larger than a ping-pong ball but they've surprised me.

I tell the Humphreys, 'Doug keeps reminding me that I promised I'd put in an entry in the Treverny show and I guess I must, since I said so, but I don't want to compete, vegetables are for eating not for showing, I feel. But I'll have to do something.'

Edna says, 'I'm sure you could win a prize for the tastiest carrots. Yours are delicious.'

I pull one up for the Humphreys' dinner that night. It's a weird shape, sort of curled one way then backing up onto itself to curve another way. Still it's edible, though it might be a bit hard to peel.

As I'm brushing the earth away from it Hector says, 'Is there a category for the oddest-looking vegetable? If so, that carrot would surely win a prize.'

With a giggle I agree it would and wonder if perhaps that's how I'll keep my promise and enter the autumn show.

It's hot today and so warm that I need to open all the windows in the house when I get home. I can't leave them wide open when no one's inside as Google gets in and causes havoc, guano everywhere and food stolen. I wonder if you can house train seagulls, though somehow I doubt it.

Going into Will's bedroom I open the window wide to get a cool breeze and turning around get a nasty shock. The snake cage is empty. No snake. I freeze, unable to move. For what seems like hours but can only be a few minutes I stand there petrified. After a time I try to calm down, telling myself that this is a corn snake, totally common, the favourite pet of little boys and weird adults who actually like snakes. Elvis will not hurt me, I say like a mantra, over and over. He slithers and slides up and down Will's arms and if he slithered and slid up my leg – but I can't imagine it and shudder just thinking about it. However, I can't stand here until Will comes home and finds his snake gone. How did he get out anyway? From where I stand I peer at the vivarium. He must have got into the thin glass shelf inside it and from there manoeuvred the sliding glass lid open. *Where is he now?*

Finally I force myself to move, taking each step slowly, watching where I tread, my eyes darting around like a feral beast looking for any sign of Elvis, though God knows what I'd have done if I'd spotted him – run hollering out of the house, no doubt. Will is devastated when he hears the news and runs upstairs to check if I'm mistaken. For a few seconds I harbour a wild hope that Elvis has returned to his happy home but Will's cry of anguish shatters that hope. He and Amy start searching the house while I try to prepare a meal. Every saucepan I get out, every cupboard I go into, I'm looking for signs of a snake.

By the time we all go to bed there is still no Elvis. My recurring nightmare is to share a house with a three- or four-foot snake on the loose. My sleep is troubled and I wake in the middle of the night needing the loo but I'm too nervous to move. I know that snakes are more active at night so Elvis might at this moment be roaming about doing whatever snakes do right under my bed. Finally I have to get up. Every step I take is torment. I turn put on the lights but every shadow I see is ominous.

The next day I phone the reptile centre to ask if they have any tips for finding a missing snake. The woman on the phone says brightly, 'Just make sure all of you check your beds before you get in at night. It could be under the blankets, or even tucked in between a duvet and its cover . . . Sorry, did you say something?'

'Uh, no, please go on,' I try not to make any more strangled noises to distract her.

'Snakes like warm, dark places. Your snake could be behind the fridge or television, or even inside the video machine.'

'But he's huge. Well, long, anyway.'

'Snakes can curl up into quite small places. Look for it in anywhere unlikely you can think of. But don't worry if you don't find it immediately. You've said that your snake is a young healthy snake with quite a bit of weight on him. It could live happily on the loose in your house for months.' I shudder.

The next thing we do is contact the RSPCA, in case Elvis gets out and goes walkabout in the village or beyond. If he's found, he'll be returned to Will. When I tell Susie at the post office, she says I should tell all my customers.

'Goodness,' I say, 'he's not going to wander that far.'

'You never know, my bird. You just never know. Cunning, snakes are.'

'Well quite honestly I hope he does go walkabout and ends up far away.'

'Aw, poor Will.'

'I mean far away so that someone will find him and bring him back to Will,' I say hastily. 'I want Will to have his snake back but I don't want to be the one to find it in my duvet one night. Or to find it anywhere. I want someone else to find Elvis.'

But no one does. Elvis becomes the favourite conversation amongst my customers, with many of them having tales to tell of their own pet snakes or those of their children/nephews/ nieces/cousins/uncles/grandparents. Everyone has a story about everything, in Cornwall. One elderly man tells me about stepping into his wellie boots one morning to find his grandson's pet snake curled up inside and someone else mentions a snake found in her handbag.

By the time I get to the village where Elizabeth and Adam, my favourite dotty second-homers, live, I don't want to hear another snake story ever again. But as freak coincidence would have it, the first thing Elizabeth says to me is, 'Oh Tessa, I'm so glad you're here. Our cat has brought a dead snake into the house and I don't know what to do with it. Adam isn't here, not that he'd know what to do. And the twins won't go near it. It's not very long, it's just a grass snake, or it must be, that's what Adam said on the phone when I rang him in London. He says there are no poisonous snakes in Cornwall only adders but he didn't think our cat would try to catch an adder. Anyway if it is an adder it wouldn't hurt would it? I mean, it's quite dead.'

She tells me all this in a rush, her voice breathless. As usual she's looking country-smart with a fine patterned skirt, definitely not from a charity shop, with a cute summery top. Even her flip-flops are a world away from my own tatty ones at home: hers are clean new leather with some trendy intricate design etched in.

She is looking at me appealingly. I grin and say, 'Sorry, Elizabeth, I don't do snakes, but how about I tell the people next door when I deliver. I'm sure they'll help.'

'Oh would you? I feel such a fool asking myself.'

Luckily the neighbour next door, a dour local woman in her late fifties, is in and I tell her about Elizabeth's dead snake. The woman sighs mournfully. 'That woman do be missing a bolt or two in her head. The snake be dead. You pick it up and toss it out. I swear she's two shillings short of a pound, like my gran used to say.'

'She's just not used to the country, that's all. She's got quite a responsible job in London.'

'Hah, fat lot of good it does her here,' the woman snorts then sighs again. 'Well, poor dear, she can't be helping it if our ways be strange to her. I'll get along over there right now and rid her of the vermin.'

I tell her that it's kind of her and she brushes me off. ''Tisn't kind, 'tis neighbourly. Besides, they two aren't a bad sort. Simple but well meaning. Poor sods, must have a dreadful life Up Country, to keep running away from it like they do.'

The next few days are nerve-wracking. There is no sign of Elvis anywhere but that doesn't mean he's not in the house. Like the woman at the reptile centre said, he's probably hiding out in some warm, dark place and roaming our house at night when everyone is asleep. I'm careful to shake out my clothes every morning before getting dressed and open cupboards slowly with great trepidation. Going to bed is a nightmare as I take my duvet cover off then put it back on again after I've made sure nothing alive is lurking there. Because all our duvet covers have poppers at the end rather than a zipper, Elvis could easily crawl between them and snuggle inside.

I talk to Ben that night on the phone, missing him even more than usual. I know he misses us too, like mad, yet he feels good acting again which is as it should be. They're doing three plays in repertoire and *The Taming of the Shrew* is one of them. He's revelling in it, playing Petruchio at last. I'm glad he's doing it but it'll be terrific to have him home again.

'So still no sign of Elvis?'

'Not a sighting. Will leaves food out for him at night, in the vivarium, hoping to entice him back, but it's untouched.'

'He's probably nibbling elsewhere, at night. In the breadbin maybe.'

'Oh God. Don't.'

Before I go to bed I do my usual shaking out of the duvet and checking under the pillows before settling in for the night. The woman at the Reptile Centre said it could be months before we found Elvis, so I've got to get used to it, though sharing a house with a snake is not my idea of an idyllic Cornish paradise.

A few days later Al, the friendly repair man from a local electrical shop, comes out to look at our washing machine. We brought it with us from London and it's been playing up again, as has our television and our freezer. All of our appliances are old now and we can't afford new ones so we keep calling Al out. His dad owns the shop and his prices are reasonable.

Al sits at the kitchen table and has a cuppa before he gets going. He's a good-looking, spiky-haired young man in his early twenties with a cheeky grin and a wide assortment of jeans fashionably torn at the knees and other places. At first I thought they were the same pair every time I saw him but I've realised that some are torn at both knees, some only at one, and some have a rip or two at the thigh as well. I do hope he made the tears himself and didn't buy them that way, as I've seen for sale in some of the more fashionable shops in Truro.

'So what's up with the washing machine then?' he asks after he's consumed two cups of tea and half a carrot cake one of my customers gave me. He's skinny as a rake and eats like a horse. Last time he came out he polished off the rest of a lasagne Ben had cooked the night before. I'd made the mistake of asking him if he was hungry, as it was an early call out and he said he hadn't had breakfast; before I knew it my dinner of leftovers for that evening had gone.

I tell him the problem and Al goes to his scruffy van, brings in his tools and begins to undo the back of the washing machine to check the electrics. As he starts to take it off and expose the insides I say, 'Uh, Al, be careful of the snake.'

He jumps back with a yell and the back of the machine drops with a great clatter. 'What? Where? Shit, man, what snake?'

'No, no, no, I mean it's probably not there, but it could be. The woman at the reptile centre said a snake could get coiled up inside a electrical appliance. We've lost a snake in the house, you see. So be careful.'

'Shit. Hell.' Poor lad, he looks white as a sheet. 'I hate snakes.'

'Oh it's only a pet corn snake and harmless,' I can't believe I'm giving the same reassurances to Al that everyone has been giving me for weeks. I'm saying the words but I know how useless they are for people who are truly frightened of snakes. Rationally we know they cannot hurt us but reason does not come in to it. I know from the look on Al's face that he feels the same as I do.

Now he says, 'Sorry but I'm not touching that machine.'

'Al, you've got to, I've got a pile of clothes that need washing, I need it fixed. C'mon, look, Elvis isn't in there.' I'm peering carefully into the coils and pipes of the machine, terrified but even more terrified of having to wash all those clothes by hand.

'Elvis? You got a snake called Elvis? Bloody hell.'

'He's my son's. He's quite sweet really,' I lie.

I persuade Al to take a step or two nearer. We both look; there's no sign of Elvis.

'Please, Al?' I whine. 'Hey, remember how much you liked my lasagne? Said your mum never cooked like that? Well, I'll make you a huge one, last you for days if you please, please, please fix my washing machine.'

He looks at me with suspicion. 'You said it was your husband's lasagne. He's away, you said.'

'I make it exactly the way he does. Honest. Cross my heart.'

He's tempted and after another close look, reaches out to touch something on one of the coils. 'Yikes!' Another shout and he pulls back his hand as if it's been burned.

'There's nothing there, Al.'

'I thought I saw something move.'

'You're imagining it.'

'Are you sure?'

I persuade him to try again. There's no sign of Elvis but at every shadow, every murky wire, Al jumps again and has to be cajoled into going back to his task.

It takes ages to replace one faulty wire. When he finally finishes I'm so relieved I offer him more tea and the rest of my precious carrot cake. It's a particularly delicious one, from a customer who is an excellent cook, but Al refuses, too nervous to sit in my kitchen with a snake on the loose. He remembers the lasagne though and I promise to drop it off at his home in the next village in the next few days.

Al still lives with his parents and they're on my round, so a couple of days later I deliver the lasagne as promised. His mum, Anthea, shouts at me to come in when I knock on her door rather than putting the post through the letterbox. The bungalow is in a cluster of half a dozen fairly new houses built on the edge of one of the tiny inland villages.

'Sorry I couldn't come to the door,' Anthea says as I go in and find her in the kitchen. 'I've been looking for my mobile phone. I'm needed at the shop, just on my way now.'

She seems in a bit of a flap so I put down the lasagne on the kitchen table and help her look, finally finding it on the floor in the corner.

'Must have been the cat knocked it down,' Anthea says, relieved. 'Thanks, Tessa.' She finally sees the lasagne. 'Goodness, that looks yummy, but you shouldn't have. Al told me how he conned you into cooking for him. It was blackmail pure and simple,' she shakes her head at her son's latest misdemeanour.

'Oh no, I was happy to do it,' I say. 'He was quite brave about it. I certainly wouldn't have wanted to investigate a machine knowing it was entirely possible a snake could be living there.'

'Well, thanks anyway. So you've not found it yet?'

I tell her quickly that we haven't then start to go, as I know she's in a hurry. As we walk out together she says, 'It's such a nuisance, the woman who works in our shop suddenly quit and gave no notice. Not that it's a surprise. She met a new man a while back from Up Country and has been hankering to go off with him. I wish she'd given us more than a few days' notice, though. It sure as hell has put us in a fine spot. I can't work every day, I got my own part-time job.'

I commiserate, 'But surely it won't be a problem finding someone else?'

'Oh, no problem, just time consuming. Advertising in the

local paper, interviewing people. And in the meantime the shop has to be shut all hours when Al and his dad are out on a job and I can't help. We need someone full-time.'

As she's saying this wheels are turning in my head and I say, 'Look, Anthea, hang on a minute. I think I know of someone.' I tell her about Ginger, who lives no more than five miles from the small town where the electrical shop is situated.

Anthea stops to listen, then says, 'Y'know, I remember her. The name especially. We were all at school together, her and her husband, that fisherman who drowned, poor lad. I've bumped into her now and again in Truro and other places over the years. Nice woman. D'you really think she'd want the job?'

I promise to find out. When I finish my round I zoom back to Poldowe, crossing my fingers that Ginger is home. She is, and I tell her about the possible job. Her drawn face is transformed and she looks ten years younger. She remembers Anthea too. I give Ginger her mobile number and even as I walk away she's making the phone call. The job satisfaction in delivering the post is sky high these days.

Chapter 12

Are you going to Penrundell Fair . . .

The exhilarating holiday atmosphere is in the air now with schools starting their summer break. Most of the second homes in all the villages are fully occupied, the shops and cafés in the seaside towns are buzzing and the harbours are filled with boats going in and out. The seabirds are in full flight and it's hard not to believe they're on holiday too, with their soaring, swooping and wild cries. It's a great time for many of the local youngsters as they can get seasonal jobs waiting on tables, helping out in restaurant kitchens and generally ministering to the wants and needs of the holidaymakers.

It takes even longer to do my rounds these days but the weather is so glorious, and the atmosphere so festive, that it usually doesn't bother me when I get held up by visitors as they crawl down narrow lanes and are too terrified of scratching their smart cars to reverse, or when they fill up the car parks in St Geraint and Morranport. I've loads more post too now that some families have moved in for a good part of the summer. This is the second busiest time of the year, after the pre-Christmas rush.

Annie comes down often and we have a great deal of fun visiting the hotel again, talking to the manager about food, seating arrangements and so on. I've found a local florist who has a reputation amongst not only the locals but with those from Up Country for her stylish, original and utterly amazing flower arrangements, so I've arranged to go see her with Annie one weekend.

Annie's less than impressed when we arrive at the woman's premises in Truro. It looks like a rather down-at-heel florist shop, with only a few wooden shelves that have been cobbled together in great haste and not a vast selection of flowers on them either. She's even less impressed when Chloe, the owner, appears in a pair of fluffy pink bedroom slippers. It looks especially odd as the woman herself is dressed elegantly in well-cut trousers and a very smart black tunic. She also can't be older than early forties.

'Maybe she has bad corns,' I whisper to Annie as Chloe leaves the room for a moment. Annie still looks dubious until Chloe shows us photos of some of the weddings she's done. The arrangements look both exquisite and original. They are stunning, and Annie is hooked. After much discussion with Chloe, and more photos, she finally decides on a 'country style' theme for the church and reception which will be all lavender and corn, greens and whites.

When we leave Annie says, 'The flowers are going to be gorgeous, I'm thrilled. And did you see those photos at the end of the book she showed us of weddings she's done the flowers for? Chloe didn't say, and I didn't want to act dumb by asking, but it was the wedding of that telly presenter, you know the one I mean.'

'I thought I recognised the bride, she's a model, isn't she?

See, Annie, I told you she had a great reputation. Anyway it's about time you learned that not everything in Cornwall is fifty years behind the times.'

Her face takes on that dreamy look it gets when she's thinking of Pete. 'I found that out a year ago, don't worry.'

We've arranged to meet Chloe at the church in Creek after a quick pub lunch of luscious, fresh crab sandwiches in St Geraint. Even though she knows the church and has done weddings there before, she'd still like to discuss with Annie how and where she'd like the flower arrangements. When we arrive, Chloe is inside the ancient stone porch, examining the arched wooden beams and the old oak door with appreciation. She's obviously been to the hairdresser while we were at lunch, for though her streaky blond hair was perfectly presentable before, she's now had a very stylish and sophisticated cut. A crimson scarf is draped casually over the black tunic and the overall effect is one of simple elegance. Except for the fluffy slippers which she's still wearing. I'm dying to ask, and I'm sure Annie is too, but though the florist is friendly enough, she maintains a professional distance which prohibits personal questions. Especially about slippers.

When we're finally on our own, Annie and I begin to giggle. 'It's so weird that she doesn't mention them. Like saying, I've got a bad foot or something.'

'And she's so elegant but her slippers are so old-fashioned and awful, the kind you'd kick under the sofa before you let anyone other than your nearest and dearest see them.'

We decide that Chloe must have her reasons, or else she's just an endearing oddball like so many we know.

That evening, Annie and Pete go with me to the opening of the new art gallery in Poldowe, the one Harry's partner, Charlie, has set up. I was hoping Ben would be able to be here but the company has several performances this weekend. Harry and Charlie both greet us as we go into the gallery. The old shop has been transformed with clever lighting and design, and it looks terrific. Charlie is buzzing with excitement. I'm particularly pleased to see his parents there, as Charlie's dad, a fisherman, was resentful for a long time that Charlie didn't want to follow in his profession but was determined to fulfil his dream to work as an artist. They've since been reconciled, and it's great to see Charlie's dad standing next to his son, his face beaming with pride. It's wonderful, too, how Charlie's family have accepted Harry, who is talking now to Charlie's mum. I look at the two men, so different in appearance with Harry tall, urban, stunningly handsome, and Charlie shorter, stockier, looking like the fisherman he might have been; yet their relationship is as solid as granite.

Annie and Pete are going about the room, Pete greeting the locals he's known for years and Annie squealing with delight as she spots London mates. Harry has asked all his old city friends and as he and Annie discovered before, they have a number of acquaintances in common. I smile to myself, watching as Annie introduces Pete to people she knows, while Pete in turn takes her to meet his Cornish friends. Visitors mingle with locals, incomers with people whose parents and grandparents were born in Cornwall, and for this one night at least, there's none of the prickly resentment that each camp sometimes feels about the other.

As I'm sipping champagne and looking at some of Charlie's latest artwork, intricate, beautiful pieces made from driftwood, Annie rushes up to me. 'Have you noticed the flowers? So discreet yet so stunning, those hydrangeas so tastefully worked in with the sea theme, those delicate shells, pebbles and seaweed. Ms Fluffy Slippers did them. Aren't they wonderful?'

*

Life is full on now, with the longer round, loads of work in the garden, feeding Google who still makes a tremendous cacophony of bird noises and protests if I don't feed him regularly and, of course, looking after the hens and taking Jake for walks. Though dogs can't go on the public beaches now that summer is here, we do know some secret coves where he can run about, and there are fantastic walks along the cliffs where I'm also looking for plants to bring home and eat, and beautiful walks through some of the most enchanting woodlands imaginable. On one of these walks I find cob nuts and later make savoury cakes for dinner, mixing the chopped nuts with leftover mashed potatoes and a couple of my hens' eggs. They are absolutely delicious so I experiment with the basic recipe. If I don't have cob nuts, I use any kind of edible plant, chickweed, sorrel or even nettles, cooking it first with lots of garlic and chopping it up when done, mixing it with the potato and egg and frying the cakes in butter or olive oil. You have a complete meal there, I tell the children: your greens, carbohydrate and protein from the eggs.

These days I also make sure that at least one of us has a look at Patch every day. His care is easy thanks to Joe but he's still our responsibility, I feel. We've all learned how to look out for the dreaded fly, the maggots that get into the back passage of a sheep and can eat the flesh out if you don't catch it in time, and for any signs of illness or weakening. Joe's a good farmer and I know he checks all the sheep but I feel it's our lamb and we need to do our bit. Besides, the three of us enjoy our visits with Patch. He's so playful, especially with Will and Amy. I'm sure he thinks they are lambs too, the way he loves to follow and run with them. He's plump and woolly, that black patch making him stand out from the other sheep in the field. I don't let myself think about the fact that we are raising him for meat but try to enjoy him each day as it comes.

I'm also getting fonder and fonder of Gruff, the billy goat that Marilyn and Dave adopted. He too has got quite playful, though unlike Patch, this billy goat is quite a rascal.

'He got out again,' Marilyn tells me next time I deliver to her. 'Went up the lane to Trelak Farm and ate all Emma's pansies by the time I got him back.' We both gaze at Gruff as he jumps up in the air and twirls around before landing in front of us then leaping up again. We can't help laughing at his antics.

I say, 'I thought Dave made that fence?'

'He did, but it was pretty makeshift. Fencing equipment is expensive so we had to make do with some spare wire and posts from up at Trelak.' She sighs. 'I could tether him up again but he hates it. Gets bored, you know? I take him for a walk when I've got time, he likes that.'

When I drive away I'm musing on yet another wonder of the countryside. Walking a pet goat, eh? Wait until I tell Annie. Maybe I'll get her a billy goat for a wedding present.

I'm harvesting loads of vegetables now but it leaves the problem of what to do with it, especially spinach as I have masses of it. I've used loads, frozen loads, and there's still more. I try giving it away to my customers but no one wants it as nearly all the locals are growing their own. In fact, giving away surplus produce becomes quite an art, I've noticed. Now that I've upset my customers by declining the extra vegetables I was avidly grateful for last year, they've become cunning. Often I get back to the post office to find my van full of vegetables that have been put there behind my back. No one likes to waste, yet with all this good growing earth and weather in Cornwall, there seems a surfeit. So people are becoming devious, trying to pass on either the guilt of wasting all these wonderful fresh vegetables, or else the effort of spending hours trying to fill an overstuffed freezer with them. Not only do I have to guard my van when I'm delivering to an avid gardener, I also have to be careful what I say. One woman enthusiastically raved about some new type of salad leaf she'd grown, saying how unusual and delicious it was. I murmured something along the lines of 'Hm, I must try it sometime,' and before I knew it she'd thrust a boxful of greenery into my arms and scuppered back into the house, shutting the door firmly behind her. I couldn't just leave it there, it would be too rude, so I had to take it home. I wouldn't have minded so much except that this rare leaf turned out to be rocket, which I have by the bucketful in my own garden.

I can tell that even the Humphreys have had enough rocket and spinach, though they seem to eat masses of it and never refuse anything that I bring them from the garden. Perhaps that's the secret of their long and healthy lives, all the vegetables they seem to consume.

They are standing talking to the hens when I arrive, and after we've collected the eggs we turn to the vegetable patch. In with the successes I've had a few disasters. Tiny cabbage butterflies have made Swiss cheese of my small cabbages and my potatoes, not much good to start with, have suffered the same fate as the lettuce and every time I cut one open there's a slug staring me in the face. There are more slug holes than potatoes but at least we have some to eat. My summer leeks are growing enormously as are the beetroot and carrots. And of course the spinach and rocket are endless.

I'm learning a dozen ways to use the spinach. I'm making wagon loads of spinach soup, and quiches filled with the stuff. I'm making sauces with a tomato base, using sieved spinach. We're eating it every day, in salads, mixed surreptitiously into curries – you name it and I've put spinach in it.

'Next year I'll try fruit,' I say, brimming with optimism. 'Some strawberries and raspberries perhaps.'

'Steady on, maid,' Hector says. 'Young girl like you shouldn't overdo it.'

Edna nods her agreement. I love it when they call me a young girl, especially when I'm stooped from pulling a back muscle while digging up leeks, when I have bags under my eyes through lack of sleep and when I haven't had time to look in the mirror for days.

She says, 'I hope you are taking time to enjoy some of this sunshine we've been having, dear.'

I tell her truthfully that I have. No matter how busy I am, I never miss a chance for a walk on the beach, usually first thing in the morning as I've done ever since moving here and then again in early evening often with the children before I take them to Daphne's to spend the night. Precious moments, all of them.

Edna also asks if we are planning a holiday this year and the question stumps me. The last holiday we had was when we lived in London and we took a cottage in Cornwall. Now we live in a cottage in Cornwall, so what do we do for a holiday? It would be fun to go to London and see our old friends, visit the city and maybe take in some shows, but no way can we afford that. We can't afford to go abroad either, and anyway, right now I don't want to; this new life still feels very much like an extended vacation to me most of the time.

Still, a holiday would be good. I decide to talk about it to Ben next time he phones, see what we can come up with. Camping would be fun. We'd want to stay in Cornwall, but in a different area, I decide, somewhere new to explore. I ask Emma about possible camping spots next day when I deliver to Trelak Farm. She suggests the Penwith area, at the tip of Cornwall.

'You've not only got the coast but the moorland around there to explore,' she tells me. 'The landscape is quite different from here. I know the perfect campsite too, owned by old friends. They had to sell their land but they kept a large field and got planning permission for a campsite.'

It sounds promising and I'm so lost in thought planning this holiday as I go on the rest of my round that I have to brake suddenly when I see a young goat in the middle of a narrow lane. The goat is lying down and in front of it there's a woman waving at me to stop. It's Marilyn and that's Gruff behind her. I pull the van into a layby and jump out.

'What's up?' I ask. 'Is he hurt?' He doesn't look it. In fact Gruff looks perfectly contented, chewing his cud placidly.

Marilyn says, 'I decided that Gruff needs to graze more, since he keeps getting out to find more interesting things to eat. So I've started taking him for more frequent walks, along the back lanes so he can nibble at all the wild stuff growing in the hedgerows. I don't even need a lead as he usually follows me quite happily, never letting me get far ahead.'

'So why is he just lying there? Is he tired or what?' I say.

Marilyn shakes her head, 'He's done that once or twice before. Just decided to stop for no reason. Usually a gentle shove gets him up but this time I can't budge him, he's been here for ten minutes now. I don't know what to do, I've been pleading and cajoling and tugging at him but nothing works.'

I've got to get down this road to deliver more post so I give her a hand. We push and tug but Gruff won't move. It's a narrow road and not much used but as luck would have it, a car zooming around the corner, nearly hits the postal van before jamming on its breaks and screeching to a stop. The driver gets out and walks towards us with a murderous look on his face. I recognise him as Mr Lander, one of the second-homers in our village and not a favourite amongst the locals. He's the one who raised hell when Joe drove through the village with a load of muck to spread on his fields something he's done regularly for twenty-five years. Mr Lander tried to get Joe stopped, complaining that it was not only a health hazard but that the smell gave his wife intense migraines. This was such a new one on the villagers that he was the laughing stock of the place for weeks. No one has laughed lately, though, as he's still fighting Joe and the other farmers, writing letters everywhere, calling meetings that no one attends, except a very few second-homers. Mrs Lander wanders around the village as if everyone is invisible and she never even looks at her neighbours, let alone speaks to us. So this is the last person we need glaring at us as Gruff sprawls stubbornly across the road.

I say brightly, 'Why, hello Mr Lander, how nice to see you. This is my friend Marilyn, and this is Gruff. Billy Goat Gruff.' I grin, hoping for even a half smile in return.

Marilyn, joining in the joke, says, 'I hope you're not a troll, Mr Lander.'

He may as well be a troll, the way he huffs and puffs out his chest and demands to know whose goat it is and why it's sprawled in the middle of a public highway when he's in a hurry to get back to the village and the bloody animal is blocking the bloody road. Marilyn is so taken aback by his vehemence that she doesn't know what do or say so I come to her rescue.

Still keeping calm and polite I say, 'Goats can be quite stubborn, and Gruff has decided he's not going to move. I'd suggest you back up a bit, turn around and go back to Treverny on the other road; it's not far out of the way and it'll be quicker than trying to move the goat.'

He's completely ignoring me, walking around Gruff and giving him a push in the back then a tug on his front legs but the goat stares reproachfully at the man and doesn't move.

Marilyn says, 'Look, it won't work, we tried everything. He's a very stubborn goat and the more you pull him about like that, the more determined he'll be to stay put.'

I say with my best diplomatic voice, 'You could have been in Treverny by now, Mr Lander. You might as well turn around, you know. I don't think he's going to move just yet.' I look at Gruff placidly chewing his cud.

Mr Lander blows. He completely loses it and starts shouting at me, Marilyn and the goat, swearing at us all and finishing by hollering, 'If you think I'm going to let a bloody goat get the better of me you're both out of your bloody heads.' With that he kicks Gruff hard on the side of his ribs.

Gruff bleats loudly with the pain but doesn't get up. Mr Lander looks as if he's going to kick him again but Marilyn shouts, 'Don't you dare!'

At the same time I cry, 'If you do that one more time I'll report you to the RSPCA for cruelty to animals.'

Mr Lander shouts back, 'And I'll report *you* to the police, causing wilful obstruction on a main road.'

This narrow lane a main road? As he jumps into his car and reverses it up the road, revving like a maniac, Marilyn and I look at one another, shake our heads and roll our eyes.

'Man that is one stressed friend of yours,' Marilyn says. 'Obviously the slow calm ways of us rural folk have not rubbed off on him.'

'He's not my friend; he's that new incomer in Treverny.'

'Ah, that explains it. I've heard talk of him. None of it good.'

'Sorry I can't stay and help any longer, Marilyn, but I've got to get going. I'll reverse and go the other way. If you're still here on the way back I'll lend a hand again.'

Even as I speak, Gruff is stirring. Moving slowly and with great dignity, he gets up and walks sedately to the edge of the road where he starts nibbling goodies from the hedgerow.

Ben comes home for good the first day of August and as part of our joyous family celebrations, we have a day out at one of our favourite events of the year, the Penrundell Fair. It's like an old-fashioned village fete and it's been going on in Penrundell since, folk say, for ever. Every antiquated game ever played seems to go on here and the place is always happily packed with both locals and visitors.

It's a breezy day when we set out, with high clouds flitting benignly above us, not interfering with the intense blue of the sky and the heat of the sun. There are already loads of people at the rugby grounds outside the village where it's held though it's not even ten o'clock. All the proceeds go towards a fund for the church roof so folk spend freely on the coconut shy, the darts game, hoopla, and guess-the-weight-of-the-pig. The prizes are just old-fashioned sweets, there are no fluffy teddy bears, or plastic trinkets. There's a huge beer tent, stalls selling local sausages and other treats to eat, and wonderful events which draw crowds either to enter or watch.

I start talking to one of my customers while Ben takes Will and Amy off to watch some men, and a couple of women, try to throw bales of hay over a crossbar which keeps being raised. I can hear their supporters cheering them on. Later there will be the donkey derby but meanwhile the sheep race has begun. This is hilarious and we watch while several sheep come out each with a knitted jockey figure perched on top. The audience roars with approval and bets are placed on favourite sheep. There are tiny jumps around the field which, led by their owners, they are supposed to leap over, though more than one refuses point blank to do so, to the consterna-tion of those who bet on them.

We wander around the fair for hours, sometimes together, sometimes separately as the children run off with mates, and Ben and I meet colleagues and our own friends. We eat the homemade sausages that are out of this world, drink ice-cold beer and lemonade, join in a few games and sit on the grass to watch others. My favourite is the terrier race. About a dozen excited yapping terriers, held on to precariously by their frazzled owners, are suddenly let loose to chase a sort of wiggly fake fox tail which stands in for the hare. It's exciting to watch. The terriers get distracted, bark frantically at each other, run the other way and start skirmishes while their owners shout and try to control them. One delightful little Border Terrier runs joyfully away in the opposite direction with its owner, a huge Amazonian woman of great weight and height, running madly after it. I don't know who is having more fun, the terriers or the spectators.

It's a lovely day all around, and on our way home we stop at the harbour town of Fowey to eat fish and chips at a cheap and cheerful takeaway, settling by the water to watch the yachts sail into harbour. The food is delicious, the sea air bliss, and there's nowhere else on earth any of us would rather be at this moment.

Chapter 13

A-camping we will go . . .

August, and Cornwall is buzzing. Holidaymakers abound, there are regattas every weekend, the beaches are full and the seaside towns and villages are filled with a festive holiday atmosphere. And now we're having a holiday too. We've never gone camping before, so it will be a huge treat. We've got an old but barely used tent a customer was getting rid of, sleeping bags and some air mattresses that Daphne lent me.

In London when we went on holidays to Cornwall, we packed children and dog in the car, a few clothes and that was it; our rented cottages were fully equipped. With camping, my list of what to bring is endless. And then there is the problem of the chickens, the seagull and the lamb – we can't take them with us, much as we'd like to.

The chickens and Patch are easy; the Humphreys will feed and look after the former, and Joe will do the same for the latter. I'm worried about Google, though. No matter where or how far he flies off, he's always at the kitchen door twice a day at least. He expects his dish of dried fishy cat food which he still loves, as well as all the other scraps we give him. Then I have a brainwave. There's been another reshuffling of part of our rounds and Eddie is now delivering to Treverny, for the summer anyway.

I find him in the Morranport post office chatting to Nell who says, 'Oh there you be, maid, Eddie and me was just talking about you, wondering whether that snake of yours be found yet.'

I shake my head, 'No, Elvis is still at large. No sign of him anywhere. We figure he's either died or slithered off somewhere. The woman at the reptile centre says we'll probably never find him now. Though I still check the bed before I get into it.'

Eddie grins. 'Mebbe it's for the best. We've all seen what happens when you spot a snake at your feet.' He's not forgotten his little joke with the fake snake and this is not the first time he's reminded me of it.

I grin. 'Yeah, Eddie, it was a great gag. Now, how about doing me a favour, since I think you owe me one for being able to laugh at the fact you nearly gave me a heart attack, throwing that thing at me.'

I explain what I want, which is basically to stop by my house every day he delivers to the village and put some food out for Google. Eddie, after making all sorts of over-the-top gestures of astonishment, rolling his eyes, grimacing and the like, reluctantly agrees. Like me and the other rural posties, he's used to feeding cats, rabbits, other small animals when the owners are away, but a seagull? I know he thinks I'm bonkers, but he's basically a good lad and he agrees to do it. So that's it, then. Animals all sorted. I can't wait until we go camping.

Unfortunately a wintry white fog settles over Cornwall for a few days and it seems more like January than August.

I'm keeping my fingers crossed that it'll go before we start our holiday. The tourists try to entertain themselves while the chilly mist envelops the beaches and the cliff tops. A wind has blown up with the fog which makes it swirl and move like something alive. Now and then the sun tries to break through but so far fails every time.

It's not only the holidaymakers who are restless but the locals, too. It's unseasonable, this weather. In summer people want to turn outward and live in the light, not huddled up inside themselves like winter, cosy by a roaring fire lit against the cold and dark. Perhaps the fog is the reason why my menagerie is getting restless too. Google hangs around the house more in this weather and sits on our roof screeching most of the day, scaring away the thrushes and other small birds. Our neighbours are getting annoyed and I don't really blame them. I keep expecting Mr Lander to report my seagull to the police, along with reporting Joe for his dung and Marilyn for obstructing the road with a billy goat.

The next morning it's still foggy. It doesn't feel like summer at all and it was hard to get up this morning, which is why I'm half asleep as I drive the empty streets to work. When I hear that raucous, familiar seagull shriek right in my ear, I nearly crash the car. I whirl around to see Google sitting on the back seat.

'How did you get in here?' I shout at him. Then I remember leaving the door open when I ran back inside for a cardigan.

It's too late to go back home and anyway I'm nearly at St Geraint. Google is getting bored with being in the car and starts flapping his wings. I step on the accelerator and get to the boatyard where my post van is.

I say loudly to my seagull, 'Well you can't come with me on my round, that's for sure.'

Mickey, materialising out of the fog, says, 'Talking to yourself, are you my lover?'

'You're here early,' is all I can think of to say. I can't, I just can't, tell him that I've got a seagull in my car, let alone that I was talking to it. I've heard Mickey's view on seagulls many a time.

'Yep, got plenty of work on today as usual. Thick old mist, ain't it?' he walks over towards my car, ready for a chat. Mickey likes to chew the fat despite always talking about how busy he is.

I open the car door, trying to get out quickly before he sees Google, but I'm in such a rush I somehow manage to trip over my own feet and land in a heap on the ground.

Mickey is with me in a flash. 'Hey, you OK?' When I nod he starts to pick me up but as he does, an almighty squawking and flapping of wings puts the fear of God into him and he drops me again. 'Shite! What is it? What the hell?'

I'm on my feet, trying to calm Google, and trying to calm Mickey who is jumping up and down severely agitated. 'God, Tessa, what the hell you got in there? A vulture? Scared the shite out of me.'

Google has calmed down so while I'm mumbling apologies Mickey calms down enough to peer into the car window. 'God Almighty. A flipping seagull. How the hell did he get in there?'

Now that Mickey knows it's a seagull and not an albatross or some such rare and dangerous creature, he becomes The Hero. 'Don't worry, Tessa, I'll get the bloody thing out. Right nuisance, those birds. Don't you fret, maid, I'll get rid of it for you. Just you stand aside now.' He picks up a shovel lying against the boatyard shed and goes towards the car.

I holler, 'No, no!'

Mickey turns to reassure me, 'Don't you worry, I won't get no blood over the upholstery. Just gonna drive it out with this, y'see?' He brandishes the shovel.

I pull on his arm. 'It's OK, Mickey, honest. He's not any

old seagull, it's my pet, it's tame. We raised him from a baby.'

Mickey drops the shovel and stares at me. 'You what?' He says it as if I've nursed a baby cobra at my breast. 'You gotta be joking.'

'Uh, no.'

He peers into the back of my car again then jumps back quickly as Google flaps his wings at him. 'You must be daft as a brush, maid,' he mutters as he walks away. 'I never heard nothing like it.'

By the time I've finished my round, all the post office workers plus half the village of both St Geraint and Morranport are talking about my domestic relationship with a seagull, taking it around for drives in my car along the seaside. And like the snake, when Elvis first came to live with us, Google is the subject of much larking about at my expense. I get comments all day like, 'Hey, me handsome, I hear tell you be keeping a home for seagulls, so how about taking away a dozen more?' and 'I done give those pesky gulls that hang out in front of me shop your car number, postie, so you can drive them all Up Country somewhere.'

When I get back to my car at the boatyard, Google is gone. I left the windows open despite the damp fog still swirling around. Everywhere is white, the sea, the sky, there's no horizon, nothing but this haze.

I jump when Mickey suddenly appears in front of me, materialising like some lanky spirit. 'He be gone, my lover. Your bloody gull. Scrabbled outa the car and flew off soon after you'd gone.'

'Oh. Well, I half expected it. I didn't think he'd stay in the car all day. Do you know where he's gone?'

'How the hell should I know? Out there somewhere with all the other gulls, stealing food, plaguing the emmetts, splattering the town with bird shit.'

'Right. Sorry I asked.'

He takes my words at face value. 'That's all right. No problem. But let me give you a piece of advice, my lover. Next time you find a baby gull, you ring its bloody neck.'

I make some kind of non-committal sound and wave goodbye. Sitting in my car, I look at the gulls sitting on some nearby rocks. They look majestic, beautiful and free, especially when they soar up from their perches or dive down after fish. Sighing, I wonder if Google will come back. Maybe he won't find his way, or won't want to come back now. I peer through my open window, hearing boat and bird noises in the fog, but I can't see anything but the swirling mist; even the gulls have gone. I wonder if I'd recognise Google with all the other seagulls but I then remember he's got a red band around his leg. Ben banded him when he was still a baby, so that if he went off we'd always recognise him amongst the other birds.

I drive home slowly, stopping every time I hear the cry of seabirds, looking out over fields and cliff tops to see if it's Google. It's daft I know, especially as the mist is so thick now I can hardly see anything, but I'm worried about my seagull. The pragmatist in me knows that if he has flown away at last, joining the other gulls on the cliffs, it would be for the best. But he's my sweetie, my baby bird that came to stay in our attic and has never left home. Not just me but the whole family would miss him if he goes now.

As I get home the first thing I see is Google, flying above the car as I slow down and park. 'I thought we'd lost you,' I say, so pleased to see him that I give him half the cheese sandwich I was saving to eat when I got home.

The unseasonable fog lifts just in time for our camping trip. August is hot and sunny and we're on our way to a campsite near the sea. We've chosen the West Penwith peninsula, still in Cornwall but a totally different landscape. The coast is more rugged and there are the moors to explore when we want a change from the sea.

We leave early in the morning so that we can ramble a bit before we set up camp. Stopping at a layby on the edge of the moors we set out for a trek. It's wild country, with craggy sheep paths, patches of yellow gorse and already purple and pink heather spreading across the hills. Then there's the granite and the incredible rock formations everywhere. We come across some prehistoric standing stones and stop, not speaking, feeling as if we've been whooshed back into some primeval time. Though it's high summer, we're the only ones on this spot on the moor and it feels as if we're the only folk in the world, just us and a lone buzzard that is circling above us making his memorable mewing call.

We walk for ages, coming across wonderful old clapper bridges across little creeks and inlets, stumbling across ancient archaeological sites – the haunting ruins of the once great copper- and tin-mining works, and the settlements that grew up alongside them. We find stone crosses and circles in the middle of nowhere, and in the expanse of lowland heath we have to find hidden sheep tracks to walk along between the gorse and brambles.

Our campsite is on the top of a cliff. There's a narrow path and rocky ledges down to a cove and a sandy beach. The children are over the moon. I'm a bit less enthusiastic. Camping is a challenge for me as I love my creature comforts especially a bed and a cosy duvet.

All goes well as we set up the massive tent. It's a perfect day and when the tent is up, the children walk to the tiny nearby village shop for freshly baked bread. I slice it for lunch, along with farmhouse cheese and tomatoes we picked up from a roadside stand. Ben spreads a blanket on the sweet-smelling grass in front of our tent and we eat with relish as we watch the sea which is still and smooth, with not a whitecap in sight. A gentle breeze prevents us from getting too hot and all my misgivings about camping vanish.

It gets better and better. In the late afternoon we walk down to the cove and spend a lovely couple of hours swimming and sunning. Because this is such an isolated beach with no access other than the fairly long, rather precarious walk down the cliff, dogs are allowed even in summer. Jake is delirious with the fun of it, bounding in and out of the shallows playing in the gentle waves. And though the walk uphill to our campsite is steep and tiring, we all feel fit, healthy and glowing when we finally reach the top. I sauté a vegetable mixture for dinner with courgettes from the garden – they are all ripening at once, as courgettes do – mixed with more fresh tomatoes, onions from the allotment and garlic. The village shop has local ham for sale and it tastes delicious with the vegetable mix.

We sleep well, after the day of fresh air and exercise, and breakfast is heaven. Emma's friends, who live in the farm-house, are friendly and helpful. We buy new-laid eggs from them and scones the woman bakes herself, as well as her own clotted cream. In the tiny shop we stock up on locally reared, cured bacon as well as more fresh bread. We take our hoard back to the campsite, delighted with our purchases.

It's another glorious day and this time we start with a walk along the cliffs, planning a good hike before lunch and an after-noon lazing on the beach. The walk takes us past stupendous views of the sea with a horizon gauzy with heat mist. The rock formations are rugged and majestic. A turning in the path leads us off the cliff top as the trail meanders through a wild meadow. It's lush with late summer foliage and I revert from holidaymaker to my foraging self and look for something we can pick to eat. While Ben and the children find a mossy spot under a shady tree at the edge of the meadow for a drink of water and an apple, I start poking about in the long grass to see what I can find.

I'm in luck. After ten minutes or so searching I find big clumps of sorrel, tucked away in a small patch of grassland. With a shriek of delight, I run back for my rucksack and start stuffing it with sorrel leaves. I'm not quite sure what to do with them but I know from my research that they're edible. And I know this really is sorrel as Edna showed me the leaves she'd collected one day.

That time she was absolutely positive what it was. 'I've been making sorrel soup for years, m'dear. Before your parents were born, I should imagine,' she had said.

That's what I'll make for our dinner this evening. We'll have sorrel soup and fresh bread, with local butter, cheese and tomatoes.

I couldn't get a recipe from Edna, though, when I asked her she looked bemused. 'Recipe, dear? Goodness, I merely throw in whatever I have to hand – maybe onions, or mush-rooms, or whatever. Anything.'

I set about making the soup while Ben kicks a ball around with Will and Amy. All that energy, after a long walk this morning and swim this afternoon, not to mention climbing back up from the beach. But we all had a siesta after lunch, Mediterranean style. The weather is so incredible we could be in Greece, Italy or the south of France.

I chop up the sorrel leaves as finely as I can with the one sharp knife I brought, toss it in a saucepan with some butter and onions and let it cook for a few minutes. From the farm I've bought local potatoes so I throw some of those in, cut into small pieces, add water and let it all simmer. When it's cooked I add a few herbs I've brought along, some salt and pepper. As the family gathers around for dinner I taste first, just to make sure.

It's not that tasty. It's too bitter for a start. For a moment I'm stumped then remember how often, when the spinach soap tastes too strong, I add a little cream to it which dilutes that strong spinach taste. We've got some of that homemade clotted cream on hand, so I slowly add a small portion to the soup before pouring it into bowls. As I stir it in carefully and not too quickly, I'm horrified as it starts to curdle. This never happened, ever, to my spinach soup. My sorrel soup is now nothing but a curdled yucky mess.

'Never mind,' Ben says as he looks at it. 'We'll have bacon butties instead.'

He doesn't look at all disappointed and the children are positively beaming with delight. I have to admit that my face lights up too and in moments we're all grinning in glee at the thought of our new dinner plans.

The smell of cooking bacon on a campsite is pure heaven and after we've rushed to the shop (which luckily never seems to close) for more bacon and fresh rolls and eaten our meal, I decide that bacon butties are my favourite camping food. I could never be a vegetarian, if for no other reason than bacon butties.

I'm chided affectionately about my occasional foraging disasters while we eat but I have the last laugh. I produce a few handfuls of wild strawberries that I also found on our walk and picked while the others hiked on ahead. They make a wonderful dessert, sweet and perfect. Everyone goes to sleep that night happy, peaceful and satisfied.

What follows is the most horrendous camping night imaginable. It begins to rain. Softly, gently, at first, so that I wake and hear soothing drops on the tent and think how cosy and dry we are inside. Then the drops get heavier and the wind comes up. Our tent moans, blows and yes, the worst scenario, it begins to leak in the children's section. They wake up and pile into our side and none of us get any sleep. I'd had the idea of making contingency plans for sleeping in the car if a storm came up but realistically it couldn't be done. Minger is old, small, and far too uncomfortable for four people to bed down. Besides, it's a dog kennel now. Jake was restless in the tent, keeping us awake, but he loves sleeping in the car. We'll just have to stick it out in the tent.

The storm is fierce with thunder, lightning, the works. I begin to worry about being struck by lightning but before my worries get too out of hand the storm seems to pass. It doesn't stop raining though, even when the wind drops. It drones on and on.

When daylight dawns having somehow found our water-proofs we stagger out in the wet to inspect the damage. We'd put the tent up at home in the front garden and left it out during a rainy day to check for leaks but it seemed fine then. Now Ben finds that the trouble is a slight tear, probably caused by the wind. It's an old tent and not as durable as some of the modern ones we've seen on the campsite. But Ben has come prepared with the stuff needed to patch it up. The trouble is, it won't stop raining. Most of the children's clothes that I couldn't rescue from the leak in time are soaking, and I have no clue where to dry them. At least they have some to last them a day or so and surely it must stop raining soon.

It doesn't. Not all day and not the next either. I finally make Will and Amy some sort of bed in Minger, one on the front seat the other on the back, and bring Jake into the tent. The rain beats on the canvas all night and Jake whimpers. Our air mattress deflates in the middle of the night, for no reason we can think of other than pure dejection. It's probably feeling as soggy as we are. But we're used to Cornwall and know that the weather can change dramatically in a couple of hours, so while the rain lasts we decide to explore a bit more of the

Penwith area and head for St Ives not far from our campsite. The only parking places are way outside the town and we're soaked by the time we have walked in. When we finally get there the place is packed with sodden holidaymakers; you can't even get into a café for a cup of warm hot chocolate, which is great for business but not for us. We look around the Tate gallery but it's packed with visitors as wet and steaming as we are.

Outside the Tate we stand in the pouring rain wondering what to do next. Porthmeor beach is right opposite, entirely empty except for the all-weather surfers. It's a wonderful beach, crescent-shaped with golden sand, and despite the weather and the choppy water, it looks amazingly tempting.

'We can't get any wetter,' I suggest. 'So why don't we go into the sea and swim?'

Like maniacs the four of us run to the beach, strip down to our swimsuits which we were wearing in case the weather changed and jump into the sea. It's such exhilarating fun that we rent body boards and do some gentle surfing. Before long we've totally forgotten that it's still raining.

I've put our waterproof jackets over our heaped pile of drier clothes and towels so we surreptitiously take off our wet swimsuits, get dressed quickly and decide on a brisk walk to warm up. From Porthmeor beach we go up the slope leading to the island, which isn't really an island but a hilly mound of grassland surrounded on three sides by the sea. We walk along the clifftop path around the island and it's fantastic, great waves crashing on the rocks below us, purple and black storm clouds above, and the noise of sea and sky thundering above and below us. It's awesome and dramatic, a theatrical performance just for us.

We walk down from the island to the end of Smeaton's Pier. The tide is in and the nineteenth-century harbour, once home to around four hundred pilchard boats, is filled with small fishing craft and motorboats. Looking over the side we're thrilled to see a seal gazing up. It's a big one and stares at us with huge brown eyes.

A man next to us says, 'That ole boy's been around for years. There be two of them seals, old'uns both, that come around every day looking for handouts from the fishermen.' He hollers down to the seal, 'Ain't that right?'

The seal cocks his head to the side then sinks under the water, bobbing up again a few minutes later. The children are enthralled and so are we. We watch the seal's antics for some time, oblivious to the rain.

We're ready for a hot drink and food now so we wander down around the maze of narrow streets and alleyways, looking at the delightful cottages once owned by the pilchard fishermen and their families but now nearly all holiday cottages and B&Bs. The cafés are still so crowded because of the consistent rain that we go back to the car and head for Zennor, not far away. The old pub there isn't crowded at this hour so we find a table, order soup and crusty bread, and begin to dry off. After we've eaten we walk across from the pub to the church of St Senara with its medieval tower, to find the mermaid that's carved into one of the wooden pews. We've never heard of a St Senara but find out that she was married to a Breton king, was wrongly accused of infidelity, put in a barrel and thrown out to sea. I'm not quite sure why that made her a saint, as I'm sure she wasn't the only ancient queen, or modern one for that matter, so wrongly accused, but what do I know?

I abandon thoughts of poor St Senara and set off with Ben and the children to find the mermaid seat. There she is, carved on a bench end, holding a comb and mirror. The legend is that a young local man fell in love with the mermaid and she lured him to a nearby cove where he drowned in the sea.

They say that on quiet nights you can still hear the two singing beneath the waves. After we've found the carving, we take a short walk along the cliff path at the top of the village to look down at the cove where the mermaid lured her man.

'I wonder if it's the same place where the Breton king threw down the barrel with poor Senara in it,' I say to Ben.

The cliffs are high and the sea with its sandy beach looks a long way down. Will and Amy are getting too close to the edge and I call, 'Get back, you two. There's been enough drama in this place to last for ever without you adding to it.' But I have to admit it's another spectacular view. The thundering rain has turned into a kind of horizontal drizzle and the waves are now more frothy than fierce.

Walking back to the car at the edge of a field, some Jersey cows follow us part of the way, intrigued by Jake as he darts along beside us. They look benign and complacent, as if nothing bothers them, not the rain, the wind, nor even our tiny group of bedraggled humans and one wet spaniel. As we walk away from them one of them moos, a deep sound that seems to amplify in the wind and follow us all the way to the car.

The next day the rain stops. It's not exactly hot and sunny but at least it's not raining. We fall out of the tent, feeling like Noah must have felt tumbling out of the arc with his animals. The children run shrieking around the campsite, despite the soggy grass and mud everywhere. The woman at the farmhouse kindly said we could dry our walking boots, saturated from days of walking in the rain, by her kitchen Aga overnight so we collect them, put them on and go for a long walk. The air smells fresh, clean and tangy. The sea is choppy and the sky is grey but it's exhilarating. There's a sharp wind now but that's fine as it'll dry out the campsite and our tent.

The weather gets better, the sun finally appears and our tent dries. As the days progress I find I'm learning all sorts of new tricks. I've learned that you have to think outside of the box, be inventive and creative to survive. Simple things like clothes pegs are an absolute necessity. Now that the rain has stopped I'm for ever pegging up clothes, blankets and towels to dry or to air. Ben has rigged up a makeshift clothesline between the tent and Minger. I've also learned to always carry a torch after tripping over the guy ropes while stumbling about in the dark one night.

Our air bed seems fine now and we never do find out why it deflated so mysteriously that night of heavy rain. As a precaution we make sure it's pumped up before dark and that our beds are all ready. I learn all sorts of tricks that seasoned campers know, like keeping a stock of 20p pieces for the shower, sticking wet clothes in the dryer next door so that when I jump out of the shower, I can jump straight into warm, dry clothes if I judge it right and there's no one around as I madly dash with just a towel wrapped around me from the shower to the laundry room.

The early mornings on a campsite are magic. Since becoming a postie I've learned to love this part of the day so still and silent, with the rest of the world asleep, or so it seems in that pre-dawn calm. On this campsite we have a wake-up call from the nearby cockerels who are vying with each other to produce the loudest cry. The dawn chorus seems louder on a campsite somehow and it's pure bliss, hearing it first thing in the morning. The only part of camping I haven't mastered yet is getting the right sleeping temperature. It's too cold at night to keep arms and legs outside the sleeping bag but too hot if it's zipped up. It'll probably take a few more camping trips for me to master the art of sleeping-bag comfort.

In the evenings we sit around the fire pit under the stars, talking, sharing stories, jokes and songs. It feels primeval, as if we're a part of a human chain that has been doing this for centuries. The fire sparks and smokes, the adults drink jugs of Scrumpy from the farmhouse and the children play games around the campsite with the new friends they've made.

On our last night I manage to make a seafood risotto on our camp stove, a feat I'm very proud of. With it we have lightly steamed marsh samphire, which I found growing in a muddy bit of ground near an estuary on our morning walk. I couldn't believe my eyes, when I spotted the bright green patch in the middle of the marshy ground; I'd never found it before. It was growing plentifully and I picked enough for a delicious accompaniment to our risotto for this last meal.

After everyone has drifted off to their tents except Ben and me, we sit watching the embers of the dying fire, a half moon and starry sky above us and the sound of the sea not far away.

'Home tomorrow,' I say contentedly.

And for the first time on holiday, home is not London and a completely different life but a short distance away on the other side of Cornwall.

Chapter 14

Wedding plans and a funeral

Annie is down here often now as she and Pete plan their wedding. The four of us have a hilarious night at Pete's house over many bottles of wine while they write out their invitation list.

'I really should invite my mother's second cousin once removed,' Annie giggled at one point. 'Or is it her first cousin twice removed? Oh dear, I've only met her a couple of times and she's quite dotty. Her husband's dotty too, and lately apparently he's become confused, lost his memory or so my mum says.'

'Well if he's lost his memory, he won't remember if you invited him or not so don't bother,' I giggle with her.

The talk rambles happily on like this for ages. There are Annie's dozens of London friends as well as Pete's many Cornish ones. Annie's parents are in New Zealand and unfortunately have health problems, which it impossible for them to travel long distances. They've given Annie and Pete their blessings, though, and the couple are going to visit Annie's parents on their honeymoon.

We are sitting outside in Pete's back garden, a small, partly terraced plot just big enough for a scruffy, but comfortable, picnic table with chairs. As we lounge around the table looking at the stars, Annie says, 'I've got this great designer and printer I know doing the invitations; he's terrific, they're going to be stunning.' Her face is shining with enthusiasm and wine and I realise she hasn't sneezed once all evening.

Pete comments wryly, 'I'm sure all my farmer friends will be impressed.'

Annie just giggles again but Ben asks Pete, 'Are a lot of your friends farmers?'

'Some. I work with them, you know, spend a lot of time with them, sitting in their kitchens talking about whether they need me to do a lime test on their fields to see what the soil's like, or whether they need to order in more silage or straw for the winter. There're two or three who have become good friends.'

While Annie and I discuss flowers for the tables, the bouquets and headdresses for bride and bridesmaids, buttonholes for groom, best man, family and ushers, Ben and Pete are mostly silent, looking up at the full moon and clear, starry sky.

The scent of some flower or blossom I can't identify wafts through the air as Annie says, 'I've got this great photographer in London, he's fantastic, takes natural shots of people throughout the day so the photos don't come out all posed and stiff. He's very funny so everyone in his pictures are captured laughing and happy.'

Pete murmurs, 'Shouldn't they be anyway, at a wedding?' His voice is low, as if he is talking to himself. 'I didn't think we needed a photographer to make us laugh and be happy on our wedding day.'

Annie smiles at him endearingly, as if he's said something wonderfully amusing, but I notice Pete's answering smile is a bit half-hearted. Perhaps all this wedding talk is boring for him. Many men hate all that kind of fuss, even for their own wedding.

And so the night wears on, getting later and later as the moon shifts in the sky and Annie, bright-eyed and animated, tells us about a great woman at the BBC who does make-up for television and is happy to do hers, as well as her hair, on the big day.

'And my Aunt Ivy, she's a professional cake maker and will make ours. Oh Pete, her cakes are gorgeous! And she's promised me that she'll put a good dollop of quality brandy in it.'

'I'm sure it'll be fantastic,' Pete says grinning. 'And all that brandy will make us all even happier and smilier.'

'Oh Pete, you're not taking me seriously.' Annie sits on his lap.

'Of course I am, sweetheart.' He kisses her lightly on the forehead. 'It's just that it seems this wedding is getting a bit much.'

She hugs him. 'Don't be silly. Tessa and I have got everything very much in hand, so you don't have to worry about a thing.'

Annie's wedding is far from my mind today for Joe tells us that he is taking one of his lambs, the same age as ours, to be slaughtered for their freezer. 'I'll take yours as well, if you like,' he says to me. 'It's a good size, quite big now and ready to go.'

I hesitate then steel myself. Of course Patch has to go. I know this, the children know this. We raised and bottle-fed him, knowing that this would be his end.

I explain this to Will and Amy who know it all anyway; I've kept reminding them about Patch's end throughout his short life. They want to say goodbye to him before he goes and so do I. I've suggested we thank him for the meat he is about to give us. We all troop over to the farm and as usual, Patch comes running, frolicking and nuzzling for food.

Amy bursts into tears. 'I don't want to eat Patch,' she howls. 'I can't. If you kill him I'll become a vegetarian.'

'Me too,' Will says, too upset to add more.

Now I'm teary, too, but try to hold them back and be sensible, calming the children and telling them that Patch has had a good life, that he's going to be humanely killed, that Joe knows the man who does the job decently and without pain. I point out that we've known all along that this would happen. They don't want to know. They just want their pet lamb.

I finally realise, after twenty minutes of this, that I can't do it. And the relief I feel is so great that I feel like letting out a huge whoop of joy. I don't quite understand it, I'm not a vegetarian and I meant every word I said to the children. I should be delighted to have our own animal humanely slaughtered; at least we know where it came from, know what went into its feed, its life. I finally decide that you can't kill something you've named. *My* family can't at any rate. I haven't given up on this idea of raising our own meat and perhaps one day we'll try it again but we can't kill Patch.

Later, when the children are in bed, I phone Daphne to try to explain. 'The trouble is, I don't know what to do with him now,' I say. 'Amy and Will want to keep him for ever, as a pet. They want to take him home to our back garden, but it's far too small.'

Daphne understands. 'I had the same thing, years ago. The children had a pet lamb they raised that was supposed to go into our freezer and they couldn't bear it, so we kept it on with the rest of our flock until it finally died of old age. We'll keep Patch. Our own kids are fond of him too, you know, so they'll be over the moon.'

The next day when I'm feeding the hens, I know I could never eat them either. I'd vaguely thought I would one day, since that is what this entire grow-find-and-raise-your-own-food project is all about. Hector told me that long ago when they kept hens, he'd wring their necks when they were old and stopped laying. Edna would boil up the plucked bird. 'Delicious, maid,' he'd told me. 'You best get Edna's recipe for chicken stew when your hens get past it.'

As the chickens come running and clucking to me I say soothingly to them, 'Y'know, you silly old things, I think you've been saved too. If we can't eat Patch, we certainly can't eat you.'

Next day I'm at the ShelterBox warehouse again. Though volunteers come and go, today there seems to be a particular influx of people.

I look around me as I fill the boxes. Next to me is a young girl who is a college student in Falmouth whom I've talked to before. There's also an elderly man who works slowly but steadily; he used to be a fisherman, he told me once. As he tenderly places an item in the box I imagine him being as tender with his catch, putting each fish carefully in the hold of his boat. The woman who lost her husband in the Argentine isn't here today but I recognise a friend she's sometimes arrives with, another well-dressed, middle-aged woman. Though we are all ages, from all walks of life, there is a camaraderie in the group that is special.

The unsettled weather of the greater part of August has calmed and the days are mostly balmy. Everything is madly hectic from delivering the post, what with all the holidaymakers clogging up the roads and towns, to keeping up with my work on the allotment. The courgettes are rampant and even Hector and Edna won't take any more, so I'm making all sorts of soups, quiches and everything else with them. My leeks are great too: huge, long and succulent. It makes up for the spring cabbage which is riddled with tiny green caterpillars. Will, Amy and I spend a whole afternoon picking the bugs off one by one and it's back-breaking work which doesn't seem to make the slightest difference although it's satisfying to work together for our food.

My potatoes aren't looking good and Daphne says it might be blight, but I've got more spinach, some fantastic radishes and cucumbers, so I'm thrilled, especially as I've got some fine parsnips coming along. I've also been preparing for winter, growing some purple sprouting and cabbage in my makeshift cold frame which I plant out now. I also have some Swiss chard and kale. I've got pumpkins, which should be ready for Halloween and delicious pumpkin soup.

Thinking about soups, I tell Edna about my sorrel soup. 'I remembered what you said about putting in whatever you had to hand. Well I had some cream I poured in and it all curdled. Had to throw the whole lot away.'

'Oh you would, dear.' Edna leans down to pet the Venerable Bede who is sprawled out under her feet. I hold my breath, making myself stay still and not grab on to Edna's shoulder as I did once when she bent over the cat. I was afraid she'd topple right over, she seemed so frail, but she shook me off as if I'd scalded her. Her and her husband's fierce and fiery independence is terrifying sometimes.

She goes on, 'Anything milky, any dairy produce, will curdle a sorrel dish. They must never be mixed together.'

Ah. Now she tells me. 'Well, live and learn,' I say. 'I seem to be doing a lot of that these days. Anyway, despite the disaster of the soup, I found some amazing marsh samphire when we were camping. It was delicious steamed.'

'Oh, now that is tasty. You can eat it raw too, has a lovely, salty taste. We practically lived off it one summer when we were roughing it up north.' She adjusts her Chinese coolies' hat which has gone a bit lop-sided on her head, nearly covering those owl glasses she wears.

Meanwhile I've got a cucumber crisis on my hand. I've got a glut and I don't know what to do with them all. It happened because I planted two seed packets of them, about a thousand too many. We've had cucumber salads till we're sick of them and I can't give them away, so I'm trying to make cucumber cosmetics having googled a recipe for face masks and a skin cream on the net. I remember the products at The Body Shop, the nettle shampoo especially. I've been making my own with the surplus of nettles around the countryside.

One morning on my round I talk to Mr Eyton, an elderly man I often stop to have a chat with. He lives halfway around a relief round I sometimes do so it fits in nicely. One of the wonderful things about Mr Eyton is that he loves cucumbers and doesn't grow his own, so I'm able to pass quite a few of my surplus to him. Talking to him one day recently, I realised what a small world this is, as we found to our mutual surprise that he employed my father-in-law decades ago when Ben's dad test drove cars for Jowett in the Yorkshire Dales. They'd lost contact, but when Ben's dad came to visit last year, they had a surprise reunion. I always seem to be finding connections between people and I rather like the idea that we're all somehow linked in this strange, wonderful, turbulent world.

Mr Eyton not only takes my cucumbers but insists on giving me a bowl of blackberries he's picked during one of his walks. The children and I have already gathered quite a few and I've been making blackberry and apple pies for the freezer. Now, out on a quick walk with Jake by a nearby creek, I discover a mass of damsons growing in hedgerow. I pick them eagerly, storing them in my rucksack that I'm never without these days. My gloves go in there for the nettles and also a Swiss Army knife to cut stems. I never take anything by the roots but am careful how I cut the plants I find, so that I don't destroy them.

My rucksack filled with damsons, I decide that maybe the quick walk I intended should be drawn out a bit. After all, my work for the day is finished and Ben is back working at the Sunflower Café for the summer. The children have gone off to play with friends. That's another important perk of living here, the fact that they can wander about the village and I don't have to worry. I would never dream of letting them do that in London.

I'm in a beech woodland, carpeted with emerald green moss, lush soft grass and a tiny gurgling stream running through it. Though I love the magnificence of the coastline, I also love these secret copses and the creeks, rivers and estuaries you find here. This woodland is like something from a fairy tale. Past the beech trees there are gnarled scrub oak, small and craggy, covered in lush moss that looks so tempting and luxurious that I wrap my arms around one of the trunks, leaning my face lightly against the moss. It smells divine, all earthy and rich. Somewhere I am sure I hear the warble of a wren which blends with the gurgling stream to make a perfect melody. Unable to resist, I lie down on my back on some thick, soft grass, a mossy bank for a pillow and before I know it, I've fallen asleep. A blackbird's call wakes me shortly and reluctantly I get up and head for home to make damson jam. Hopefully I'll have enough not just for us but to give as Christmas presents.

Feeling both tranquil and energised from my walk and catnap, I'm practically bouncing down the road towards home when a familiar voice hollers, 'Hey, my lover, you be full of beans today. You been working in your allotment? I ain't forgot what you said about competing with me in the harvest show.'

'Oh hi, Doug,' I grin. 'I didn't say competing with you, I said I'd be joining you by entering a vegetable.'

He's fairly close now and I notice he's staring at me, looking at me up and down. Never having taken much interest in what I've looked like before, I'm wondering what he's looking at. I'm wearing my usual digging in the garden and foraging clothes, nothing startling.

'What's up, Doug? You're looking like you've never seen a woman before.'

He leaps back as if I've bitten him, 'Oh, uh, I never, I wasn't . . . I didn't mean nothing. I mean, you ain't a woman.'

'What?' Now I'm the one looking at him oddly. Has he flipped? I mean, I know I'm not a pretty sight right now, blond hair dark with sweat and pulled back with a clip, pale blue cotton trousers, eons old, loose and baggy, the better to dig and pick things in and old white T-shirt, but it's obvious I'm female. Well, I hope so anyway.

His jowly face has turned bright red and I see he's writhing with embarrassment. He's a bachelor, I remember, still living with his mum though middle-aged, and I realise that other than her and Daphne, he probably doesn't have much contact with women.

He's mumbling on, 'I mean, course you be a woman, but I wasn't looking at you like that. I be staring at you because you've gone all green and twiggy.'

'*What?*' Now I'm disconcerted and it shifts the balance.

He's no longer embarrassed but has regained his smug composure. I look down and see that I'm covered with grass stains, bits of foliage and quite a lot of moss stuck to my trousers and T-shirt. While Doug shakes his head and tuts as if I were some recalcitrant child, I put my hand to my hair and pull away bits of twigs and blades of grass.

Doug guffaws. 'What you been up to, anyway? Even your face got a greenish tinge.' He stares at me almost with admiration then repeats beguilingly, 'C'mon, me lover, tell ole Dougie what you've been up to.'

I smile at him serenely, making no attempt to brush away the grass and debris. 'I'm getting in practice, Doug, for Halloween. I'm dressing up as the Jolly Green Giant to go trick or treating with the children. D'you think I've got enough greenery on me or do I need more?'

He peers at me with a nod and a sombre look, and in that moment I know he believes me. I said it without thinking, as a joke, but he's taken me seriously. 'You need to wear something green too, y'know. To be authentic, like.'

Now I too solemnly nod, 'Good point, Doug.' As I say goodbye and skip off I'm thinking what a barmy thing to say. Now not only will Doug be telling everyone in the pub that the adult incomer is prancing about in a Halloween get-up two months early, but worse, come the time, it will be hard getting out of dressing up with Will and Amy if Doug has anything to do with it.

With all the summer activities, harvesting the vegetables and work, enjoying the beach with the family, snorkelling, crabbing and evening picnics on the shore, I don't notice at first that Google Gull has disappeared. During the summer months with the long light evenings, often I've been in bed ages before darkness, even before twilight. When you get up at four, you need early nights, so I've been used to not seeing him before locking up for the night although he's nearly always there in the morning. Suddenly I realise I've not seen him for over twenty-four hours, the longest he's been away. It's the lack of noise that alerts me. In the wee hours of the morning the dawn chorus contains no harsh seagull shrieks. He's not back that day when I return from work. A consultation with Ben and the children reveals that no one has seen him in the last twenty-four hours.

Ben says, 'Perhaps he's found a mate and gone off with her.'

'It's the end of summer. Wouldn't he have done that in spring?'

We don't know. That day I start asking around. First I ask folk in the village if they've come across a sick or wounded gull anywhere. Somehow I can't believe he's just flown off without warning.

I end up at Joe and Daphne's farm, standing by the field where the sheep are grazing. Patch comes bounding up for his usual nuzzle as I say, 'I don't mind if Google has flown off to live on the cliffs or with the other gulls, but I'd hate to think of him injured or ill. He could have got hit by a car; he's fearless around vehicles. I've nearly run him over myself.'

Daphne says she'll keep an eye out for Google, but Joe has gone quiet. His face is troubled, concerned. Daphne is about to say something more but he looks at her, shakes his head, an almost imperceptible gesture meant for her alone that I pick up.

'What do you know, Joe? What is it you don't want to tell me?'

He hesitates but I push him.

'I don't know if it was your seagull. It was a young one, still with its grey feathers, but huge as they are. This one was even bigger than usual.'

'That's him. He's grown enormous. Where was he?'

'You can't be sure it was yours.'

'Google has a red band around one of his claws.'

Joe looks away from me, not speaking.

I say, 'You've seen him. Do you know where he is now?'

He hesitates so long I think he's not going to answer, but finally he says, 'He's dead, Tessa. I'm sorry.' He blurts the rest out quickly. 'I shot him. I didn't mean to, but I did.'

I'm so shocked I can't speak. Daphne says, 'Oh no. Was that the gull you told me about last night? The one attacking the ewe?'

'I didn't know it was Tessa's gull. Not that it would have made any difference.'

I find my voice. 'Not made a difference? I can't believe you're saying that.' I'm struggling with tears. 'What are you doing shooting a seagull anyway? Aren't they a protected species?'

Joe shakes his head. I go on, the words tumbling out incoherently. 'You shot him just because you think gulls are a bit of a nuisance, a bit troublesome, is that what happened? How can you? You farmers . . . ' I can't speak any more as the tears win, half grief, half fury.

Joe's face has turned from concern to anger. 'You're talking just like some of the incomers from Up Country, the ones who move down here knowing bloody sod all about country life, the ones who think all farmers are alike, shooting everything that moves if we don't like the look of it.' He breaks off, puts his hand to his head in a gesture of both anger and helplessness. 'D'you think I or any of the farmers around here would deliberately kill a seagull? God knows they're a pest but I don't go around killing things, Tessa, whatever you think. I got my shotgun out because I looked out over that field there and saw one of my ewes, a weak sick one lying on her side, being attacked by some gulls. Yes, and your bloody gull amongst them, though I didn't know it then.'

He pauses, too upset to go on for a moment. I'm still too stunned to say another word. Joe goes on, more quietly now, 'It happens, y'know. You haven't a clue how vicious gulls can be sometimes; I've seen them peck the eyes out of a lamb when it wasn't even dead yet.' He presses his fingers to his eyes in a gesture of helplessness. 'That's why I ran for the gun. I wasn't about to let them kill or maim my ewe.'

I stammer, 'It couldn't have been Google. He wouldn't.'

Daphne intervenes, gently, 'It's a wild creature, Tessa. They always stay wild no matter how you try to tame them.'

'But . . .' I start crying again. 'You didn't have to kill it.'

Joe lets out an exasperated, frustrated sigh and says, 'I wasn't trying to bloody kill it. I hate killing things. God, Tessa, don't you know me by now? I shot up in the air to scare them away and it was one of those one in a million fluke accidents that the shot hit your bird.'

Daphne confirms this. 'Joe was ever so upset when he told me. And that was before we knew it was your gull.'

I'm struggling to take all this in, but finally I pull myself together and apologise to Joe for the things I said. I know he is not only a good farmer but a good man. When I try to tell him this he says brusquely, 'Don't go the opposite way and romanticise us farmers, Tessa. Much as I hate killing, I'd shoot at anything that was savaging my sheep, even a dog. I had a dog once, one I thought was a soppy Golden Retriever, but one night he got out with another dog and killed and savaged a ewe in lamb. Viciously, horribly. The farmer shot and killed my dog. I was heartbroken but I understood why he did it. I'd have done the same.'

I nod, not knowing what to say. The longer I live here, the more I'm learning about rural living, about the cruelty, too, of the nature I love. And I know I have to accept the harshness and pain of it as well as the idyllic bliss. Finally I say, 'Where is he? My seagull?'

Joe looks miserable now and I finally realise how hard this is for him and how courageous of him to tell me. I'd never have known what had happened to our seagull otherwise. For a moment though I wish he hadn't. I could have imagined Google Gull soaring the skies over the cliff tops and over the sea, free and light as the wind with the other gulls, but I know in my heart it wouldn't have been that way. Instead I'd have fretted over the other scenario, Google run over, injured, dying slowly and painfully in a ditch somewhere. After all, he'd never flown off for good before. Knowing was, after all, better than not knowing. Joe was right to tell me.

He says, 'The gull is in the woods at the edge of the field where the sheep are. I saw it fall, saw it was dead, but had to leave it there as I needed to see to the ewe. I was going back there just as you came.'

'Can I have him? I'd like to bury him in the garden.'

Which is what we do. We put Google in a cardboard box, have a small family ceremony, just me, Ben and the children. Joe dug the hole in the back garden; he said he wanted to, to make amends. I took Will and Amy down to the beach beforehand and they picked the best seashells they could find to adorn the grave, and some silvery luminous strands of seaweed to drape around the body. Laid to rest, Google looks every bit the splendid bird he was as he lies covered with all the treasures of the sea.

As each of us solemnly shovels dirt over his coffin, a tear or two falling, we hear a familiar raucous cry from the rooftop of our house. Three seagulls are perched there, two adult gulls and one young one the same size as the parents but with those unmistakeable grey feathers. They are watching us intently, making their haunting cries as we complete the burial.

Later, Will asks if I think they were Google's friends. Amy says, 'I think they were his mother, father and sister. Or maybe brother. We never did find out where Google came from.'

For days afterward, I can't hear a seagull's cry without feeling my eyes prick with tears. And then one day I make my way groggily down to the kitchen just as the dawn light is filtering through the darkness and as I look out the window I'm sure I see a seagull sitting on the old outdoor table. I blink, look again, and seem to see it soar away over the trees, towards the sea. It was probably a shadow, I say to myself. A trick of that iridescent morning light. But why should it be? Why not believe in a little magic on this ancient stretch of ground renowned for its Celtic myths, its tales of enchantment and mystery. As I make my way to work, driving through silent roads, seeing the sea change colour as the sun works its way up the horizon, I decide to believe I saw the ghost of my beloved seagull, making one last visit to the home he was brought up in before finally flying away for ever over the sea.

Chapter 15

My cabbage is bigger than your cabbage

It's the day of the Treverny autumn show and the village is in a fever of excitement bordering on hysteria. This normally placid, easy-going village is seething with competitive spirit. It's all in good fun, though, or rather I hope it is. It's surprising how serious folk can get over a carrot.

The list of categories for the different produce are listed and studied by all. There are nearly two hundred of them along with numerous classes – vegetable, fruit, dairy, flowers and children's among others. There are photography, art and floral arrangement competitions as well as cookery categories. I consider entering my damson jam into No. 76, the Jar of Jam (Any Kind) competition; I have had many compliments on it and it's absolutely delicious, if I do say so myself. Then I remember all the stones in it, the ones I couldn't get out, so I quickly discard that idea. Amy is going to enter her sunflower in the children's flower competition, the Tallest Sunflower in the Show. She got some seeds out of a Beano comic of all things and her sunflowers, growing proudly in the front garden, appear to be amongst the tallest in the village.

I have been pondering my leeks for some time, toying with the idea of entering them as to me they look absolutely perfect. I could enter the No. 9 category, Three Leeks (Trimmed). I look at the other vegetable categories to see if there's anything else I can enter. I could do Three Round Beet (With Tops) or Two Garden Cabbage. Or Four Courgette. As my beets, though perfectly round, are small, I forget that idea and my cabbages are full of slug holes. My courgettes, though tasty and plentiful, are not the prettiest I have to admit.

I put down the catalogue, laughing at myself because my veg are for eating not for competing, except that I made that silly promise to Doug that I'd enter something. I'd hate not to keep it.

I've been preparing dinner while pondering the harvest fair and reading the brochure, and there staring me in the face is the answer to my dilemma. *A cucumber.* It is not any cucumber, it's the strangest, most peculiar-looking cucumber I've ever seen, all twisty, lumpy and odd. Actually, thinking about it, nearly all my cucumbers are a bit peculiar.

Odd. There's a category for the Oddest Vegetable, probably invented for the likes of me who can't grow perfectly shaped produce. I'll enter one of my cucumbers. Honour will be satisfied.

I forget all about the Treverny show the next day when I'm delivering to one of the farms on my route and run into Pete, on his way out. We leave our respective vans to greet each other while the farm sheep dog barks frantically in tail-wagging welcome and the two white geese run about the place honking. We fuss over the dog and ignore the geese, which though loud are not aggressive, unlike some other geese on my rounds.

I say to Pete, 'You're not a secret postman, are you? Delivering mail on the sly?'

'Not likely. One postie in the family is enough.' I'm so overcome by this remark, including me in the extended family, that I give him an impulsive hug. He gives me a big bear hug back and as we break apart, I see the farmer and his wife staring open mouthed at us from the front door.

I wave merrily at them, rush over with the post and say, 'Isn't it lovely? Pete is marrying my very best friend.'

I tootle off with another jolly wave to find Pete waiting for me at our vans, shaking his head, but with a grin on his face. 'Well that was great, Tessa. I'll now be put down as a bounder who snogs the postie while engaged to her best friend.' The geese begin raucously honking again, as if confirming this.

'Oh dear. Ah well, I'll put it right next time.'

He rolls his eyes in mock despair. 'No, don't, just leave everything be.'

'You haven't told me what you're doing here. I thought you were working.' I'm tickling the dog's tummy as we speak, give him one of the biscuits I keep in my van.

'This *is* working. Part of my job is to visit farmers to see if they need anything for their animals or land. I just tested the soil on one of the farms here for a lime deficiency.' He too makes a fuss of the black and white dog which is nuzzling me for more treats.

We talk a few more minutes and I mention some more wedding plans Annie told me about on the phone last night. 'And when she's here this weekend, she wants to go over the menu again for the reception, the drinks and food, plus some other stuff you've got to decide.'

Pete, who has been looking quite boyish and jovial, suddenly changes demeanour. His body language is now tense and strained. When he doesn't speak I say, 'What is it? Annie *is* coming this weekend, isn't she?'

He nods, 'Look, Tessa, I'd better get on.'

I've known Pete now for some time. Since Annie met him, well over a year ago, I've seen him not only with her, but on our own, stopping for a quick coffee when we've met in St Geraint, inviting him over for meals now and again with Ben and the children. I like him more and more each time we meet; he's open, honest and there's certainly something bothering him today.

So I stop him before he gets into his van. 'Pete, it's none of my business, but as soon as I mentioned Annie and the wedding, you froze. Is something wrong, and if there is, do you want to talk about it? Tell me to buzz off if you don't, I won't be offended.'

He turns back to me and I drop my hand from his shoulder. I'm aware, and no doubt he is too, of the farmer now ambling out towards his milking parlour but practically walking backwards to gape at us and his wife throwing some corn to the geese but also staring surreptitiously.

Pete says, 'We're not far from Creek and I've got to see a farmer near there now but if you've got time we could talk after that?'

I agree to meet him at the estuary in about half an hour. I often stop at Creek anyway, sitting on the sea wall to eat my lunch, so it's perfect timing for me.

He's there when I arrive, watching an oyster catcher walking along the edge of the water, making little claw marks on the shiny, wet sand. The tide is at the halfway mark and a few old boats bob about in the tiny harbour. A cormorant perches on a rock, still as a statue, looking out to sea. Pete comes over to the sea wall where I've perched and sits down as well. He doesn't speak for a few moments.

Finally, I break the silence. 'Pete, you're not having second thoughts, are you? About this wedding? About Annie?' I hate saying the words but I can tell he needs to talk. My heart sinks as I think how heartbroken Annie will be if this falls through. I know how much she loves him.

All my worse fears are confirmed when he says, 'I guess I am.' Then he looks at my stricken face and says quickly, 'Oh not about Annie, never. God, she's the best thing that's every happened to me. No, it's this damn wedding. I'm growing to hate the thing before we've even had it.'

'Have you talked to Annie about it?'

'How can I? All these plans . . .'

He begins to talk then, haltingly at first then faster as his thoughts formulate. 'You know this isn't my first marriage. Maybe if it were I wouldn't mind so much, but a second time around . . .' He breaks off then goes on, 'It seems wrong somehow. And all this fancy stuff, the London make-up artist, the posh invitations, the fancy reception at that fancy hotel. It's not *me*, it's not my family, not the way I live.' He looks at me, his face pained. 'I wish we could have a simple exchange of vows, with a few close friends and family, then a drink and maybe a bite to eat at a pub afterwards. Not all this fuss.'

The cormorant suddenly dives into the water after a fish and the splash it makes silences us for a few moments. Then I say, 'Pete, you've got to tell Annie. You can't keep this in, you'll resent it more every day. Talk to her tomorrow when she comes down.'

For the next twenty-four hours I brood on what Pete said. As I deliver my morning rounds my mind races, wishing Annie had been more receptive to Pete's feelings, then wishing Pete had been honest with Annie instead of letting his resentment build, and finally berating myself for not seeing the signs earlier.

My worst fears are confirmed when I get home. Annie is

sitting in the kitchen with Ben, crying her eyes out. Ben looks so relieved to see me, scuttling away quickly to leave us alone, that I know it's not good.

I ply her with tissues, hug her and try to comfort her until the sobbing stops and she can talk coherently. 'It's over, it's finished. The wedding is off.'

I murmur some banal words to the effect that it can't be, I'm sure they'll sort it out. Annie goes on, 'Pete said he'd talked to you. I'm glad he did, he might never have told me otherwise.'

There is a commotion at the door and Ben says, 'Pete's here,' at the same time as the two men walk in.

Pete rushes to Annie, 'Why did you drive off like that? I didn't know where the hell you'd gone.'

Annie sobs, 'Go away. Just leave. It's best we don't see each other.'

'What're you talking about? Annie, be sensible. It's just a bloody wedding; we've got the rest of our lives.'

'Go away!' she's starting to sound hysterical so Ben says, 'Look, Pete, leave her to Tessa until she calms down, then you can talk.' He steers a bewildered Pete into the living room.

Annie, still in tears, tells me that she's driving back to London as soon as she stops crying. Luckily she drove down this time, she gulps, but could I do her a favour next week and gather all her stuff still at Pete's and send it up to her?

I say, 'Annie, this is crazy. Just because he doesn't want a great big fancy wedding is no reason to break everything off. Can't you compromise somehow?'

She looks up at me with swollen eyes. 'You don't understand. Pete's agreed to the wedding. He told me how he felt, and I understood, I really did.'

'I hope you told him that.'

'Of course I did. I was so sorry for not realising before.

Then I told him I'd always wanted a big proper wedding, it's a once-in-a-lifetime thing for me. And he understood. Said he was being selfish and of course we'll have the wedding and he won't mind at all now we've talked about it.'

I stare at her as she begins to cry again. Ben creeps into the kitchen trying not to be seen, grabs the coffee pot from the counter and two cups, then dashes out again. Before he disappears we look at each other and roll our eyes.

'Annie,' I say, 'What's the problem? You've talked, you both understand each other now, and Pete is happy for the wedding to go ahead as planned. What are you talking about going back to London for?'

It all comes rushing out in a gush of sporadic words, tears and a fair amount of tissues. Annie has realised, by this conflict over the wedding, that she and Pete are worlds apart, that their lives and backgrounds are too different to be compatible, that she'll always be a Londoner and Pete an agriculturalist and never the twain shall meet. She goes on in this vein for nearly an hour, going over the same things again and again while I ply her with coffee and more tissues, trying to make her see sense. In the meantime Ben whisks Pete away, 'for a walk', he says, but no doubt he'll take Pete to the local pub and give him a stiff drink or two. Annie still won't let Pete near her.

'Annie,' I say finally. 'Does Pete agree with this? That you're incompatible?'

It appears he doesn't, as I knew, of course. As is obvious, the way Pete has followed her here and is trying to talk to her.

Annie says, 'That's why it's up to me, you see? One of us has got to see clearly.'

I try to tell her that she's the one not being lucid. Long before she and Pete got engaged, they talked about her leaving London, about the life they both wanted to live in Cornwall. Despite their superficial differences, Annie and Pete share a similar core of values and that's the important thing, as I remind her now.

She won't hear it. I'm about to despair when Pete and Ben come back. Annie tries to retreat to the bathroom but Pete firmly takes her arm, tells her she owes it to him to talk to him before flying back to London, and settles down with her at the kitchen table as she refuses to go back to his house.

Now it's Ben and my turn to leave. 'Thank goodness Will and Amy aren't home,' I mutter as we call Jake and take off towards the nearby beech woodland for a walk. Ben and I take off our sandals, paddling in the creek with Jake who chases sticks and races madly about, delighted to be here even though he's already had a long walk with Ben while I was working.

When we get back, Annie's car is gone, as is Pete's. 'Oh hell,' I mutter, 'She's gone back to London.'

But there's a note on the table. It's from Annie, saying that she and Pete have thrashed it out, that all is fine, the marriage is on, the wedding's on, that God's in his heaven and all's right with the world. Well, she didn't write that last bit but that's what the note implied. Pete had added a postscript, apologising for descending on us so dramatically and adding they hoped it was OK if they came to us for dinner that night as planned.

Which they do. Both looking gloriously, madly in love. Pete is fine about the wedding now that he knows how much it means to Annie, and Annie is overwhelmed with love and gratitude for his understanding. We end up having a hilarious night, all of us flicking through hymn books and searching the Internet trying to decide what songs to have at the wedding, falling about laughing as we belt out 'Jerusalem' at the top of our lungs.

Now that that traumatic weekend is over, my thoughts turn to the autumn show again, as everyone in the village is talking about it. The locals have been checking up on other people's gardens for days trying to see how they are faring. I must say it's catching, for I find myself peering into the odd vegetable patch alongside the lanes to see if I can spot a weird-looking cucumber.

I start fantasising about entering a proper vegetable next year. Maybe potatoes? There are four categories: Four Round Potatoes (White); Four Kidney Potatoes (White); Four Coloured Potatoes (Round); and Four Coloured Potatoes (Kidney). There are no categories for Potatoes With Slug Holes. Perhaps I should suggest it to the committee for next year's show.

The event takes place in the village hall where long trestle tables are set up, covered with pristine white cloths. The produce and other items have to be delivered in the morning, and I'm amused to note a kind of military air about the place, a buzz and alertness as if waiting for the moment of victory. All morning long there are people, mostly men I've noticed, marching up to the village hall carrying huge parsnips, turnips, onions and other produce. They carry them as if they were a cross between a precious infant and an explosive, holding their prizes slightly away from their bodies as if not wanting to tarnish the cleaned and polished vegetables by contact with a pullover or jacket. As they march through the village they glance furtively at their rivals, checking out whether some other man's turnip might be bigger than theirs. You can feel the testosterone driving them on. I can't help smiling, feeling like I'm in an Agatha Christie thriller, and I invent titles as I watch like, 'Murder on the Allotment Express' or 'The Case of the Missing Cabbages'. I can see Hercule Poirot finding clues amongst the courgettes, or better still Miss Marple. In fact I can see someone just like her, carrying a basket with fresh eggs into the village hall. Miss Marple, ordinary villager, will be the one to solve 'The Mystery of the Poisoned Parsnip'.

I try out my little joke about Miss Marple to Doug who is on his way back from delivering his entries and I'm severely reprimanded. "Tis no laughing matter, my lover. Growing stuff is a serious business, not for the likes of folk who laugh.'

Oh dear. Suitably chastised, I bring my ugliest, funniest cucumber and hand it in to the organisers who will arrange the produce for display after everything has been given in.

When it's all set up I and the children, alongside just about everyone else in the village, go in to look. The first thing I'm struck by is the weird symmetry of the displays. The vegetables and fruit look unreal; they've been cleaned, washed and polished so that they look nothing like my produce ever looked. Most are in groups of threes and I see that they are all not only large but uniform in size. There's not a nobbly parsnip in sight, nor a smallish beetroot or a lettuce with even the slightest hole or blemish. There's no room here for wonky organic carrots or uneven sets of onions or crooked runner beans. Doug wasn't kidding when he said folk took their vegetables seriously.

We move over to the parsnips, which are long, straight and perfect. 'The winners will have grown them in lengths of drainpipes, to get them like that,' Daphne says.

'You're joking.'

'Not at all. I've seen Doug do it and he's not the only one. He also sieves the soil very finely for them.'

I'm learning about a type of garden totally alien to the way I work. This seems to me more like controlling nature rather than just letting it all grow as it comes. It's only when we get to the 'Oddest Vegetable' category that I see produce which has a similarity to my own. Here there are carrots shaped like half moons, parsnips with legs and arms sticking out and all sorts of weird shapes and sizes of every kind of vegetable. I'm proud of my cucumber; it looks at home here.

We wander over to the egg section where I've never seen so many varieties, all displayed on earthenware saucers with straw to give it some atmosphere. I recognise the amazing brown eggs that could almost be mistaken for chocolate; my Maran hen lays ones like that. The Arauncanas eggs are a pale blue-green. As with the other produce, the idea is to have the three eggs on display identical in size and shape.

We stroll around the jams and marmalades, which the judges will select for taste and consistency, and then look at the cakes, the bouncy sponge cakes and fruity farmhouse slab cake. All are beautifully presented and look professionally baked. People have worked long and hard for this show.

After the judging everyone in the village troops in again to see who has won. You don't even have to look at the cards by the side of the entrants, with the handwritten First, Second, or Third prize and 'Highly Commended', like personal invitations to some exclusive party. All you have to do is look at the faces of the competitors, especially the men. Those that haven't won look either crestfallen or miffed, but you can tell they're already thinking of next year's blue ribbon. Those that did get a coveted prize try to look modest but fail utterly. People crowd around them telling them how exquisite their onions are, their brown papery tops bound up sweetly with brown string, or how big their turnips are, how huge their parsnips. Once again the testosterone in the air is nearly tangible.

I giggle to Daphne in a whisper, 'I don't see the female gardeners strutting around like that.'

She laughs, 'They don't take it as seriously.'

At the cabbages we see Doug, gloating over his blue ribbon. He's grown the most humongous cabbage I've ever seen. I go to congratulate him and he surprises me by saying, 'Well my lover, I needs be congratulating you too.'

'What for?'

'Why your cucumber, 'tis the ugliest the judges have seen for years, apparently. You got the blue ribbon for it.'

I rush over to have a look and sure enough, there it is, first prize for the oddest-looking vegetable. I couldn't be more chuffed if I'd grown a hundred perfect leeks and a bigger cabbage than Doug's.

'So, my lover, what's your secret then?' Doug has followed Daphne and me to see my blue ribbon. 'How you be growing such an ugly thing?' He snorts with laughter.

I just grin but Daphne says, 'What about you, Doug? What nasty things did you use to grow that monster of a cabbage?'

He scowls at her. 'That's a slander I thought I'd never hear. Others may do wicked things with their cabbages, ply them with chemicals and such like, and I know for a fact they do, but not Dougie here, no way.' He straightens his back and glares at her. 'I got me own secret ingredient.'

When we're out of earshot Daphne says, 'I can't resist winding him up sometimes; he does get far too cocky. But it's true, he's about the only one who wins prizes without using artificial stuff. He thinks I don't know it but his secret ingredient is nothing more than good old dung. It works a treat for him every year.'

A tiny seed of elation begins to plant itself inside me. Dung, eh? Dung is good, dung is organic. Daphne and Joe can supply me, I'm sure. My mind is racing ahead to next year, to huge cabbages, monster onions. Maybe I'll even grow one bigger than Doug's, enter it in the show, win the blue ribbon.

Luckily I stop myself before I get too carried away, and I remember that growing food is not a competition but a way to feed my family the way I want to. And besides, the competitive side of my nature has been mollified, what with my cucumber and now, with another victory. As Daphne and I approach the children's section I see Amy, waving at me and holding up the card in her hand which says her sunflower has won second prize for the tallest sunflower.

When all the gaping and gawping over the produce and the prize winners has finished we sit down for a massive Cornish cream tea. Life in London was never like this, I think, as I bite into my second homemade scone and ladle the clotted cream on it as thick as I dare.

'Tuck in, my lover.' Doug, passing my chair, gives me a nudge on my shoulder. 'You be a proper gardener now. Mebbe next year you can grow the most peculiar radish. Especially if you talk to it.' He roars with laughter at his joke, as he always does. Then he adds, 'I even might be persuaded to give you a gardening tip or two for the future.' He gives me a smug wink, taps the side of his nose and puffs up his chest on which he's pinned his blue ribbon.

'Oh you have already,' I say. 'Given me a huge tip.'

He looks at me suspiciously, 'Have I?'

'Maybe,' I say, all innocent and mysterious. He stares at me then shrugs and goes to get his cream tea, plonking down with it in the seat opposite me and Daphne, the one I've been saving for Ben who is somewhere around talking to the locals.

'I have to say, my lover, despite all your peculiar ways, your garden ain't looking half bad.' He consumes an entire half scone covered with jam and cream, in one huge mouthful.

I'm ridiculously gratified. I feel as if I've passed some enormous test and have come out with flying colours.

Chapter 16

Happy endings

In October, the country is plagued with storms and ferocious gales. With the autumn tides the sea is fierce, pounding over the sea wall as it is doing today, washing over the road in Morranport where I'm on my walking round. I fear I'm going to be blown away into those monstrous waves, never to be heard of again. Despite being dressed in waterproofs from top to bottom, I'm pretty wet when I reach Archie and Jennifer's house at the end of the sea wall.

'Come in, quickly,' Jennifer says, hauling me into the house. 'Get something warm in you and dry off a bit in the kitchen.'

I take up her offer gratefully. Archie is in the kitchen, already putting on the kettle. I admire some new paintings of Jennifer's – she does exquisite portraits of local people, and in fact sold a couple of them at Charlie's gallery – then comment on the storm.

'It's a bad one, a south-easterly, and lasting longer than it should. They'll be more call outs for the lifeboats yet, you wait,' says Archie.

Jennifer puts a hand on his shoulder. 'Wayne will be fine. You worry too much about him.'

'Has the lifeboat already been called out from Falmouth?'

Archie nods. 'Early this morning, ages ago when it was still dark. The all-weather boat, there's a freighter in trouble. An old mate who lives in Falmouth rang to tell me. He knows I like to know when Wayne's out there.' He looks at Jennifer, tries to smile as he says to her, 'You think it is best I don't know until he's back safe, but I like to hold him when he's out there.' He turns to me, 'Hold him in my mind, is what I mean. In my heart, you know? Like praying, I guess. I like to feel something, some strength or good wishes or whatever, are going from me to him and all the others, out there in this.'

He looks out of the kitchen window and my eyes follow, seeing the spray lash against it. I've never seen the sea this high. 'The freighter's got some sort of engine problem I think, and it's perilously close to some rocks, not sure exactly where, my mate didn't know.'

The three of us are silent, listening to the wind and the lashing rain. I go back out, uncomplaining about the weather. Walking in it is a doddle compared to what Wayne and the rest of the lifeboat crew are doing.

When much later I deliver some post to Belle, she asks me in and I accept, hoping to spend a few minutes in front of her wood-burning stove warming up again. Batman stops barking when I shout, 'Ham,' and lies down like a lamb in front of me. As usual he accepts my ham gracefully and wags his long, thick, furry tail at me; we're slowly learning to be friends now.

Belle says, 'You've heard the lifeboat be out?'

'Archie told me. His godson Wayne is on it. I guess Blake, your grandson, is there too?'

She nods. 'His mum just rang. 'Tis monstrous rough out

there.' We sit quietly for a few minutes, listening to the storm. 'It don't get easier, y'know. Not for his mum, nor me, nor any of us who love him. No matter how many times that lifeboat gets called out.'

Much later I see Nell in the post office, ask if she's heard anything about the Falmouth lifeboat. 'Back safe, only just heard. Freighter still out there though, anchored down but they took the ten man crew off, too dangerous for them. Storm's the worst I've seen in a dozen or more years, I'm telling you.'

I stay a while, drinking more tea with Nell, before going out in it again and heading home. I think of Belle and Archie and Jennifer, the relief on their faces as they learn that their loved ones are safe home from the sea yet another time. I hope and pray it will always be so for the lifeboat crew.

The weather stays unpredictable for the next couple of weeks and now I'm getting worried about the wedding. It's the last Saturday in October, not far away now, and it's more like winter than autumn. We've hardly had a chance to admire the splendour of the turning leaves and many have blown away prematurely in the gales. The autumn chrysanthemums in the village gardens look bedraggled and sodden, and everywhere you stand your feet squelch in the soggy grass and mud.

By coincidence some of our rounds have been slightly altered and for the last few weeks I've been delivering to Pete's parents who live in a bungalow in one of my new villages. I've got to know them quite well as either Bernie or Miranda, and often both, are outside in their garden when I arrive. They are a good solid Cornish couple who like Annie but can't help viewing her with a hint of suspicion, as I've come to realise. Today, as we chew the fat and watch their tabby cat stalking what looks like a beetle in the front lawn, we are, as usual, talking about the wedding, about Annie and Pete.

Suddenly, as if making up his mind at last to speak, Bernie

says, 'I tell'ee, maid, I'm fond of that girl of his. I truly am.'
There's a *but* in that sentence, you can tell. I wait for him to
go on. 'But she do be sneezing all the time. 'Tis a worry, that
is. 'Tis not normal.' He shakes his head which is square, stocky
and bald, sitting on his short squat body. The only resemblance
to Pete is the warm twinkle in his clear blue eyes.

'It's only an allergy, Bernie,' I tell him. 'She can't help it,
she has lots of them. They're starting to ease, though, now
that she's coming here more often, getting acclimatised to
the different types of plants and things that can cause her
allergies.'

He doesn't look convinced but shakes his head worriedly.
A chilly wind is whipping around the garden though the rain
has stopped at last. Pete's mum, Miranda, who has been listening
to us, now shakes her head as well. It too is square, full jawed.
Her hair is grey and permed tightly and does nothing for her,
but her face is open and kind. They are good people and I
know they've tried to welcome Annie into their family. I've
grown fond of them both, and more importantly, so has Annie.

Miranda says, ''Tisn't good for childbearing. All them sneezes.'

Ah, so that's what this is all about, I think. I assure her that
Annie's health is spot on, that truly her allergies are only allergies and won't affect any pregnancy she might have.

Miranda looks doubtful. 'She's a good maid, I be fond of
her too, like Bernie is. But a city maid like she be won't want
to be bothered by infants now will she?' Her face is so woeful
my heart goes out to her. Pete is their only child. Have this
kind couple been worried all these months that they are to be
for ever deprived of grandchildren?

I reassure them with words I know to be true. 'Annie loves
babies and would love children.'

The look of relief doesn't come as I expected. 'But, maid,'
Miranda begins then hesitates.

'What is it?'

Bernie takes up the challenge as his wife falters, lowering her eyes in embarrassment. 'The thing is, she ain't a young'un, is she? Now don't get me wrong, we like her well enough, but she be not a young maid for sure.'

I'm flabbergasted. Annie's not even forty yet, not for another year or so. Plenty of women these days get pregnant in their late thirties or early forties for the first time; I could name a few I know straight off. I'm starting to feel indignant for Annie's sake when I realise how they must be feeling. Pete's first childless marriage and divorce, long before he met Annie. All their hopes dashed. Then Pete finding another woman at last but one who perhaps doesn't want, or is too old to have, a child. I look at their kind, concerned faces and my heart goes out to them.

Miranda is saying, 'The thing is, Pete do be wanting kiddies; he'd hope for one with his first wife but they broke up before any little'uns came along. All for the best in hindsight, but . . .' her voice trails off.

I do my best to let them know that there is a good chance that one day they'll have the grandchild they so long for.

Reassured on that front, Bernie now says, 'But 'twill be hard on the maid, adjusting to our ways.'

Miranda nods sagely, ''Twill be terrible hard.'

'How do you mean?' I mumble the words but I know what they are saying.

They look at each other. Miranda says, 'Pete be a country lad. Annie be city.'

I open my mind to say something glib and meaningless, like I'm sure they'll work it out, they'll be fine. Looking at their serious, concerned faces I realise I owe them more than shallow words meant to reassure. They are too intelligent for that, and too caring.

So I say, 'You're right. It will be hard, very hard, for them both. Pete will find Annie difficult and strange at times I'm sure.'

They look relieved to hear me say this. Annie has told me this herself, has admitted some things will be tough for both of them.

I go on, 'It's going to be hard on Annie too, leaving the only environment she's ever known, and she'll find some things extremely difficult.' I think back to my first year in Cornwall, the times I felt I was living in an alien place whose customs I'd never understand, let alone master. I remember the times I missed all the things London has to offer: the theatre, music, variety of shops and restaurants, the vibrancy of a huge cosmopolitan city. I go on, 'But she'll be compensated by all the other things, like I was. The gentler, easier way of life for a start. The friendliness of the people. She's finding out these things already, you know.'

We're silent for a few moments. Then Miranda says, 'So long as they're happy, the both of them.'

Bernie agrees. 'There's not a thing else we want for either of them.'

'They will be,' I promise, for I'm as sure of that as one can be sure of anything. Annie and Pete love each other and if anyone can make a go of it, they can.

A couple of days before the wedding I take my checklist to make sure everything is as we've planned. The weather looks promising for a golden Indian Summer has arrived and is predicted to last through the weekend.

First I go to the hotel overlooking the sea to check with the manager that all is ready for the big day. Standing in the room where the reception will be held, I look out through the massive picture windows to the sea beyond. A perfect view, and it should still be light enough for everyone to admire for some time after the guests arrive. The wedding is midday and the reception straight afterwards.

The manager, who has followed me into the room, says, 'All seems to be in order. In fact, the woman who is doing the flowers was here not long ago, to check the table arrangements again and so on.'

'Ah, Ms Fluffy Slippers,' I say without thinking.

He looks relieved. 'Oh, so you've noticed too? It is most peculiar. This sophisticated and, if I may say so, very attractive woman, wearing what look like an extremely old pair of slippers.'

I nod. 'I've never seen her without them. She must have terribly bad feet, poor thing.'

'It was raining cats and dogs the day she came, and I saw her get out of the car. She was wearing boots but took them off as soon as she got to the door. She was so well dressed that I was sure she'd be putting on some elegant footwear and then she came in with those slippers.' He shakes his head in wonder. 'Amazing, isn't it? People, I mean. The types I've met in this business . . .' He trails off and looks at me. 'And that reminds me, Mrs Hainsworth, about the dancing at the reception.' He has a faint smile on his face and I know, I just know, he's remembering Annie and me lunging around the room in a parody of a dance and ending up in a heap on the floor.

We adjust some details about the music and dancing, parting in a jovial mood. He says as I leave, 'I do hope the groom is as energetic a dancer as his bride.' His voice is solemn but his eyes are twinkling.

After this I take a quick drive around to the half dozen hotels and B&Bs where the guests will be staying, the ones Annie and I found ages ago. I want to reassure myself that all is fine and there are no unforeseen problems.

I don't really need to visit Trelak Farm because I know Emma and Martin do a great B&B, but as I'm passing by I call in. Emma is outside feeding the goats but stops to talk about the weekend.

'We're booked solidly,' she tells me. 'All folk from London; Annie's friends I suppose.'

She doesn't look too happy about it so I ask her if something is wrong.

'Oh no, not at all, and we're thrilled, financially it's a great boost this time of year.'

'So what it is? C'mon, Emma, you're worried about something, I can tell.'

After a slight hesitation she says, 'Well, a couple of the bookings are in names I recognise. Like, on the telly. I know they're only staying with us because the posher places were booked up early.'

Martin has joined us, coming along with a bale of hay to put in the goat feeder. He's heard Emma's comment and adds, 'To be honest, Tessa, we are both worried that Trelak won't be good enough for them. That they'll find fault.'

I assure them that if they're Annie's friends, they'll be decent people who will find nothing to fault at Trelak Farm. I leave them with their goats, thinking how lucky these minor celebrities are, to see something of the real honest rural Cornwall in the shape of Trelak Farm, its owners and animals.

Chapter 17

Wedding bells

The day is as beautiful as promised. I wake up on the morning of the wedding looking out over a golden landscape. The sun is shining on the yellow beech leaves making them glow like jewels, turning the other leaves coppery, red and a deep bronze colour. Slanting sun beams dice through the few fluffy clouds and everything is as near perfect as can be.

Annie is staying with me and wakes early as I do. 'Shall we sneak out and walk on the beach?' she says as we meet in the kitchen over coffee.

No one else is up so we quietly dress and head for the cove. The tide is far out and the sand smooth. Jake runs in circles chasing seabirds who hover, tantalising him, then fly off exuberantly, crying their triumphant caws. Barefoot, Annie and I make footprints in the pristine sand.

'The first footprints in the whole world,' I say.

'The first day of my new life,' she smiles. We hug, there's no need for any more words.

Before we make for home I take her to my special rock pool where I most often find the cowrie shells, hoping there is one for Annie today. There is and she holds it in the palm of her hand. 'I'll tuck it into my bra, under my wedding dress, for luck.'

The cars arrive on time to pick up the bridal party. Ben is going to give Annie away, standing in for her father in New Zealand. I'm her maid of honour, and Will and Amy will be her page and flower girl. They look wonderful, Will grown up in his new suit and Amy beautiful in a new dress.

After I've admired them I turn to Annie. She looks stunning. A designer friend who is a stylist for the BBC made the dress which is an elegant creation of natural silk and lace. I smile when I see her veil perfectly framing her lovely face, her dark hair, longer now, is worn up for this special day. The veil is an antique silk one that I wore for my own wedding to Ben. In a mad, impulsive moment, justifying the expense by telling myself I'll only be married once, I bought it in Harrods after falling in love with it at first sight. Now Annie is wearing it, thrilled that I'd offered it to her for her 'something borrowed'. The cornflowers in her hair are blue and, she whispers to me as we get ready to go, the cowrie shell is her 'old' item, for who knows how long it was there waiting for her to pick up on her wedding day.

As we leave the house, there's a crowd outside, waiting to see Annie, waving and wishing her luck. Word gets around quickly in a village like ours so there are not only the people Annie has actually met on her visits here, but others who are happy to come out on such a fine day to contribute to a joyous event. There are dozens of children who cheer when Annie appears plus a few dogs, including Old Yeller, who has ambled up to see what all the fuss is about. Annie's smile when she waves back at them is radiant.

It's a short drive to Creek and when we turn off the main

road down the narrow lane that leads to the church, I check my watch and see that the timing is exactly right. I feel a glow of satisfaction that we remembered to check the tides before deciding on the time of the wedding. When the tide is in, the view from the church is spectacular, but when it's out, it's mud flats. Today, when we arrive it will be high tide, the sea placid and awesomely beautiful on this windless October day.

Suddenly our car stops and I realise that never, in rural Cornwall, can you be precise about some things, like time, for instance. For in front of us, ambling down the hilly road, is a huge herd of dairy cows. They're being moved from one field to another by a farmer and his son, and we've arrived at the very start, just as the cows are leaving their first field.

It takes ages. The sweet scent of wedding bouquets is replaced by the warm rich smell of earth and animal. One independent cow decides to go her own way and darts past the car, mooing in the window as she does so.

'Ah, Annie,' I smile to myself, 'Welcome to country living.'

And so the wedding is held up for what feels like a long ten minutes or so thanks to the cows and Annie nearly trips on her gown as she steps perhaps a little too fast into the stone porch of the old church.

'Steady on,' I say. 'He's still waiting for you. Take a couple of deep breaths first.'

She does, holding up her bouquet of lavender, mingled with fine greenery and small white daisies, to inhale its scent. Within seconds she starts sneezing.

'Oh God, why did I do that?' she whispers, while Ben gropes for the antihistamines he's in charge of and hands her a hand-kerchief. She swallows a pill without water while I'm murmuring warnings about overdosing.

'I took one first thing this the morning, ages ago,' she mutters back.

It takes another few minutes for Annie to get over her attack which is only a blip. She still looks gorgeous and, despite everything, serene.

'Keep those flowers at waist level,' I hiss as the familiar strains of Handel's 'The Arrival of the Queen of Sheba' signals the beginning of this wedding we've all been waiting for.

It's a beautiful wedding. Ms Fluffy Slippers has done a sterling job; the lavender at the heart of each arrangement at the pew ends sends wafts of delicate scent which mixes with the ancient aroma of old stone and candle. I wonder what the vicar thought, seeing Chloe adjusting the elegant flowers in her worn slippers.

All goes smoothly and I shed happy tears when Ben reads Annie's favourite Shakespeare sonnet. We catch each other's eye as he says the words 'Love alters not when it alteration finds', remembering our own wedding vows all those years ago.

And then it's over. Annie and Pete leave the church to the wedding march and the pealing bells to be congratulated, photographed and showered with organic confetti of rice and dried lavender.

There is a moving moment as, in the midst of this happy commotion, a man dressed in a tartan kilt stands solemnly on a mound of grass between church and estuary to play the bagpipes. Everyone falls silent, listening to the haunting sound of the pipes rising and falling, drifting across the still deep waters of the bay.

It's such an enchanted, magical late autumn afternoon that everyone lingers at the church for quite some time. Annie and Pete are cocooned in a constant group of friends and family, the photographer mingling takes photos of everyone and everything. Amy and Will are running about with other children, their happy shouts adding to the joyful atmosphere. Pete's best man, an old school friend, is talking to the bagpiper, who is a mate of his just moved here from Inverness. Ben is over there too, talking to some of the ushers. It's like a lovely dance, with groups forming, dissolving then re-forming into other patterns.

For a few moments I'm alone. I gaze at the medieval church and think about a funeral I attended here, in October also. It was the funeral of one of my customers, an old Cornishman named Mr Hawker who lived and died alone but whose basic goodness filled the church with those who mourned him.

And now that memory is superimposed by this day, this glorious wedding. As the afternoon changes slowly into evening and people start to leave for the reception, I watch the sea darken from pale turquoise to a royal blue, and the sky grow amber as the sun begins its downward journey.

'Come on, everyone,' I finally call to my family. 'Time to go on. There's still loads more to come, you know.'

And there is. With a full heart, I'm thankful that there is always more to come.